Civil Procedure in the European Union

Civil Procedure in the European Union

Third Edition

Carlo Rasia

This book was originally published as a monograph in the International Encyclopaedia of Laws/Civil Procedure.

Founding Editor: Roger Blanpain
General Editor: Frank Hendrickx
Volume Editor: Wannes Vandenbussche

Wolters Kluwer

Published by:
Kluwer Law International B.V.
PO Box 316
2400 AH Alphen aan den Rijn
The Netherlands
E-mail: lrs-sales@wolterskluwer.com
Website: www.wolterskluwer.com/en/solutions/kluwerlawinternational

Sold and distributed by:
Wolters Kluwer Legal & Regulatory U.S.
7201 McKinney Circle
Frederick, MD 21704
United States of America
E-mail: customer.service@wolterskluwer.com

ISBN 978-94-035-0206-9

e-Book: ISBN 978-94-035-0396-7
web-PDF: ISBN 978-94-035-0406-3

The Author

Carlo Rasia (Venice, 1977) is an associate professor at the University of Bologna, Department of Legal Studies, where he teaches Civil Procedural Law and Domestic and International Arbitration Law.

He has written more than fifty works, including books and articles. Among his books, *Tutela giudiziale europea e arbitrato* (Bologna, 2010) and *La crisi della motivazione nel processo civile* (Bologna, 2016) are to be quoted. For his first work, in 2015, he won the 'Mauro Cappelletti Prize' to a young scholar for the best procedural book from the International Association of Procedural Law. He has participated in national and international research projects and conferences. He is a member of the Italian Association of Civil Procedure Law and a member of the International Association of Procedural Law. He also practices civil and commercial law in Bologna. He can be contacted at: Università di Bologna, Dipartimento di Scienze giuridiche, via Zamboni n. 22, Bologna, Italy. E-mail address: carlo.rasia@unibo.it.

The Author

Table of Contents

Table of Contents

List of Abbreviations

Cah. Dr. Eur.	Cahiers de droit européen
CFI	Court of First Instance
CFSP	Common Foreign and Security Policy
CJ	Court of Justice
Comm. M. L. Rev.	Common Market Law Review
CST	Civil Service Tribunal
Dir. com. sc. internaz.	Diritto comunitario e degli scambi internazionali
Dir. comm. internaz.	Diritto del commercio internazionale
Dir. Un. eur.	Il diritto dell'Unione europea
EAEC	European Atomic Energy Community
ECB	European Central Bank
ECHR	European Convention on Human Rights
ECJ	European Court of Justice
ECR	European Court Report
ECSC	European Coal and Steel Community
EEC	European Economic Community
EES	European Economic Space
EFTA	European Free Trade Association
EIB	European Investment Bank
ESCB	European System of Central Bank
EU	European Union
Eu. R.	Europa Recht
Eur. L. R.	European Law Review
Foro it.	Foro italiano
GC	General Court
Giur. it.	Giurisprudenza italiana
Giust. civ.	Giustizia civile
OHIM	Office of Harmonization for the Internal Market
OJEU	Official Journal of the European Union

List of Abbreviations

Ord.	Order
Rev. intern. dr. comp.	Revue international de droit comparé
Rev. trim. dr. eur.	Revue trimestrielle de droit européen
Riv. dir. eur.	Rivista di diritto europeo
Riv. dir. internaz.	Rivista di diritto internazionale
Riv. dir. internaz. priv. e proc.	Rivista di diritto internazionale privato e processuale
Riv. dir. proc.	Rivista di diritto processuale
Riv. it. dir. pubbl. com.	Rivista di diritto pubblico comunitario
Riv. trim. dir. proc. civ.	Rivista trimestrale di diritto e procedura civile
RP	Rules of Procedure
TEU	Treaty on European Union
TFEU	Treaty on the Functioning of the European Union

Foreword to the Third Edition

More than a decade ago, I was requested by the Directors of the International Encyclopaedia of Laws to draft a monograph about civil procedure before the European Courts in Luxembourg. I accepted with great pleasure, and the first edition of the book was published in 2011.

When the second updated edition had to be prepared, I asked my pupil Prof. Carlo Rasia to take part in the work with me. So, we signed the second edition together in 2019.

This new 2022 third edition is the perfect moment for further change. Carlo Rasia has undertaken the task of correcting and updating the text. In this way, thanks to the work of a young and brilliant scholar, the procedural law school of Bologna may adequately ensure the continuation of the studies related to the EU proceedings, with a hopeful glance towards the future.

Bologna, January 2022
Paolo Biavati

General Introduction

§1. Historical Outlines and Sources of Law of the Jurisdiction and Legal Proceedings of the European Union

I. The Treaties Establishing the European Communities

1. The treaties are the main source of the procedural law of the European Union (EU). Reference is made here to the three treaties establishing the European Communities (Paris, 18 April 1951, European Coal and Steel Community (ECSC) and Rome; 25 March 1957, European Economic Community (EEC); and European Atomic Energy Community (EAEC)). From the beginning, the Court of Justice (CJ) was considered the judicial organ. The ECSC Court started its activity in 1954 and the single CJ on 6 October 1958.

The European Community (EC) Treaty has been, of course, the basic source, taking into account that the ECSC Treaty expired on 23 July 2002 and the application of the EAEC Treaty is more and more limited. The EU Treaty (Maastricht, 7 February 1992) started the extension of the jurisdiction also to subjects not related to the EC pillar.

It has to be considered that, in the meanwhile, the treaties have been modified several times due to both the enlargement of the community and the progressive expansion of the EU (with reference, in particular, to the Treaty of Amsterdam, signed on 2 October 1997[1] and the Treaty of Nice dated 26 February 2001).[2]

1. F. Dehousse, 'Le Traité d'Amsterdam, reflet de la nouvelle Europe', *Cah. dr. eur.* (1997): 265 et seq.; H. Labayle, 'Le Traité d'Amsterdam. Un espace de liberté, de sécurité et de justice', *Rev. trim. dr. eur.* (1997): 813 et seq.; P. Wachsmann, 'Le Traitè d'Amsterdam. Les droits de l'homme', *Rev. trim. dr. eur.* (1997): 883 et seq.; R. Adam, 'La cooperazione in materia di giustizia e affari interni tra comunitarizzazione e metodo intergovernativo', *Dir. Un. eur.* (1998): 481 et seq.; A. Albors-Llorens, 'Changes in the Jurisdiction of the European Court of Justice under the Treaty of Amsterdam', *Comm. M. L. Rev.* (1998): 1273 et seq.; P. Biavati, 'Prime note sulla giurisdizione comunitaria dopo il trattato di Amsterdam', *Riv. trim. dir. proc. civ.* (1998): 805 et seq.; C. Curti Gialdino, 'Schengen e il terzo pilastro: il controllo giurisdizionale secondo il Trattato di Amsterdam', *Riv. dir. eur.* (1998): 41 et seq.; B. Nascimbene, 'Tutela dei diritti fondamentali e competenza della Corte di giustizia nel trattato di Amsterdam', in *Scritti in onore di G.F. Mancini*, vol. 2 (Milan: Giuffrè, 1998), 683 et seq.; E. Tezcan, 'La coopération dans le domaine de la justice et des affaires intérieures dans le cadre de l'Union européenne et le traité d'Amsterdam', *Cah. dr. eur.* (1998): 661 et seq.; C.D. Classen, 'Die Jurisdiktion des Gerichtshofs der Europäischen Gemeinschaften nach Amsterdam', *Eu. R.* (1999): 73 et seq.; Tavassi, 'Nuove prospettive nei rapporti fra giudici comunitari e giudici nazionali dopo il trattato di Amsterdam', *Dir. com. sc. internaz.* (2000): 463 et seq.; M. Chavrier, 'La Cour de justice après le Traité d'Amsterdam: palingénésie ou palinodies?', *Revue du Marché commun* (2000): 542 et seq.

II. From the Treaty of Lisbon to the UK Withdrawal from the EU

2. Following the failed introduction of the constitutional treaty, European integration continued its way, even if with more limited goals. The Treaty of Lisbon was signed on 13 December 2007. After the favourable exit of the Irish referendum (October 2009), the new Treaty entered into force on 1 December 2009.[3]

Within the framework of Lisbon, the subject of the treaties is divided into two texts: the Treaty on European Union, which is enhanced with new content, and the Treaty on the Functioning of the European Union (TFEU), which replaces the EC Treaty. The distribution of the rules between the two treaties has implied a new numbering.

The Member States confer competences on the Union to attain objectives they have in common. The use of the Union competences is governed by the principles of subsidiarity and proportionality.

The legislative and budgetary functions are exercised by the European Parliament (whose members are elected by the Union's citizens by direct universal suffrage for a term of five years) and the Council (which consists of a representative of each Member State at the ministerial level, who may commit the government of the Member State in question and cast its vote). The ordinary legislative procedure shall consist of the joint adoption by the European Parliament and the Council of regulations, directives and decisions, on proposal by the Commission. The Commission is the main executive body of the EU.

After the Treaty of Lisbon, the European Council shall define the general political choices of the EU. It shall consist of the Heads of State or Government of the Member States. It elects its President, who exercises the external representation of the EU on issues concerning its common foreign and security policy (CFSP).

3. The initial structure consisting of pillars created in Maastricht has been superseded and the EU is given a single legal personality (which replaces and supersedes the EC: Article 1 EU). When the ECSC was dissolved, the EC was replaced by the Union. However, it should be mentioned that the Protocol in the annexed Treaty of Lisbon annuls most of the provisions in the treaty referring to the jurisdictional function and states that the provisions in the TFEU (Article 106a EAEC) apply to the EAEC. The Charter of Fundamental Rights is recognized as legally binding as the treaties, even if it remains a separate document (Article 6 EU); as a consequence, the principles of the Charter can be immediately implemented within the jurisdictional bodies. Among the various human rights, the Charter includes those

---

2. B. Nascimbene (ed.), *Il processo comunitario dopo Nizza* (Milan: Giuffrè, 2003).
3. J.V. Louis, 'Bilan d'une réforme. De l'acte unique européen à la CIG 2007', *Cah. dr. eur.* (2007): 559 et seq.; S. Van Raepenbusch, 'La réforme institutionelle du traité de Lisbonne: l'émergence juridique de l'Union européenne', *Cah. dr. eur.* (2007): 573 et seq.; K. Lenaerts, 'De Rome à Lisbonne, la Constitution européenne en marche?', *Cah. dr. eur.* (2008): 229 et seq.; R. Baratta, 'Le principali novità del Trattato di Lisbona', *Dir. Un. eur.* (2008): 21 et seq.; M. Fragola, 'Osservazioni sul Trattato di Lisbona tra Costituzione europea e processo di «decostituzionalizzazione»', *Dir. com. sc. internaz.* (2008): 205 et seq.; S.M. Carbone, 'Le procedure innanzi alla Corte di giustizia a tutela delle situazioni giuridiche individuali dopo il Trattato di Lisbona', *Studi sull'integrazione europea* (2008): 239 et seq.

relative to jurisdictional protection (Article 47). At the same time, the Union adheres to the ECHR, according to the instructions of the attached Protocol No. 8. Furthermore, the fundamental rights, guaranteed by the EHRC and resulting from the mutual constitutional traditions of the Member States, form part of the Union's law as general principles. The European policies are organized on the basis of three spheres: those exclusively belonging to the Union, those exclusively belonging to the Member States, and those with shared competence, which include freedom, security, and justice (Article 4(2) TFEU) and, therefore, cooperation in civil matters, which is dealt with in Article 81 TFEU.

4. The above-mentioned enlargement of the community of Member States took a step back in 2017 when the UK formally manifested its intention to leave the EU. The UK's intention to withdraw from the EU came after the referendum on the UK membership of the EU which took place on 23 June 2016.[4] Following long negotiations, on 31 January 2020, forty-seven years after its accession to the EU, the United Kingdom left the EU (so-called Brexit withdrawal agreement).[5]

The withdrawal of the UK from the EU created an unprecedented situation so that in response to this unique circumstance, the EU has consistently attempted to create a new partnership between the Union itself and the UK, embracing trade and many other areas of cooperation.

During the Brexit negotiations, the role that the CJ would have played after the withdrawal was a major matter of principle, because the UK considered it necessary in the process of regaining independence and control over its own laws. Although the UK left the EU, the CJ continued to have jurisdiction in any proceedings brought by or against the UK and give preliminary rulings on requests from UK courts and tribunals made before the end of the transition period,[6] which was set for the end of 2020.[7]

4. On 29 Mar. 2017 the UK notified the European Council of its intention to leave the EU, thus formally triggering Art. 50 of the Treaty on European Union.
5. Council Decision (EU) No. 2020/135 of 30 Jan. 2020 on the conclusion of the Agreement on the withdrawal of the United Kingdom of Great Britain and Northern Ireland from the European Union and the European Atomic Energy Community, O.J.E.U., L 29, 1, 31 Jan. 2020. On 31 Jan. 2020, the withdrawal agreement entered into force and the UK left the EU. This marked the start of a transition period which lasted until 31 Dec. 2020. On 24 Dec. 2020, the EU and UK agreed a trade and cooperation agreement, reshaping their future relations. All 27 remaining Member States approved the Agreement on 29 Dec. 2020. *See* 'Declarations referred to in the Council Decision on the signing on behalf of the Union, and on a provisional application of the Trade and Cooperation Agreement and of the Agreement concerning security procedures for exchanging and protecting classified information', O.J.E.U., L 444, 1475, 31 Dec. 2020.
6. According to Art. 86 of the Agreement, the ECJ continued to have jurisdiction in any proceedings brought by or against the United Kingdom before the end of the transition period. Such jurisdiction applied to all stages of proceedings, including appeal proceedings before the Court of Justice and proceedings before the General Court where the case is referred back to the General Court.
7. In 2020, the General Court issued its first rulings on the consequences of the referendum of 23 Jun. 2016. In this respect, it should be highlighted that in *Schindler v. Commission* (T-627/19, EU T 2020, 335), delivered on 14 Jul. 2020, the General Court held that the European Commission did not possess any competence to adopt an act allowing British citizens residing in Member States other than the United Kingdom to retain their European citizenship after the date of their country's withdrawal

This means that the Court of Justice of the European Union has no legal powers on new disputes any longer and, consequently, courts and tribunals of the UK will not be bound by future decisions of the European Court of Justice (ECJ). It must be pointed out that according to Article 87 of the Agreement, if the European Commission considers that the United Kingdom has failed to fulfil an obligation under the Treaties or under Part Four of the above-mentioned Agreement before the end of the transition period, the European Commission may bring the matter before the ECJ under Article 258 TFEU or the second subparagraph of Article 108(2) TFEU. The agreement provides that the Commission shall apply the same principles in respect of the United Kingdom as in respect of any Member State; moreover, it defines the procedural rules applicable to the proceedings before the ECJ.[8]

III. The EU's Approach in Tackling the Pandemic Crisis

5. The last few years have been characterized not only by the UK withdrawal from the EU, but also by the spread of the coronavirus and the resulting pandemic crisis, which has caused an economic and social breakdown. Since the beginning of 2020, due to the spread of the coronavirus, States and institutions have had to react to the economic and health crisis that followed. As well as other continents, Europe was hit by the coronavirus pandemic and in response to the economic and health crisis, the EU institutions had to demonstrate their capacity to adapt and innovate.[9] The restrictions adopted by the Member States made the preparation of the parties' statements and the consultations between their representatives a much more complex task than expected.

Accordingly, the institution had to minimize people-to-people contacts and to encourage – as far as possible – remote working and electronic communications. Therefore, on 13 March 2020, given the global extent of the health crisis, the Court requested all staff of the institution to work from home, in collaboration with the members of the Courts and administrative staff of the institution. As the national restrictions were introduced, all hearings that had been scheduled to take place after 16 March 2020 were cancelled and then rescheduled.[10]

Moreover, the Court received a significant number of requests for deferral of the time limits for lodging statements or written observations and initially granted those requests on a case-by-case basis. Consequently, on 19 March 2020, the Court took the decision to extend all the time limits prescribed in pending proceedings by one month, except for the time limit in cases of particular urgency, such as those subject to the urgent preliminary ruling procedure or the expedited procedure.

---

from the Union. The UK withdrawal from the EU is also at the origin of the judgment *Brown v. Commission* (T-18/19, EU T 2020, 465), delivered on 5 Oct. 2020.

8. Article 88 of the Agreement and seq.
9. Statistics show that in 2020 1582 cases were brought before both EU Courts, which is lower than the record number for the previous year (1905 cases in 2019), but comparable to the statistics for 2018 (1683) and 2017 (1656).
10. *See* Press release No. 46/20, 3 Apr. 2020.

Although the measure slightly increased the length of the overall proceedings before the ECJ, it nevertheless allowed the parties to take part in the procedure under more convenient conditions.

The impossibility of ensuring that hearings be held in person has led to the introduction of a new type of hearing, with undeniable effects on the oral part of the procedure. It should be pointed out that the conduct of oral hearings has not changed, except for the fact that Member State officials and representatives of the parties can remain in their country and participate remotely.

This kind of hearing was made subject to consent of the lawyers and agents on behalf of the parties in each case, in order to guarantee compliance with the requirements of a fair trial and to maintain the high level of quality of simultaneous interpretation.

6. Statistics[11] highlight that in 2021, 131 hearings were held by videoconference before the CJ and the General Court (GC), some of which entailed the remote participation of up to four parties. Furthermore, due to the introduction of widespread remote working arrangements as a result of the need to ensure social distancing, both courts and departments have introduced paperless document and decision-making processes, resulting in many cases of simplification and streamlining of approval processes.

IV. The Statute of the Court of Justice

7. A protocol on the Statute of the relevant CJ (Article 245 EC, Article 160 EAEC, Article 45 ECSC), covering both relevant organizational matters (so to speak regarding the judicial system) and procedural rules, was attached to each of the original treaties establishing the Community. The Treaty of Nice introduced a single protocol on the Statute of the CJ annexed to the EU Treaty, EC Treaty, and EAEC Treaty.

The Treaty of Nice also simplified the procedure for amending the Statute. According to Articles 245 EC and 160 EAEC, the Statute could be modified by a Council Act (except for title I, regarding the status of the judges and of the Advocates-General, and for Article 64, subject to the rules on the modification of the treaties), with its unanimous approval upon request of the CJ and after consultation of the European Parliament and of the Commission, or upon request of the Commission and after consultation of the European Parliament and of the CJ.

8. After the Treaty of Lisbon, based on Article 281 TFEU, the Statute of the CJ of the EU can be modified by the Parliament and by the Council through the ordinary legislative procedure, except for title I and Article 64, which still require the ordinary procedure for the modification of treaties. Moreover, due to the abrogation of the previous law, the substitution of the Statute of the Court with a new Statute, attached, as Protocol No. 3, to the EU and TFEU treaties and to the EAEC Treaty,

11. *See The Year in Review, Annual Report 2021*, available on http://www.curia.europa.eu.

had become necessary. The new protocol is not different from the one prior in force, except for the adaptations and the changes strictly required by the new structure of the treaties.

The Statute is now applicable to the CJ, to the General Court, and includes an annexe dedicated to the previously established first specialized court, that is to say, the Civil Service Tribunal (CST), which ceased to operate on 1 September 2016 after its jurisdiction was transferred to the General Court in the context of the reform of the EU's judicial structure.

Modifications of the Statute are frequent. To date, the Statute has been amended five times, the last one by Regulation (EU, Euratom) No. 2019/629 of the European Parliament and of the Council of 17 April 2019 amending Protocol 3 on the Statute of the CJ of the EU.[12] The amendments to the Statute resulting from the adoption of the previously mentioned Regulation can be summarized as follows.[13]

First, the Court was given general jurisdiction to rule on actions for annulment concerning the payment of lump sums or periodic penalty payments imposed on a State, pursuant to Article 260(2) or (3) TFEU. Second, in the light of the constant increase in the number of cases brought before the Court and in the interest of the administration of justice, the aim of the above-mentioned reform is to prioritize the establishment of a procedure whereby the Court allows an appeal to proceed only where it raises an issue that is significant with respect to the unity consistency or development of Union law. Lastly, the legislator amended certain provisions of the Treaty in order to coordinate the Statute with the corresponding provisions of the TFEU and to provide for appropriate transitional provisions for cases pending at the date of entry into force of the regulation.

V. Rules of Procedure of the Judicial Bodies

9. One of the most significant characteristics of European procedural law is that relevant sources of law come from the institutional initiative of the judicial power. The CJ,[14] the General Court (together with the CJ),[15] and the specialized courts[16] have to issue their own Rules of Procedure (RP). The rules have to be approved by the Council with a simple majority.[17]

12. Regulation (EU, Euratom) 2019/629 of the European Parliament and of the Council of 17 Apr. 2019 amending Protocol No. 3 on the Statute of the Court of Justice of the European Union, in O.J.E.U., L 111, 1, 25 Apr. 2019.
13. *See* C. Rasia, 'L'introduzione del "filtro" nel giudizio di impugnazione avanti alla Corte di Giustizia dopo la riforma del 2019', *Riv. trim. dir. proc. civ.* (2020): 699 et seq.; C. Amalfitano, 'Note critiche sulla recente riforma dello Statuto della Corte di giustizia dell'Unione europea', in *Dir. Un. eur.,* (2019): 29 et seq.
14. Article 253 TFEU.
15. Article 254 TFEU.
16. Article 257 TFEU.
17. Articles 253, 254, and 257 TFEU.

Due to this characteristic, the Rules of Procedure of the judges in Luxembourg can often be modified and therefore the courts provide progressive adjustments as the need arises.[18]

The Rules of the CJ were completely renewed on 25 September 2012 and the new text entered into force on 1 November 2012, with some modifications made in June 2013, in July 2016 and on 31 July 2018. A total renewal was also made for the Rules of the General Court, which are dated 31 July 2018.

Lastly, the Rules of Procedure of the CJ were amended on 9 April 2019 and on 26 November 2019.[19] The latest reform replaced Article 14 of the Rules of Procedure concerning the election of the First Advocate General and introduced, after Article 159, Article 159a regarding the manifestly inadmissible or manifestly unfounded requests and applications. The updated version can be found on the Court website.

The Instructions to the Registrar of any court are attached to the corresponding rules and, for the CJ, there is an additional set of supplementary rules.

VI. Other Sources of the Procedural Law of the EU: The Charter of Rights – The European Soft Law

10. The general law principles common to the systems of the Member States represent sources of the EU procedural law. Fundamental human rights, as guaranteed by the European Convention for the Protection of Human Rights and Fundamental Freedoms (signed in Rome, 4 November 1950) and as they result from the constitutional traditions common to the Member States, shall constitute general principles of the Union's law.[20] Among these principles, the right to a fair trial within a reasonable time by an independent and impartial tribunal (Article 6 of the Convention) has to be recalled.[21]

The Charter of fundamental rights of the EU (Nice, 7 December 2000), which is now immediately binding, recognizes a series of human rights, including the right to an effective remedy before a tribunal (Article 47).[22] In fact, pursuant to the new

---

18. J. Biancarelli, 'Le règlement de procédure du Tribunal de première instance des Communautés européennes: le perfectionnement dans la continuité', *Rev. trim. dr. eur.* (1991): 543 et seq.; G. Koutsoukou, 'The Court of Justice's New Statute and Rules of Procedure', in E. Guinchard & M-P. Granger (eds), *The New EU Judiciary* (Alphen aan den Rjn: Wolters Kluwer 2018), 277 et seq.; P. Iannuccelli, 'La réforme des règles de procedure de la Cour de justice', *Dir. Un. eur.* (2013): 108 et seq.
19. Amendments of the Rules of Procedure of the Court of Justice, in O.J.E.U., L 316, 103, 6 Dec. 2019.
20. *See* Art. 6(3) EU and also Art. 340 TFEU and 188 EAEC.
21. *See* GC, 14 May 1998, T-348/94, *Enso Española v. Commission*, ECR, II, 1875; GC, 20 Feb. 2001, T-112/98, *Mannesmannröhren v. Commission*, ECR, II, 729.
22. In a recent case law, the CJ found that provision of domestic law which, according to national case law, does not allow individual parties to challenge the conformity with EU law of a judgment of the highest administrative court (Council of State) by means of an appeal before the Supreme Court of Cassation does not conflict with the EU. In accordance with the principle of procedural autonomy, the national legal order of each Member State to establish procedural rules for the remedies on condition, however, that those rules are not – in situations governed by EU law – less favourable than in similar domestic situations (so-called principle of equivalence) and that they do not make it

Article 6 EU (introduced by the Treaty of Lisbon), the Union recognizes the rights, freedoms, and principles set out in the Charter of Fundamental Rights of the EU, as adapted at Strasbourg on 12 December 2007, which shall have the same legal value as the Treaties. Moreover (what is very important from the point of view of jurisdiction), the rights, freedoms, and principles in the Charter shall be interpreted in accordance with the general provisions in Title VII of the Charter governing its interpretation and application and with due regard to the explanations referred to in the Charter, that set out the sources of those provisions.[23]

At the same time, the Union adheres to the ECHR, according to the instructions of the attached Protocol No. 8. However, to date, adhesion has not been achieved yet. What is more, a first adhesion agreement project was not deemed to be compliant with the EU law by the CJ, with opinion No. 2/13, dated 18 December 2014.[24] In December 2021, the negotiations concerning the adhesion of the EU to the ECHR have been resumed and they are still on.

It has to be stressed that the European Charter and the European Convention on Human Rights (ECHR) are not perfectly identical. Even if the basic rights are equally protected, it will be a task of the CJ to solve any possible question arising from this difference.

11. The case law of the courts of the Union, and above all of the CJ, is not technically deemed as a law source; however, judicial precedent forms part of the *acquis communautaire* and maintains significant effective relevance in determining the law in force.[25]

It is in any event useful to refer to the published Reports, which include the text (often the complete version) of the decisions of the European courts. This traditional tool is now supported by the Court website, which gives users quick and complete information.

---

impossible in practice or excessively difficult to exercise the rights conferred by EU law (so called principle of effectiveness). The Court found that in this case both requirements are fulfilled; moreover, it does not conflict with the provisions of Directive No. 89/665 either, under which, in the field of public procurement, the Member States are obliged to guarantee the right to an effective remedy. On this matter *see* CJ, 21 Dec. 2021, C-497/20, *Randstad Italia SpA*, ECR, 1037.

23. G.F. Mancini, 'La tutela dei diritti dell'uomo: il ruolo della Corte di giustizia delle Comunità europee', *Riv. trim. dir. proc. civ.* (1989): 1 et seq.; L.P. Comoglio, 'Diritti fondamentali e garanzie processuali nella prospettiva dell'Unione europea', *Foro it.* (1994): V, 153 et seq.; P. Wachsmann, 'L'avis 2/94 de la Cour de Justice relaif à l'adhésion de la Communauté européenne à la Convention de sauvegarde des droits de l'homme et des libertés fondamentales', *Rev. trim. dr. eur.* (1996): 467 et seq.; M. Waelbroeck, 'La Cour de Justice et la Convention européenne des droits de l'homme', *Cah. dr. eur.* (1996): 549 et seq.; F. Chaltiel, 'L'Union européenne doit-elle adhérer à la convention européenne des droits de l'Homme?', *Revue du Marché Commun* (1997): 34 et seq.; F.G. Jacobs, 'Human Rights in the EU: The Role of the Court of Justice', *Eur. L. R.* (2001): 331 et seq.; N. Trocker, 'La Carta dei diritti fondamentali dell'Unione europea e il processo civile', *Riv. trim. dir. proc. civ.* (2002): 1171 et seq. *See* in case law: GC, 12 Nov. 2010, C-339/10, *Asparuhov*; GC, 1 Mar. 2011, C-457/09, *Chartry*; GC, 14 Mar. 2013, C-555/12, *Loreti;* GC 8 May 2014, C-483/12, *Pelckmans*).
24. *See* I. Pernice, 'L'adhésion de l'Union européenne à la Convention européenne des droits de l'homme est suspendue', Cah. dr. eur. (2015): 47 et seq.
25. A. Arnull, 'Owning Up to Fallibility: Precedent and the Court of Justice', *Comm. M. L. Rev.* (1993): 247 et seq.; C. Charrier, 'L'obiter dictum dans la jurisprudence de la Cour de Justice des Communautés européennes', *Cah. dr. eur.* (1998): 79 et seq.

12. The European procedural soft law has become increasingly more important and interesting. Single judiciary bodies are authorized to issue practical instructions or information notices to the parties, which are likely to exert a deep influence over the management of proceedings. It should be mentioned that recent case law tends to attribute relevant consequences when these indications are not complied with.

13. Lastly, it should be stressed that the Agreement on the European Economic Space (EES) aimed at economic harmonization between the former Communities and the twelve Member States, on the one hand, and the European Free Trade Association (EFTA) Member States, on the other, was signed in Oporto, 2 May 1992, and Brussels, 17 March 1993. The EES Agreement, together with the attached protocols and declarations, contains relevant provisions in relation to procedure. The signatory States who are currently not members of the EU are Iceland, Lichtenstein, and Norway.

VII. Relations Between Different Sources

14. The rules of the Treaty of the Union and of the founding treaties (following subsequent amendments; and so, now the TFEU) are positioned at the highest level. The Statute of the CJ is a single protocol added to the EU, the TFEU, and the EAEC treaties, forms an integral part of them, and is formally positioned at the same level.[26] However, due to its simplified modification procedure (except for the provisions of title I and of Article 64), it is in reality a source which is only partly at the same level. Also the legal principles common to the Member States are positioned at the same level as the treaties and of the Charter of Rights. Below that, it has positioned a subordinate (or secondary) legislation (and therefore the Rules of Procedure of the CJ, of the General Court, and of the specialized courts).

The case law, on the other hand, strongly influences the interpretation of European law at different levels, according to the level of the source of the judgment in question.

As regards the relationship between the Statute of the Court (higher, but less complete source) and the Rules of Procedure (lower ranked, but more detailed source), one must recall that, at law, the Rules include not only the provisions foreseen by the Statute but also provisions required for its application and, insofar as necessary, its completion.[27] Surely, the Rules add something to the provisions of the Statute; but this phenomenon has not been considered a conflict.

26. Article 7 of the Treaty temporary and final provisions.
27. Article 63 of the Statute provides that: 'the Rules of Procedure of the Court of Justice and of the General Court shall contain any provisions necessary for applying and, where required, supplementing this Statute'. *See also* Art. 2 RP CJ; Art. 2 RP GC.

§2. Nature of Jurisdiction of the EU

15. The special feature of the legal system arising from the European treaties is that the treaties not only set rules which are binding for the Member States (and, therefore, compulsory for the citizens of those States after the ratification of the international provisions within the internal legal system), but they also set rules and acknowledge subjective positions (even if only for some effects) directly on individuals. The legal relationships coming from the treaties as a whole represent an autonomous system, characterized by the great two principles regarding the immediate applicability of its rules and its supremacy over the system of the Member States. Rather, following the development of the Union, the division between the European and the national sphere has to be taken into consideration.

This special feature of the Union affects the nature of the jurisdiction, which has to ensure that the law is observed through the interpretation and the implementation of the treaties and of the secondary law sources (regulations, directives, decisions) according to Articles 19 EU. The jurisdiction represents, within the European system, the power to check and guarantee the proper functioning of the mechanisms set up by the treaties. It is therefore the jurisdiction of the special and autonomous system of the Union.

It certainly has limited functions because the relevant system to which it refers is limited and incomplete and because it only takes effect on certain relations and not on the totality of the legal relations developing within the Member States. So, while the national jurisdictions are complete, the Union jurisdiction is limited; while the national jurisdictions are supported by the strength of the coercion in implementing their decisions, the European jurisdiction has to rely on the cooperation between the Member States (both for the jurisdiction and the administration and, sometimes, for the legislation) for the effective implementation of its decisions.

Nevertheless, the Union has a real jurisdiction; perhaps this jurisdiction is weak from an enforcement proceeding perspective, but surely it is very strong from a political point of view and therefore its decisions are enforced just as the Member States' ones.

16. Functions of the European judges are those typical of international justice (such as the actions for failing to fulfil an obligation brought by a Member State against another Member State) and of constitutional justice (in every instance where the division of powers between the Member States and the Union, or the different bodies of the Union, is under discussion). However, they are also judges of last instance for the interpretation of the EU law (and the CJ plays a role similar to a supreme national court), administrative judges (e.g., when annulling unlawful acts of the institutions), and judges with unlimited jurisdiction on subjective rights (in EU non-contractual liability matters or in legal relationships regarding the EU servants). These three functions (the most important in terms of quantity) put the European jurisdiction in direct contact with situations of damage suffered by individuals. Therefore, even if only in certain sectors, the jurisdiction of the Union is an instrument for natural and legal persons to enforce European law (or in any event in direct reference to the claims they raise).

Certainly, cases of litigation between individuals are still excluded from the Union's jurisdiction. However, there are already some contrary indications; for example, questions referred for preliminary ruling or certain aspects of the litigation on intellectual property rights (as it will be more deeply stressed afterwards). Moreover, according to Article 262 TFEU, the Council, acting unanimously in accordance with a special legislative procedure and after consulting the Parliament, may adopt provisions to confer jurisdiction on the EU courts in disputes relating to the application of Acts creating European intellectual property rights. Behind this approach, there is the assignment of the capacity to take decisions in litigation between individuals, for example, in European patent matters.

17. After the Treaty of Amsterdam, the jurisdiction of the CJ broadened, for the first time, to the former third pillar of the Union, beyond EC protection in the strict sense. The Treaty of Nice emphasized this phenomenon.[28] Lastly, after the Treaty of Lisbon, the restoration of the European system based on the two Union treaties overcomes, *inter alia*, the pillar structure of the Treaty set in Maastricht. There is no longer a distinction between the Community and the intergovernmental jurisdictions in the second and, especially, in the third Union pillar. The judicial power of the CJ of the EU now covers all the matters ruled by the Union system, save some limited and specified exceptions.

In fact, some specific situations, to be interpreted narrowly, do not lie within the general jurisdiction of the European judicial system. The jurisdiction of the Kirchberg's bodies does not include CFSP. However, the Court has jurisdiction in any procedure provided for by the treaties about CFSP and decides the appeals brought by natural or legal persons within the limits of actions for annulment, regarding the legality of European decisions, which provide for restrictive measures vis-à-vis natural or legal persons, adopted by the Council on the basis of Chapter II of Title V of the EU Treaty (regarding CFSP).[29]

In the sector of freedom, security, and justice, only the validity or the proportionality of operations carried out by the police, or by other law-enforcement services of a Member State or the exercise of the responsibilities incumbent upon Member States with regard to the maintenance of law and order and the safeguarding of internal security, are not included in the jurisdiction (also as regards preliminary procedures) of the European judicial system.[30]

Laws and special conditions of judicial protection, through which the Treaty of Amsterdam extended (exceptionally, at that time) the jurisdiction of the CJ outside the Community pillar, are abrogated (save the provisional rule settled by Protocol No. 36 attached to the Treaty of Lisbon) so, the procedure for the judicial interpretation pursuant to Article 35 EU; the action for special avoidance, ruled by paragraph six of the same provision; the procedure for the settlement of disputes pursuant to Article 35(7), EU; the main application for interpretation, pursuant to Article 68(3), EC.

28. *See* prior Arts 7 and 46 EU.
29. Article 275 TFEU, Art. 24 EU, Art. 40 EU.
30. Article 276 TFEU.

§3. The Jurisdiction in the Constitutional Framework of the Union

18. The judges of the Union have the following functions:

(a) to control the institutions (especially the Commission, the Council, and, ever increasingly, the Parliament), to ensure that their activity is compliant with the treaties and, in any event, with the proper hierarchy of the law sources of the Union;
(b) to ascertain that the Member States fulfil their obligations set by the system of the Union;
(c) finally, to complete the system of the Union both setting out principles of the system (making clear the content of the already existing rules, especially of the treaties) and developing and filling in the gaps due to the limitations of the system.

The first two duties are quite similar to those pertaining to judges in a national system. The third duty – interpreting, integrating, and creating the system – is peculiar to the European jurisdiction and, especially, to the CJ. This duty can be examined from two perspectives: historical and systematic.

19. From a historical perspective, it is clear that the CJ has been the institutional driving force for the European system. In a situation characterized by frequent political paralysis, the extensive and valuable activity of the Court replaced the inertia of the governments of the Member States, setting out basic principles for the system's identity, from the direct applicability of European law to its supremacy over national systems. In this regard, it has been said that to date, the CJ has been the institution least affected by political balance problems and which can be better described as a truly supranational body.

20. From a systematic perspective, this special duty of European jurisdiction affects in many ways the interpretation of the procedural rules. The statement of European law represents the main and essential duty pertaining to the judges in Luxembourg and it comes first, but does not exclude the settlement of the disputes, the re-establishment of the individual rights, and fact-finding. Due to the organization of the Union's jurisdiction in different bodies, the CJ has a creative and declaratory function, while the General Court (even if often innovative, especially in competition and intellectual property matters) and the specialized courts act as judges of the facts.[31]

---

31. A. Arnull, 'Judging the New Europe', *Eur. L. R.* (1994): 3 et seq.; P. Biavati, 'La funzione unificatrice della Corte di giustizia delle Comunità Europee', *Riv. trim. dir. proc. civ.* (1995): 273 et seq.; J.L. Da Cruz Vilaça, 'Le système juridictionnel communautaire', *Revue du Marché Unique europeén* (1995): 243 et seq.; T. Tridimas, 'The Court of Justice and Judicial Activism', *Eur. L. R.* (1996): 199 et seq.; C. Timmermans, 'The European Union's judicial system', *Comm. M. L. Rev.* (2004): 393 et seq.; K. von Papp, 'The Role and Powers of the Court of Justice of the European Union', in E. Guinchard & M-P. Granger (eds), *The New EU Judiciary* (Alphen aan den Rjn: Wolters Kluwer 2018), p.101 et seq.

§4. Roles of the Judges of the Union

I. Outline

21. The European judges (CJ, General Court, and the specialized courts, within their respective competence) have the essential role of guaranteeing the observance of the interpretation and of the enforcement of the treaties and, in general, of the European system. Pursuant to Article 19 EU, they shall ensure that in the interpretation and application of the Treaties, the law is observed, while Member States shall provide remedies sufficient to ensure effective legal protection in the fields covered by Union law.[32] In fact, the aim of Article 19 of the EU Treaty is to establish a complete system of legal remedies and procedures designed to ensure judicial review of the legality of EU acts as well as to entrust such review to the Courts of the EU.[33]

So, the European judges have to interpret and apply the treaties, the protocols, the subsequent Acts and amendments, the agreements entered into by third-party States, and the legislative instruments issued by the European institutions. It has to be outlined that according to the two founding principles of the supremacy of the European system with respect to the national systems and of the direct applicability in the Member States of the rules of European law, the norms provided by European sources prevail (for matters governed by the treaties) over the norms of the national law systems (including those at constitutional level), both preceding and subsequent and, therefore, the national judges have to directly apply European law without giving effect to all the provisions (also subsequent) arising from the national legislation, which might be in conflict with European law. Therefore, not only the European judicial bodies but also the national judges are required to enforce European law.[34] Nowadays, Article 19 EU affirms that Member States shall provide remedies sufficient to ensure effective legal protection in the fields covered by Union law.

22. However, in addition to the widespread enforcement of European law, one must refer to European jurisdiction narrowly defined, which is granted to the judicial bodies of the Union, for the matters and for the powers specified by the treaties (the CJ, the General Court, and the specialized courts, which are of such nature both from a functional and a structural point of view). In this book, reference to European jurisdiction shall, unless otherwise specified, mean in the structural sense.

---

32. F.G. Jacobs, 'Recent and Ongoing Measures to Improve the Efficiency of the European Court of Justice', *Eur. L. R.* (2004): 823 et seq.; C. Harding & A. Gibbs, 'Why Go to Court in Europe? An Analysis of Cartel Appeals 1995–2004', *Eur. L. R.* (2005): 349 et seq.; J. Komàrek, 'Federal Elements in the Community Judicial System: Building Coherence in the Community Legal Order', *Comm. M. L. Rev.* (2005): 9 et seq.; P. Mengozzi, 'I giudici CE e l'equilibrio istituzionale comunitario', *Contratto e Impresa: Europa* (2006): 117 et seq.; K. Lenaerts, 'The Rule of Law and the Coherence of the Judicial System of the European Union', *Comm. M. L. Rev.* (2007): 1625 et seq.; H. Rasmussen, 'Present and Future European Judicial Problems after Enlargement and the Post-2005 Ideological Revolt', *Comm. M. L. Rev.* (2007): 1661 et seq.
33. *See* CJ, 25 Feb. 2021, C-689/19 P, *VodafoneZiggo Group v. Commission*, ECR, 142.
34. Opinion No. 1/17 of 30 Apr. 2019, *EU-Canada Agreement*, ECR, 341.

23. While both national and EU courts have to apply European law, the latter are exclusively entitled to interpret the EU law. In fact, the uniform interpretation of European law not only by the EU courts but also, and mainly, by national judges is essential in order to maintain and strengthen the unity of the system. The national judges, therefore, for proper interpretation of the norms of the Union's system must refer to the European judicial bodies, which, from this perspective, also act as supervisory regulators.

II. Different Content of the Jurisdiction of the Union

24. The jurisdictional powers of the Union are exercised in three different ways:

(1) unlimited (i.e., full substantive) jurisdiction;
(2) jurisdiction of annulment;
(3) declaratory jurisdiction.

A. Unlimited Jurisdiction

25. The following fall in this category:

(1) actions for damages for non-contractual liability of the Union (Articles 268 and 340 TFEU and 188 EAEC);
(2) disputes between the Union and its servants (Article 270 TFEU, 91 of the Staff Regulations), unless referred to the annulment of unlawful Acts;
(3) actions against pecuniary penalties (Articles 261 TFEU and 144, lett. b) EAEC), also on the basis of specific secondary sources (i.e., Article 31 of the regulation 1/03 on competition);
(4) litigation settled with arbitration clauses (Articles 272 and 273 TFEU);
(5) actions governed by Article 260 TFEU, regarding defaulting Member States sentenced to the payment of a lump sum or penalties;
(6) all litigation that the treaties recognize under the full jurisdiction of the Court (such as the appeals ex Article 144 lett. a) EAEC).

In these cases, full powers are granted to the European judges; they examine both fact and law, decide on the merits, evaluate the opportunity of the measures under examination (both in terms of annulment and amendment), and issue decisions establishing the breach and imposing the payment of monetary damages. Under the rules mentioned above, the EU courts are granted the same powers, as the national courts in their legal orders.

B. Jurisdiction of Annulment

26. Actions for annulment of the Acts of the institutions are included in the jurisdiction of annulment.[35] A particular place has to be given to actions concerning the intellectual property rights, which can lead both to the annulment and to the modification of the contested decision.[36]

In these cases, the European judges are entitled not to re-examine the merits of contested decisions but only their compliance with the EU law, according to the following grounds: (i) lack of competence; (ii) infringement of an essential procedural requirement; (iii) infringement of the treaties or of any rule of law relating to their application; and (iv) misuse of powers. The reasoning of the judges regards both points of fact and of law. The final decision can annul an Act, so withdrawing it from the system; however, it does not extend to the rules following the annulment.

Within the framework of jurisdiction of annulment, there is also the situation provided for by Article 7 EU and Article 269 TFEU, in relation to the reaction by a Member State to a finding by the Council that a material and continued breach of one or more fundamental rights, as well as the consequent decisions (even if only limited to the procedural issues).

C. Declaratory Jurisdiction

27. European judges, even if by means of a knowledge in law and in fact, have to express their valuation about the compliance or compatibility with the system of acts and conduct, as well as to set the correct interpretation of European rules. No Act is set off the EU system, nor any condemnation is made.

This jurisdiction includes:

(1) preliminary rulings of interpretation and validity (Article 267 TFEU), also in the framework of some conventions providing for the assignment of an interpretative function to the CJ;
(2) actions for failure to fulfil an obligation against the Member States (Articles 258, 259, 271 lett. a) TFEU);
(3) incidental submissions to ascertain the illegality of general Acts (Article 277 TFEU);
(4) actions for failure to act (Article 265 TFEU);
(5) actions for the fulfilment by national central banks of obligations under the Treaties and the Statute of the European System of Central Bank (ESCB) and of the European Central Bank (ECB) (Article 271, lett. d) TFEU).

The declarative functions of the European judges are at the same time the most primitive and the most important aspect of European jurisdiction. They represent the

35. Articles 263, 264, and 271, lett. b) and lett. c) TFEU; Art. 18 EAEC.
36. *See* Art. 72 of Regulation No. 1001/17 on the EU trademark; Arts 73 and 74 of Regulation No. 2100/94 on the European plant variety rights; Art. 61 of Regulation No. 6/02 on the EU design.

most primitive aspect, since it is the more limited and less compulsory (and therefore more respectful of the sovereignty of the Member States) form of the jurisdiction of the Union. This is the area most affected by international profiles. However, at the same time, these functions have the greatest importance (especially through the preliminary rulings) within the activity of the Luxembourg courts, above all as far as it concerns the building of the EU legal order, by means of the case law.

III. Other Aspects of the Jurisdiction of the Union

28. The jurisdiction of the Union can also be considered for its role in conflict resolution. From this point of view, a difference between contentious and non-contentious jurisdiction can be set. The activity of the EU courts is included in the former, where the parties bring matters directly before the judges, who decide on a true dispute. The second type comprises only the preliminary rulings (relating to interpretative issues and the validity of the Acts), where the parties do not bring a claim, but the EU courts are invested with a national judicial authority and they do not decide on the litigation but only set the right interpretation of one or more aspects of the EU law. Opinions might also be included in the non-contentious jurisdiction, even if it is better to hold that they are quite outside the jurisdictional function. In the first hypothesis, one speaks of direct actions; in the second, of preliminary questions.

29. Another relevant distinction concerns the mandatory or optional character of the jurisdiction of the Union. Usually, as mentioned above, European jurisdiction is mandatory; however, there are examples (mainly those related to arbitration clauses) of optional jurisdiction. In this regard, it has to be specified that only specific and particular matters can be voluntarily brought by the parties before the European judges.

It is opportune to recall that beyond the tasks attributed to the EU jurisdiction, other disputes in which the EU institutions are parties are submitted to national jurisdiction.[37]

30. The CJ can be asked to perform duties according to special Conventions or Protocols, concluded between the Member States of the Union and sometimes extended to other third States, and not on the basis of the law system set by the treaties. It has to be said that this kind of competence is getting less and less important, while the common powers of the EU courts are greatly extending, also from a substantive point of view.

On the basis of the EES Agreement (which also deals with EU-EFTA relationships), the CJ interprets those provisions of the agreement which are substantially identical to European rules. All the contracting parties and the EFTA Surveillance Authority may bring matters before the Court, both directly and by way of preliminary ruling, also at the request of judges of countries acceding to the EES Agreement, which are not Member States of the Union.

37. Article 274 TFEU.

The expansion of the jurisdiction of the CJ out of the matter of the treaties grew very fast especially during the last two decades of the last century, but now it seems that this trend has halted. This does not mean a reduction in the competence of the Court but that, as a consequence of the Europeanization of certain sectors, new tasks are performed by the EU jurisdiction. Nevertheless, as for material jurisdiction, it is outlined that the CJ in any event has the role of acting as the European Supreme Court and as a crucial reference point for all the issues concerning, also indirectly, the EU law.

In particular, judicial cooperation in civil matters represents the most important area from this perspective. The European regulations concerning civil procedure, with regard to Article 81 TFEU, now grant the interpretative power to the CJ on the basis of the treaties and not on the basis of specific protocols.[38]

The CJ has jurisdiction in any dispute between Member States which relates to the subject matter of two important Treaties between groups of Member States. It is about the so-called Fiscal Compact Treaty signed on 2 March 2012 and the Treaty establishing the European Stability Mechanism agreement, originally signed by finance ministers of the 17 Eurozone countries on 11 July 2011.[39] These treaties do not belong, in a strict sense, to the EU System: here the EC Court is the competent judge and it decides, according to Article 273 TFEU, by virtue of an arbitration clause between Member States.

§5. The CJ, the General Court, and the Specialized Courts

I. Outline

31. The judicial role has been practised for a long period only by one body: the CJ ECSC, first, and then the single CJ of the three Communities. The Court has represented for almost thirty-five years the whole of the judicial power of the former Communities, gathering very different roles and functions and working at the same time to integrate and to set out the principles of the European law.

This situation, which dates back to the original stage of development of the system and resulted from the treaties of Paris and Rome, lasted until 1989, when the first relevant structural change within the European jurisdictional structure was enacted. In particular, we refer to the division of European jurisdiction between two different bodies (the CJ and the Court of First Instance (CFI)), so that the judicial structure was definitely no more identified as a single body.

After the Single European Act (Luxembourg, 17 and 28 February 1986), the CFI had jurisdiction to hear in first instance a certain category of actions brought by

38. *See*, for example, Regulation (EU) No. 1215/2012 of the European Parliament and of the Council of 12 Dec. 2012 on jurisdiction and the recognition and enforcement of judgments in civil and commercial matters.
39. A modified version of the Treaty was signed in Brussels on 2 Feb. 2012.

natural or legal persons (appealable only for reasons of law) and under the conditions laid down by the Statutes. The first session of the CFI was held on 25 September 1989.[40]

32. Due to the increasing workload of the Court and the introduction of new areas under the Union's jurisdiction (e.g., the very relevant area regarding intellectual property litigation), a new and more radical adjustment of the judicial European legal system was needed.

The Treaty of Nice granted the CFI the same role as the CJ, but without the extension of the Court's jurisdictions. In fact, Articles 220 EC and 136 EAEC specified that the CJ and the CFI guarantee, within their jurisdictions, that the interpretation of the law and the enforcement of the treaties are compliant with law.[41]

Second, the Treaty of Nice conferred to the Statute a more flexible source than the treaties, the duty to divide the jurisdictional competence between the CFI, the

---

40. E. Van Ginderachter, 'Le tribunal de première instance des Communautés européennes', *Cah. dr. eur.* (1989): 63 et seq.; T. Kennedy, 'The Essential Minimum: The Establishment of the Court of First Instance', *Eur. L. R.* (1989): 7 et seq.; T. Millett, 'The New European Court of First Instance', *International and Comparative Law Quarterly* (1989): 811 et seq.; H. Jung, 'El Tribunal de primera instancia de las Comunidades europeas: aspectos de la ampliacion a dos organos de la jurisdiccion comunitaria', *Revista de Instituciones Europeas* (1989): 339 et seq.; C.O. Lenz, 'The Court of Justice of the European Communities', *Eur. L. R.* (1989): 127 et seq.; Y. Galmot, 'Le Tribunal de première instance des Communautés européennes', in *Revue française de droit administratif* (1989): 567 et seq.; R. Joliet & W. Vogel, 'Le tribunal de première instance des Communautés européennes', *Revue du Marché commun* (1989): 423 et seq.; J. Biancarelli, 'La création du Tribunal de première instance des Communautés européennes: un luxe ou une necessité?', *Rev. trim. dr. eur.* (1990): 1 et seq.; A. Saggio, 'Osservazioni sul giudice comunitario nel contesto attuale: natura del ruolo e novità istituzionali', *Riv. dir. eur.* (1990): 245 et seq.; K. Lenaerts, 'Das Gericht ester Instanz der Europäischen Gemeinschaften', *Eu. R.* (1990): 288 et seq.; N.J. Weidner, 'The Court of First Instance of the European Communities', *Syracuse Journal of International Law and Commerce* (1991): 241 et seq.; A. Saggio, 'Prospettive di evoluzione del Tribunale di primo grado delle Comunità europee', *Riv. dir. eur.* (1992): 3 et seq.; L. Daniele, 'Profili istituzionali del Tribunale di primo grado delle Comunità europee', *Riv. dir. eur.* (1992): 21 et seq.; H. Jung, 'Das Gericht erster Instanz der Europäischen Gemeinschaften: Praktische Erfahrungen und zukünftige Entwicklung', *Eu. R.* (1992): 246 et seq.; C. Curti Gialdino, 'Tribunale di 1° grado', *Enciclopedia giuridica Treccani*, vol. XXXI (Roma: 1994), 1 et seq.; M. Condinanzi, *Il Tribunale di primo grado e la giurisdizione comunitaria* (Milan: Giuffrè, 1996); P. Mengozzi, 'Le Tribunal de première instance des Communautés Européennes et la protection juriridique des particuliers', *Dir. Un. eur.* (1999): 181 et seq.; K. Lenaerts, 'Le Tribunal de première instance des Communautés européennes: regard sur une décennie d'activités et sur l'apport du double degré d'instance au droit communautaire', *Cah. dr. eur.* (2000): 323 et seq.; M.C. Reale, *Il Tribunale di primo grado e la litigiosità comunitaria* (Milan: Giuffrè, 2000).
41. J. Wouters, 'Institutional and Constitutional Challenges for the European Union: Some Reflections in the Light of the Treaty of Nice', *Eur. L. R.* (2001): 342 et seq.; D. Ruiz-Jarabo, 'La riforme de la Cour de justice opérée par le traité de Nice et sa mise en œuvre future', *Rev. trim. dr. eur.* (2001): 705 et seq.; R. Mastroianni, 'Il Trattato di Nizza e il riparto di competenze tra le istituzioni giudiziarie comunitarie', *Dir. Un. eur.* (2001): 769 et seq.; A. Johnston, 'Judicial Reform and the Treaty of Nice', *Comm. M. L. Rev.* (2001): 499 et seq.; O. Tambou, 'Le système juridictionnel communautaire revu et corrigé par le traité de Nice', *Revue du Marché commun* (2001): 164 et seq.; R. Calvano, 'Verso un sistema di garanzie costituzionali dell'UE? La giustizia comunitaria dopo il Trattato di Nizza', *Giurisprudenza costituzionale* (2001): 209 et seq.; F. Salerno, 'Giurisdizione comunitaria e certezza del diritto dopo il trattato di Nizza', *Riv. dir. internaz.* (2002): 5 et seq.

Court, and the judicial panels. In this manner, the decision of the Council on 26 April 2004 modified such competence for the first time since 1993.[42]

Third, it gave the CFI the opportunity to act as preliminary interpreter of European law, even if only limited to specific subjects to be identified by the Statute and subject to the controls of the CJ, to be determined as well by the Statute.[43]

Fourthly, it started a second structural enlargement of the European judicial bodies by setting up judicial panels.[44] This reform also modified the role of the CFI, which became a judge of appeal and gave rise, in some cases, to three judicial instances. The programme of Nice was first implemented through the foundation of the CST, as decided by the Council on 2 November 2004.[45]

33. With the Treaty of Lisbon, a further implementation was made, without modifying the philosophy of the Treaty of Nice. A provision of the EU Treaty, the new Article 19, is dedicated to the European judicial system, providing that the judicial institution is named CJ of the EU. It includes the CJ, the General Court (dropping 'of first instance', which was no longer consistent with its new and broader functions), and specialized courts (new name of the judicial panels). It has the role to ensure that in the interpretation and application of the Treaties the law is observed.

An important clarification of terms has so been achieved. When the European judicial system is mentioned without specifying the competence of each body, reference is made to the CJ of the EU; while, when the CJ is mentioned without specifications, the reference has to be made to the higher European judicial body, as a separate entity from the General Court and specialized courts.

Also after Lisbon, it should be focused on the possibility of founding new specialized courts, according to the new ordinary legislative procedure. Furthermore, the potential assignment of the jurisdiction for Acts establishing European rights of intellectual property remains. Yet, it must be said the EU judiciary is recently going towards a different direction: the Regulation (EU, EAEC) 2016/1192 of the European Parliament and of the Council of 6 July 2016 amended the Statute, abolishing the CST and transferring to the General Court the matter of the disputes between the EU and its servants.[46]

---

42. Articles 51 and 54 of the Statute were changed.
43. *See* former Art. 225(3) EC and former Art. 140A EAEC.
44. R. Schiano, 'Le "camere giurisdizionali" presso la Corte di Lussemburgo: alcune riflessioni alla luce dell'istituzione del Tribunale della funzione pubblica', *Dir. un. eur.* (2005): 719 et seq.; M. Borraccetti, 'Le Camere giurisdizionali nel sistema giudiziario dell'Unione europea: il Tribunale della funzione pubblica', *Dir. com. sc. internaz.* (2005): 525 et seq.
45. This court was dissolved on 1 Sep. 2016. The prior rules here referred to are Arts 225 and 225a EC.
46. Articles 50a and 62d of the Statute. *See* a critical approach about the new deal of the EU judiciary in E. Guinchard & M-P. Granger, 'Conclusion: Sisyphus in Luxemburg', in E. Guinchard & M-P. Granger (eds), *The New EU Judiciary* (Alphen aan den Rjn: Wolters Kluwer 2018), p.375 et seq.

II. Competence of the CJ and of the General Court

34. The EU jurisdiction is now divided into many bodies: the CJ, the General Court, and (in theory) specialized courts, each of them having jurisdiction on specific matters. As mentioned above, the CST was the first judicial panel founded: but in 2015, in view of the increase in litigations and the excessive length of proceedings in cases being dealt with in the General Court, it was established to gradually increase the number of judges at the General Court to fifty-six and to transfer to it the jurisdiction of the CST, which was dissolved on 1 September 2016.

Therefore, the different spheres of competence have to be pointed out.

35. The CJ has general jurisdiction. Even if its functions are similar to those of a national Supreme Court, mainly as interpreter and guardian of the EU law, it still, however, covers all matters not expressly assigned to the General Court or to the specialized courts.

Practically, at the moment, the jurisdiction of the CJ covers: (a) preliminary issues on interpretation and validity, except those which might be transferred to the General Court, according to a future provision of the Statute; (b) proceedings for failure to fulfil an obligation; (c) actions for annulment and against failure to act of the EU institutions that are not transferred to the General Court; (d) part of the actions brought in force of arbitration clauses; (e) appeals against the decisions of the General Court; (f) specific assignments from the EAEC Treaty; (g) specific competence pursuant to Articles 269 TFEU and 7 EU; (h) the assignments from specific conventions.

36. Pursuant to the treaties, the jurisdiction of the General Court is set up, both directly and with a cross-reference to future determination of the Statute.[47] A distinction between jurisdiction at first instance, jurisdiction upon the appeals, and preliminary jurisdiction has to be made.

At first instance, the General Court has jurisdiction to hear and determine actions or proceedings referred to in Articles 263, 265, 268, 270, and 272 TFEU, with the exception of those assigned to a specialized court (if any) and those reserved in the Statute for the CJ. Furthermore, the Statute may provide for the General Court to have jurisdiction for other classes of action or proceedings.

At the moment, the General Court is entitled to determine the following actions:

(a) annulment of Acts of the EU institutions, including those referring to penalties imposed by the European authorities;[48]
(b) actions against the failure to act of the EU institutions,[49] both when filed by:
    (i) natural or legal persons in any case;
    (ii) Member States, against decisions taken by the Council under Article 108(2), third par., TFEU; against Acts of the Council adopted pursuant to a council regulation concerning measures to protect trade within the

47. Article 256 TFEU.
48. Article 263 TFEU.
49. Article 265 TFEU.

meaning of Article 207 TFEU; against Acts of the Council by which the Council exercises implementing powers in accordance to Article 291(2) TFEU;

(iii) Member States, against acts of or failure to act by other institutions;[50]

(c) actions for damages for non-contractual liability of the EU institutions;[51]
(d) matters assigned to the EU jurisdiction on the basis of an arbitration clause;[52]
(e) civil service disputes (since 1 September 2016, after the dissolution of the CST);
(f) intellectual property rights.

Jurisdiction sub (c) and (d) pertain to the General Court, without any exception with regard to the nature of the applicant (therefore, both natural and legal persons, both States or institutions).

As for the subjective profiles of the division of the jurisdiction between the CJ and the General Court, the EU case law has specified that the notion of State has to be interpreted restrictively and it does not include bodies like regions or autonomous communities, even if, according to their national and constitutional law, they are entrusted with legislative powers for the direct enforcement of European law.[53]

With the purpose of making the sharing of jurisdiction clearer, it has to be outlined that the actions for annulment and against the failure to act of the EU institutions lie within the competence of the CJ when:

(a) brought by a Member State against a legislative act, an act of the European Parliament, of the European Council or of the Council, or against a failure to act by one or more of those institutions,[54] an act of, or a failure to act by the Commission under Article 331(1) of the TFEU;
(b) brought by an institution of the Union against a legislative act, an act of the European Parliament, of the European Council, of the Council, of the Commission or of the ECB or against a failure to act by one or more of those institutions;[55]
(c) brought by a Member State against an act of the Commission relating to a failure to comply with a judgment delivered by the Court under the second subparagraph of Article 260(2), or the second subparagraph of Article 260(3), of the TFEU.[56]

---

50. Article 51 of the Statute.
51. Article 268 TFEU.
52. Article 272 TFEU.
53. CJ, 21 Mar. 1997, ord., C-95/97, *Région wallonne v. Commission*, ECR, I, 1787; CJ, 1 Oct. 1997, ord., C-180/97, *Regione Toscana v. Commission*, ECR, I, 5245; GC, 10 Feb. 2000, T-32/98 and T-41/98, *Nederlandse Antillen v. Commission*, ECR, II, 201; CJ, 2 May 2006, C-417/04 P, *Regione Sicilia v. Commission*, ECR, I, 3881.
54. Articles 263 and 265 TFEU, except for decisions taken by the Council under the third subparagraph of Art. 108(2) TFEU, b) acts of the Council adopted pursuant to a Council regulation concerning measures to protect trade within the meaning of Art. 207 TFEU, c) acts of the Council by which the Council exercises implementing powers in accordance with Art. 291(2) TFEU.
55. Articles 263 and 265 TFEU.
56. Article 263 TFEU.

With the adoption of Regulation (EU, Euratom) No. 2019/629 of the European Parliament and of the Council of 17 April 2019, the legislator amended Article 51 of the Statute on the division of jurisdiction between the CJ and the General Court, conferring general jurisdiction (therefore, at first and sole instance) on the CJ under Article 260(2) and (3), ensuring the exclusive intervention of the highest court on the matter.

The decisions of the General Court on matters where it has competence are subject to a right of appeal to the CJ on points of law only and upon the conditions and to the extent provided for by the Statute.

The Treaty of Nice, for the first time, had entrusted the CFI with appeal jurisdiction. The General Court has the appeals against the decisions of the specialized courts (on points of law only in the case of the dissolved CST[57] or when it is provided for in the regulation establishing a future specialized court, also on matters of fact). The decisions of the General Court delivered after appeal proceedings are subject to be exceptionally reviewed by the CJ, under the conditions and within the limits laid down by the Statute, where there is a serious risk of the unity or consistency of Union law being affected.[58]

Lastly, after the Treaty of Nice, the General Court may have competence to hear and determine questions referred for a preliminary ruling under Article 267 TFEU, in specific areas, which may be laid down by the Statute. This provision has not been enacted yet.[59]

37. After the Treaty of Nice, according to Article 257 TFEU and Article 140 B EAEC, the European Parliament and the Council, acting in accordance with the ordinary legislative procedure, by means of regulations either on proposal from the Commission after consultation of the CJ or at the request of the CJ after consultation of the Commission, may establish specialized courts attached to the General Court to hear and determine at first instance certain classes of action or proceedings brought in specific areas. These judicial bodies have a specialized jurisdiction on subjects having a large impact but usually not affecting the founding principles of the European legal system. The regulations establishing a specialized court shall lay down the rules on the organization of the court and the extent of the jurisdiction conferred upon it. Unless otherwise provided for in the regulation, the provisions of the treaties relating to the EU jurisdiction and the Statute shall apply to the specialized courts. Each court sets its Rules of Procedure in agreement with the CJ; those rules shall require the approval of the Council (the qualified majority is no longer required). As mentioned above, the decisions of the specialized courts are subject to the right of appeal before the General Court, on points of law or, when provided for by the institutive decision, also on matters of fact.

38. It should be stressed that the design of the EU judiciary, as it came out from the Treaty of Nice, has been strongly contradicted in the recent years. The case of CST has been perhaps the most evident example.

---

57. According to the repealed Art. 11 annex I to the Statute.
58. Article 256(2) TFEU.
59. Article 256(3) TFEU.

The EU CST was the first specialized court (former judicial panel). It was established by a decision of the Council on 2 November 2004. The body was ruled by annexe I of the Statute (in addition to its specific Rules of Procedure and the related secondary law) and, as mentioned, its jurisdiction covered disputes between the Union and its servants, pursuant to Articles 270 TFEU and 152 EAEC, including disputes between European bodies, offices and agencies, and their employees (such as Eurojust, ECB, or Office for Harmonization in the Internal Market). They represented around 150 cases a year for a staff of approximately 40,000 individuals in all the institutions, bodies, and offices and agencies of the EU. The CST included seven judges appointed by the Council for a renewable period of six years, following a call for applications and after consulting a committee established for that purpose. When appointing the judges, the Council ensured a balanced composition of the CST on as broad a geographical basis and as broad a representation of the national legal systems as possible. The judges of the CST elected their President from among their number for a term of three years, which could be renewed. It sat in Chambers of three Judges or, whenever the difficulty or importance of the questions of law warranted it, as a full court. Appeals, limited to points of law, could be brought before the General Court against decisions of the CST within a period of two months, and decisions delivered by the General Court on appeal could, in turn, be reviewed by the CJ in exceptional circumstances. Over the period of its existence (almost eleven years), the CST delivered 1.549 judgments.

Litigation on intellectual property might be another area of possible future intervention, taking into account the preliminary debates and the content (which are not univocal, but open) of Declaration N° 17 annexed to the Treaty of Nice, according to which the Grand Duchy of Luxembourg accepts not to claim the location within its borders of the Board of Appeal for the harmonization in the internal market, currently at Alicante, also in the case that, as explicitly considered, they would be transformed into judicial panels.

39. Nowadays, the General Court plays a central role, but above all as common judge for direct actions (since most competence at single instance still pertaining to the CJ are founded on provisions of the Statute and not on rules set by the treaties), more than as appeal judge against the decisions of the specialized courts and as a body having the jurisdiction to hear, even if limited to certain sectors, preliminary proceedings.

In terms of quantity, the institution of the former CFI allowed an initial transfer of a number of pending claims (equal to approximately one-quarter of the workload of the Court). In the subsequent years, the Court's workload did not decrease but rather increased significantly (379 pending claims in 1990, 443 in 1997, 741 in 2007, 1102 in 2019, 1,045 in 2020, 1,113 in 2021), while at the same time the General Court's workload also increased sharply (164 pending claims in 1989, 644 in 1997, 1,154 in 2007, 1398 in 2019, 1,497 in 2020, 1,428 in 2021).

The CJ maintains many functions mainly focused on the safeguarding of the EU law and on the control of the relations between the institutions and the institutions and the States.[60] As a matter of fact, the Court has the exclusive function to assess the failure to fulfil the obligations of the Member States and, above all, to set and create the European system. In fact, the Court still has the task to give its opinion on preliminary issues of interpretation and validity and has the power to intervene, upon certain conditions, to correct the preliminary decisions of the General Court. Furthermore, the Court is entitled to quash the judgments of the General Court, stating the principle of law which the General Court should apply when the case is referred back to it.

The jurisdiction pursuant Articles 269 TFEU and 7 EU, regarding the judicial control of the matter of the procedural declaration of the existence of a serious and persistent breach by a Member State of the fundamental values of the Union (like human dignity, freedom, democracy, and so on), also pertains to the CJ. The assignment of these functions exclusively to the highest court can be considered totally logical; it deals with politically very sensitive questions, which touch the national sovereignty.

§6. The Role of Case Law Within the European System

40. Formally, case law is not a source of law within the EU legal system. The principle of *stare decisis* does not apply and the CJ is not bound by its precedents. Previous judgments only set examples of the enforcement of the law sources, with a higher or a lower influence.

Where a judgment is quashed in appeal proceedings, the lower courts, to which the case is referred back for the decision, are bound to the enforcement of the law principles set by the higher court (such as the General Court in respect to the CJ and, in the past, the CST with respect to the General Court). However, this rule is internal to the procedure and it aims at keeping the contents of the judgment issued by the higher court.

With regard to the decisions on preliminary questions, national judges are exempted from referring cases to the Court, where it has already stated on the same issue; the Court itself is entitled to decide on such questions by an order, with reference to its settled case law. However, the Court might change its opinion by specifying or reviewing its case law, even if that is absolutely rare. Therefore, the rule of precedent is highly influential even if it is not strictly binding on the Court.

Moreover, the above observations about the role of the European jurisdiction in the constitutional framework of the Union have great consequences on the evaluation of the efficiency of case law in the European system. The unity and coherence (also for the case law) of European law are promoted as guidelines for any potential review of the decisions of the General Court either given upon appeal against the decisions of the specialized courts or in preliminary proceedings. In the same way, a reference to the 'established case law' is considered as an element which makes

60. C. Iannone, 'La Cour de justice: une Cour de cassation et une cour constitutionelle à 25?', *Dir. Un. eur.* (2005): 159 et seq.; T. Horsley, 'Reflections on the Role of the Court of Justice as the "Motor" of European Integration: Legal Limits to Judicial Law-Making', *Comm. M. L. Rev.* (2013): 931 et seq.

possible the delegation of cases to a single judge in the General Court; that is the chance to clearly deduce the reply to a question from existing case law, as a reason to allow the CJ to solve, by orders, preliminary ruling questions.[61]

It is commonly known that the decisions of the judges set the pace of the development of European law. The statement on European law supremacy over national law is one example;[62] the statement about the direct applicability of European law to individuals, without the mediation of the Member States is another;[63] reference to fundamental human rights as heritage of the European system has also origin in the case law, much before the recent developments.[64]

However, making reference to the names of the parties in historical decisions of the Court (*Costa-Enel*, *Simmenthal*, *Nold*, etc.), which are emblematic in the establishment of the European system, is not the aim of these lines. On the contrary, it should be recalled that the classical law sources do not include the explanation of relevant principles, which can be only found on the grounds of one or more decisions of the CJ. It is true, on the one hand, that these principles of law do not enter the operating part of the judgments, but it is also true, on the other hand, that the real dimension of the EU 'living law' can be verified only by taking into consideration case law. After all, in this sense, the European System is the heyday of a historical phenomenon (i.e., the progressive growth of jurisprudence) which is clearly present in all modern legal systems of Roman-Germanic origin.

In other words, a realistic vision of the Union's constitutional structure has to take into account the judicial power, which set *praeter legem* rules and played a very similar role to the legislator. Moreover, it is easy to understand that all the above affects the European proceedings which are the necessary instrument of the creative contribution of the judges to the establishment of the system.

---

61. *See* Art. 29(1), lett. a) RP GC; Art. 99 RP CJ.
62. CJ, 15 Jul. 1964, 6/64, *Costa v. ENEL*, ECR, 1127; CJ, 9 Mar. 1978, 106/77, *Simmenthal*, ECR, 629.
63. CJ, 5 Feb. 1963, 26/62, *Van Gend & Loos*, ECR, 1; CJ, 8 Apr. 1976, 43/75, *Defrenne*, ECR, 455.
64. CJ, 17 Dec. 1970, 11/70, *Internationale Handelsgesellschaft*, ECR, 1125.

Part I. Competences of the European Judges

Chapter 1. Direct Actions

§1. The Mandatory Jurisdiction of the European Courts

41. Not all the disputes with aspects of Union law can be submitted to the Luxembourg courts; the Kirchberg judges have jurisdiction to hear cases only in the hypothesis laid down by the treaties or specifically assigned by the law. So, at the moment, the EU jurisdiction does neither include cases brought by individuals or legal entities against other individuals or legal entities nor include actions having the aim to abrogate or to assess the illegality of national measures; and this is also true for those matters which require the direct enforcement of European law. As it has already been stressed, national judges and not the EU courts are the most common applicators of the EU law.

In this regard, it can be said that the EU actions are tendentially a *numerus clausus*. As a matter of fact, a difference between declaratory and annulment jurisdiction, on the one hand, and unlimited jurisdiction on subjective rights, on the other, may be pointed out. In fact, while declaratory and annulment jurisdiction include only some typical classes of actions, unlimited jurisdictions include actions having different and somehow undeterminable content.

Unlimited jurisdiction includes, *inter alia*, actions brought by EU servants, cases concerning compensation for non-contractual liability of the Union, and claims against penalties fixed by the European institutions. Each of these groups does not identify a typical individual action, but many potential actions which may have, also in an abstract sense, a different content. The employees of the EU institutions are entitled either to claim sums of money or a promotion or simply bring an action for the declaration of the existence of a right; the individual injured by the conduct of an institution is entitled both to claim for damages and simply to get liability established.

It seems clear that within the many different competences of the Kirchberg judges are included both jurisdiction (and the related actions) with limited powers to verify the compliance of acts or conducts with the legal system or to annul unlawful Acts and full and unlimited jurisdiction, where the courts' power is extended to state on the merits of facts. The former represents a lower level in the development of the European system and the fixed number of actions allowed is the consequence of the limits binding the judicial power. The latter expresses a legal order able to set rules affecting the legal situations of individual citizens or undertakings, who are entitled to challenge such rules and are endowed with a judicial protection similar to that existing in a national system.

§2. The Subject Matter of EU Proceedings

42. It has to be specified that when talking about the subject matter, reference is made to the real matter under the jurisdiction of the courts operating at the Kirchberg Plateau, without considering the nature of the judicial powers exercised from time to time and the classification of the actions brought by the parties on the basis of the scope of the application (what will be studied in the following paragraphs).

Due to the development of European integration, the judgments on fundamental rights are more and more frequent. However, since the former EEC matters in the strict sense of the expression are still predominant, the EU proceedings (both within the direct actions and the preliminary rulings) are focused on the functioning of the complex economic system ruled by the treaties. The ruling submitted by a national judge about the interpretation of a regulation, the claim to annul a decision, the control on a potential infringement by a Member State setting administrative provisions clashing with the European law: all the above – but there could be many other examples – imply litigation relating to the main pillars of the economic integration, pursued by the treaties.

In other words, the judges of the Union are above all focused on the (public) law of the economy, that is to say, a way to control the legality applied to the economic administration. Few kinds of action may be considered out of this scenario: the claims brought by the servants of the institutions, which follow the traditional labour litigation scheme, the actions based on arbitration clauses; usually about contractual matters of private law; and (to some extent) the disputes on intellectual property rights. Also the claims for damages for non-contractual liability of the EU institutions often require a previous evaluation of the economic mechanism of the common market in order to identify the potential damage.

43. Consequences of this peculiar aspect of the EU proceedings have a great impact on many points.

First of all, the control of the judges on the legality of Acts, which mainly affect the administration of the economy, implies a delicate link with the discretion of the European institutions. As a consequence, the extension of the powers entrusted to the parties is greatly limited. The parties are entitled to get the declaration of the illegality or, at the most, to annul an Act without anyway having the control on the measures adopted by the EU institutions in order to change the measure which has been declared void or has been annulled.

Second, the EU proceedings become very complex, due to the specific macroeconomic nature of many disputes, when an investigation of the facts is required.

The increasing application of European law and the more and more frequent contact points with the national judicial systems, also in the sphere of private law, outline a new different trend: not only public law but also private law is getting an important subject matter in the EU cases. The preliminary rulings are the preferential area for the development of case law regarding such new issues.

§3. Actions for Failure to Fulfil an Obligation Against a Member State

I. General Features

44. The claim for failure to fulfil an obligation against a European Member State is governed by Articles 258 and 259 TFEU. It is a remedy that can be utilized both by the Commission and an individual Member State against breaches (as well as omissions) of the Member States to meet obligations with regard to the enactment of the European law.[65]

Pursuant to Article 258 TFEU, the Commission, when it considers that a Member State has failed to fulfil an obligation under the Treaties, delivers a reasoned opinion on the matter after giving the State concerned the opportunity to submit its observations. If the State concerned does not comply with the opinion within the period laid down by the Commission, the latter may bring the matter before the CJ of the EU.

According to Article 259 TFEU, a Member State which believes that another Member State has failed to fulfil an obligation under the Treaties may bring the matter before the CJ of the EU. Yet, before a Member State brings an action against another Member State for an alleged infringement of an obligation under the Treaties, it shall bring the matter before the Commission. The Commission shall deliver a reasoned opinion after each of the concerned States has been given the opportunity to submit its own case and its observations on the other party's case both orally and in writing. If the Commission has not delivered an opinion within three months from the date on which the matter was brought before it, the absence of such opinion shall not prevent the matter from being brought before the CJ.[66]

Moreover, the CJ has jurisdiction in disputes concerning the fulfilment by Member States of obligations under the Statute of the European Investment Bank (EIB); in this connection, the Board of Directors of the Bank shall enjoy the powers conferred upon the Commission by Article 258 TFEU. In the same way, the Court is called to decide the disputes on fulfilment by national central banks of obligations under the treaties and the Statute of the ESCB and of the ECB. As mentioned above, the Governing Council of the ECB in respect of national central banks has the same powers as those conferred upon the Commission in respect of Member States by Article 258.[67]

---

65. A. Dashwood & R. White, 'Enforcement Actions under Articles 169 and 170 EEC', *Eur. L. R.* (1989): 388 et seq.; A. Mattera Ricigliano, 'La procedura per inadempimento prevista dall'art. 169 Cee e la sua attuazione da parte della Commissione', *Dir. com. sc. internaz.* (1989): 267 et seq.; A. Mattera Ricigliano, 'Le procédure en manquement et la protection des droits des citoyens et des opérateurs lésés', *Revue du Marché Unique Européen* (1995): 123 et seq.
66. Other cases of action for failure to fulfil obligations are provided by specific rules (i.e., Arts 108, 114, 348 TFEU).
67. Article 271 TFEU, lett. a) and d).

While a claim for failure is very seldom raised by a State, those raised by the Commission against the individual Member States are quite frequent.

The judgment about the failure belongs to the declaratory jurisdiction of the EU because it only states that the conduct of the State concerned is unlawful, and no direct condemnation to do anything is provided. Yet, pursuant to Article 260 TFEU, a subsequent claim to obtain the condemnation of the unfulfilling State to pay a lump sum or a penalty is possible.

II. Standing

45. The standing to begin these kinds of procedure is mainly assigned, even if not exclusively, to the Commission, since it is the supervising body on the enactment of the treaties by the Member States. The action of any Member State for the recognition of an infringement by another State is possible only after the request for the intervention of the Commission. This request, which is a compulsory prerequisite to submit the action, is clearly aimed at avoiding, as far as possible, the beginning of a case brought to the Court by a Member State. In the special cases mentioned above, also the Board of Directors of the EIB and the Council of ECB have standing to bring the action.

Usually the Commission, by means of a non-contentious procedure, invites the State concerned to interrupt the illegal conduct and, if the State is still defaulting, acts directly. It has to be outlined that the Commission has the full discretion on the decision of whether or not to start the procedure. In particular, individuals cannot oppose the refusal to start a procedure on the part of the Commission.[68]

Only the Member States have standing to be sued pursuant to the treaties. In fact, should any legal or natural person and even a public body, different from the State, act in conflict with the EU legal system, any interested party may submit its claim before the national courts, which shall apply the European law, always prevailing over any different national rule. The standing to be sued of the national central banks, in the specific case laid down by Article 271, lett. d), TFEU, has also to be remembered.

III. Pre-litigation Phase

46. As previously mentioned, before the Commission brings an action pursuant to Articles 258 and 259 TFEU, there is a non-contentious phase aimed at a preliminary solution of the dispute.

This phase starts with a formal letter from the Commission to the Member State, which defines the subject matter of the case and specifies the infringement of which the Member State is accused. The Member State is invited to reply to this letter, within a certain time limit, submitting its observations. After this first phase of consultation, if the State challenges the point of view of the Commission, the latter issues a reasoned opinion on the point at discussion, with a detailed explanation of

68. CJ, 22 Jun. 2011, C-521/10, *Grúas Abril Asistencia c. Commissione.*

the claims, and invites the State to comply with it. At this stage, if the State is compliant with the opinion of the Commission, the procedure ends. If the State is not compliant, the Commission is entitled to bring the case to the Court to have the breach declared. For the purposes of identifying the matters at issue, the object of the claim pursuant to Article 258 TFEU during the judicial phase has to be the same as that already identified during the pre-litigation procedure; any possible extension of the subject matter is not admissible.

The same procedure applies when a State asks for the recognition of the infringement of another State.

IV. Breach

47. The CJ has extensively interpreted the concept of 'obligations under the Treaties'. The obligation may arise both from a rule of the treaties and from a provision of secondary Union law (directives, regulations) or from a decision itself of the EU courts.

The breach potentially arises from the adoption of an internal legal Act infringing the European law, from the refusal to adopt the required measures (which may consist in legislative as well as in administrative Acts) or from any conduct against European law.

It has to be noted that failure does not only concern the States' governments but also exists if the body who made the breach is a constitutionally independent institution. Therefore, the State may also be declared defaulting for the conduct of legislative authority or national courts.[69]

V. The Consequences of the Declaration of Breach

48. In most legal systems, claims for breach typically presume the assessment of the breach and an order to remedy. Within the European system, the decision is limited to the first aspect, having only declarative effectiveness. The judgment cannot be enforced by coercion, even if the defaulting States have to comply with the decision of the CJ and, if the breach continues, they are subject to the payment of a sum which represents also an indirect penalty for the persisting breach of the rules of the Union system.

According to Article 260(1) TFEU, if the CJ finds that a Member State has failed to fulfil an obligation under the treaties, the State shall be required to take the necessary measures to comply with the judgment of the Court. If the State does not comply, consequences mainly have a political character, since a State systematically refusing to fulfil would be actually outside the Union.

69. The matter has been definitively settled by the decision of the Court of Justice, 9 Dec. 2003, C-129/00, *Commission v. Italy*, ECR, I, 14637.

49. In particular, it has to be clarified that the European judges are not entitled to annul the national rules (laws, Statutes, regulations, or even judgments) which constitute the breach by Member States, because that would directly affect their sovereignty.

Yet, the Treaty of Maastricht and the Treaty of Lisbon have strengthened, even if indirectly, the potential coercion of the EU judgments in the matter of failure to fulfil obligations.

According to Article 260(2) TFEU, if a Member State has not taken the necessary measures to comply with the judgment of the CJ, the Commission may bring the case before the Court after giving that State the opportunity to submit its observations. It shall specify the amount of the lump sum or penalty payment to be paid by the Member State concerned which it considers appropriate in the circumstances.[70] After Lisbon, the Commission is no longer required to issue a reasoned opinion in order to have access to the EU courts.[71]

In the framework of this kind of action, the Commission not only has the continuity of the breach declared, but it is also entitled to claim for the order to pay a lump sum or a penalty. If the Court finds that the Member State concerned has not complied with its judgment, it may impose a lump sum or penalty payment on it.[72]

Furthermore, according to Article 260(3), if the claim regards the failure to transpose a European directive into national law, the Commission can specify the amount of the lump sum or penalty payment to be paid by the Member State concerned which it considers appropriate in the circumstances; if the claim is upheld, the Court can impose the payment of the penalty, not exceeding the amount specified by the Commission. The payment obligation shall take effect on the date set by the Court in its judgment.

VI. Breach of the State and Protection of Individuals

50. Breach of EU law by the Member States has also to be considered with regard to the protection granted to individuals.

On the one hand, individuals are entitled to seek the remedies provided for by the national legal systems, which are obviously completely different from the action for failure to fulfil an obligation pursuant to the EU treaties.

---

70. S. Heidig, 'Die Verhängung von Zwangsgeldern nach Art. 228 Abs. 2 EGV', *Eu. R.* (2000): 782 et seq.; M. A. Theodossiou, 'An Analysis of the Recent Response of the Community to Non-compliance with the Court of Justice Judgments: Article 228(2) CE', *Eur. L. R.* (2002): 25 et seq.; B. Masson, '"L'obscure claret" de l'article 228 par. 2 CE', *Rev. tr. dr. eur.* (2004): 639 et seq.; L. Clèment-Wilz, 'Une nouvelle interprétation de l'article 228-2 CE favorisée par le dialogue entre la Cour et son Avocat général', *Cah. dr. eur.* (2005): 725 et seq.; T. Van Rijn, 'Non-exécution des arrêts de la Cour de justice par les États membres', *Cah. dr. eur.* (2008): 84 et seq.
71. L. Pignataro, 'La politica della Commissione in materia di sanzioni per inadempimento delle sentenze della Corte', *Contratto e impresa – Europa* (2006): 129 et seq.
72. *See* CJ, 4 Jul. 2000, C-387/97, *Commission v. Greece*, ECR, I, 5047; CJ, 12 Jul. 2005, C-394/02, *Commission v. France*, ECR, I, 6263 (which states that it is possible to cumulate the penalty and the lump sum to the State's detriment); CJ, 31 Mar. 2011, C-407/09, *Commission v. Greece,* ECR, I, 2467.

On the other hand, individuals have the right to request the national courts to start proceedings for preliminary interpretation, pursuant to Article 267 TFEU, in order to obtain from the CJ the verification of conformity of the national legislative instruments with European law. In this way, there is the possibility to get a preliminary ruling which interprets the EU law, and, as a consequence, specifies the contrast between the EU and the national system. Therefore, any individual may obtain an internal judicial decision which directly enforces European law.[73]

The CJ decided that judgment for failure by a Member State to fulfil the obligations arising from European law gives standing to the individuals, potentially injured by such conduct, to sue that State in front of the national judicial authority to seek compensation for damages. According to the case law of the Court, the infringement of the defaulting State has in any event to be sufficiently 'serious and clear'.[74]

The court also tried to prevent Member States from making internal compensation claims excessively difficult. So in the 'Traghetti del Mediterraneo' case, it decided EU law precludes national legislation (like the Italian one), which limits the liability of the Member State solely to cases of intentional fault and serious misconduct on the part of the court.[75]

---

73. *See* in literature M. Wathelet & S. Van Raepenbusch, 'La responsabilité des États membres en cas de violation du droit communautaire. Vers un alignement de la responsabilité de l'État sur celle de la Communauté ou l'inverse?', *Cah. dr. eur.* (1997): 12 et seq.; G. Anagnostaras, 'The Allocation of Responsibility in State Liability Actions for Breach of Community Law: A Modern Gordian Knot?', *Eur. L. R.* (2001): 139 et seq.; M. Breuer, 'State Liability for Judicial Wrongs and Community Law; The Case of Gerhard Kobler *v.* Austria', *Eur. L. R.* (2004): 243 et seq.; A.S. Botella, 'La responsabilité du juge national', *Rev. trim. dr. eur.* (2004): 283 et seq.; Z. Peerbux-Beaugendre, 'Première consécration expresse du principe de la responsabilité de l'État membre pour les jurisprudences de ses cours suprêmes dans le cadre de l'article 226 CE', *Rev. trim. dr. eur.* (2004): 208 et seq.; E. Scoditti, '"Francovich" presa sul serio: la responsabilità dello Stato per violazione del diritto comunitario derivante da provvedimento giurisdizionale', *Foro it.* (2004): IV, 4 et seq.; M. Miglioranza, 'Il ricorso di annullamento tra verifica della legittimità degli atti comunitari e garanzia degli interessi dei cittadini', *Riv. it. dir. pubbl. com.* (2004): 1512 et seq.; O. Pallotta, 'Interpretazione conforme ed inadempimento dello Stato', *Riv. it. dir. pubbl. com.* (2005): 262 et seq.; P. Baumeister, 'Effektiver Individualrechtsschutz in Gemeinschaftsrecht', *Eu. R.* (2005): 1 et seq.; C. Rasia, 'Il controllo della Commissione europea sull'interpretazione del diritto comunitario da parte delle corti supreme degli Stati membri', *Riv. trim. dir. proc. civ.* (2005): 1025 et seq.; P. Biavati, 'Inadempimento degli Stati membri al diritto comunitario per fatto del giudice supremo: alla prova la nozione europea di giudicato', *Int'l Lis* (2005): 62 et seq.; E. Scoditti, 'Violazione del diritto comunitario derivante da provvedimento giurisdizionale: illecito dello Stato e non del giudice', *Foro it.* (2006): IV, 418 et seq.; C. Rasia, 'Responsabilità dello Stato per violazione del diritto comunitario da parte del giudice supremo: il caso Traghetti del Mediterraneo', *Riv. trim. dir. proc. civ.* (2007): 661 et seq.; R.A. Jacchia & M. Frigo, 'Responsabilità extracontrattuale degli Stati membri, effettività e rimedi giurisdizionali nella giurisprudenza della Corte di giustizia', *Riv. dir. internaz. priv. proc.* (2008): 643 et seq.
74. CJ, 19 Nov. 1991, C-6/90 and C-9/90, *Francovich*, ECR, I, 5357; CJ, 5 Mar. 1996, C-46/93 and C-48/93, *Brasserie du pêcheur*, ECR, I, 1029; CJ, 30 Sep. 2003, C-224/01, *Köbler*, ECR, I, 10239 (which extended the liability of the State also to the infringements of the EU law by a national judicial body of last instance).
75. CJ, 13 Jun. 2006, C-173/03, *Traghetti del Mediterraneo*, ECR, I, 5177, para. 46.

§4. The Action to Annul Acts of the Institutions

I. General Features

51. On the basis of Article 263 TFEU,[76] the EU courts (according to the levels of jurisdiction mentioned above) exercise judicial review of the legality of legislative Acts, of Acts of the Council, of the Commission and of the ECB, other than recommendations and opinions, and of Acts of the European Parliament and of the European Council intended to produce legal effects vis-à-vis third parties. They shall also review the legality of acts of bodies, offices, or agencies of the Union intended to produce legal effects vis-à-vis third parties.

The treaties specify that for this purpose the judges have the competence to decide in such actions brought by a Member State, the European Parliament, the Council, or the Commission, on grounds of lack of competence, infringement of an essential procedural requirement, infringement of the Treaties or of any rule of law relating to their application, or misuse of powers. They also have jurisdiction, under the same conditions, in actions brought by the Court of Auditors, by the ECB, and by the Committee of the Regions for the purpose of protecting their prerogatives.

52. Any natural or legal person may, under the same conditions, institute proceedings against an act: (a) addressed to that person or (b) which is of direct and individual concern to them, even if it apparently regards another party, and against a regulatory act which is of direct concern to them and does not entail implementing measures.[77] Such wording is wider than the text of former Article 230 EC.

Therefore, the Treaty of Lisbon has filled a lack of protection as far as it concerns the individuals. The regulatory acts may now be reviewed and challenged even if they are not of 'individual' (but only direct) concern to the persons affected by them. At the same time, Acts entailing implementing measures are out of the sphere of the review, because in these cases actions may be brought against such (European or national) measures, while it is necessary to grant immediate protection against those acts, which bring about prejudices automatically (for instance, because they introduce new prohibitions).

The time limit to submit the applications pursuant to Article 263 TFEU is two months, as the case may be, of the publication of the measure, or of its notification to the plaintiff or, in the absence thereof, of the day on which the measure came to the knowledge of the plaintiff.

53. A specific hypothesis of action for annulling acts is provided for by Article 271 TFEU. According to this rule, any Member State, the Commission and the Board of Directors of the EIB have the right to bring an action, under the conditions of Article 263 TFEU, against the decisions of the Board of Governors of the EIB; moreover, Member States and the Commission are entitled to seek the annulment, upon the same conditions, of the decision of the Board of Directors of the EIB (but

76. *See also* Art. 146 EAEC.
77. Article 263(4) TFEU.

only on the grounds of non-compliance with the procedure provided for in Articles 19(2), (5), (6), and (7) of the Statute of the Bank).[78]

54. The purpose of the remedy is close examination by the European judicial authority on the legality of any Act made by the EU institutions binding on third parties, to annul unlawful Acts and, lastly, to force the institutions that issued the unlawful Acts, to take the necessary measures to restore the legal framework existing prior to the decision.

All the Acts with binding legal effects issued by a European institution (including the Acts of bodies, offices, or agencies of the Union intended to produce legal effects vis-à-vis third parties) are subjects to review.[79] Even if the recommendations and the opinions are expressly excluded by Article 263 TFEU, the substantial matter of the Act has to be taken into account and not the formal requirements. In fact, also certain non-standard acts, such as letters or communications, even if not formally included within the contestable acts, can be compared to binding acts due to their content and effects. The point has been confirmed by uniform case law. In this way, a system of complete judicial protection has been formed without the gaps deriving from the original wording of the treaties. Moreover, after the Treaty of Lisbon, the end of the distinction of the EU system in separate pillars has as a consequence the right to claim for the review of any Act of the EU institutions, save the exceptions laid down in Articles 275 and 276 TFEU.

55. It should be noted that Article 8 of Protocol No. 2 alleged to the Treaty on the application of the principles of subsidiarity and proportionality introduces a specific action for annulment, which may be brought by the Member States and, in some cases, by the Committee of the Regions, against any infringement of the principle of subsidiarity made by means of a legislative Act. Such action is brought in accordance with the rules laid down in Article 263 TFEU.

II. Standing

56. The rules of the Treaties distinguish between two different categories of applicants having the right to bring actions to annul Acts: the EU institutions and the Member States, which may be called privileged applicants or constitutional operators, on the one hand, and natural and legal persons, other than States and institutions, called ordinary (or not-privileged) applicants, on the other hand.

57. The Council, the Commission, the Member States, and the European Parliament are not subject to any restriction regarding the Acts which they may challenge; in fact, they have the right to challenge all the binding Acts which have illegal

78. Article 271 TFEU, lett. b) and c).

79. *See* Arts 263(1) and (5) TFEU. *See* CJ, 25 Jun. 2020, C-14/19 P, *European Union Satellite Centre (SatCen) v. KF,* ECR, 492, where the Court stated that the SatCen's decisions fulfil the requirements of Art. 263(1) TFEU, because they are able to have binding effects towards KF, a member of the contrast staff.

aspects, without the obligation to demonstrate a specific interest in bringing the proceedings. The Court of Auditors, the ECB, and the Committee of the Regions may challenge any unlawful act, for the purpose of protecting their prerogatives.

58. On the contrary, individuals have the right to claim for the annulment of Acts only upon special conditions. As mentioned, Article 263 TFEU states that any natural or legal person has the right to submit a claim against a decision taken in their respect that is of direct and individual concern to them, even if it apparently regards somebody else, and against a regulatory Act which is of direct (and no longer individual) concern to them and does not entail implementing measures.[80]

59. The extension of the latter category of applicants has been progressively specified by the case law. The main problem arose above all to defining when individuals (in the prior wording of the rule) were directly and individually affected by a regulation.

Originally, the CJ clarified that: (a) a measure must be considered as a decision if it refers to a particular person and binds that person alone; (b) the wording and the natural meaning of the rule (the former Article 173 EEC) justify the broadest interpretation; (c) the provisions of the treaties regarding the right of action of interested parties must not be interpreted restrictively, and where the treaties are silent a limitation in this respect may not be presumed; (d) persons other than those to whom a decision is addressed may only claim to be individually concerned if that decision affects them by reason of certain attributes which are peculiar to them or by reason of circumstances in which they are differentiated from all other persons, and by virtue of these factors distinguishes them individually just as in the case of the person addressed.[81]

Then the judges of Luxembourg made another distinction, by recognizing that, in some cases, Acts bearing regulatory measures, having general application to all economic operators, may contain provisions that individually concern specific operators. Therefore, the latter are entitled to submit an action to annul an Act.[82] From a

80. F. Von Burchard, 'Der Rechtsschutz natürlicher und juristicher Personen gegen Eg-Richtlinien gemäss Artikel 173 Abs. 2 EWG-Vertrag', *Eu. R.* (1991): 140 et seq.; P. Nihoul, 'La recevibilité des recours en annulation introduits par un particulier à l'encontre d'un acte communautaire de porté générale', *Rev. trim. dr. eur.* (1994): 171 et seq.; M. Canedo, 'L'intérêt à agir dans le recours en annulation du droit communautaire', *Rev. trim. dr. eur.* (2000): 451 et seq.; P. Cassia, 'Continuité et rupture dans le contentieux de la recevabilité du recours en annulation des particuliers', *Revue du Marché commun* (2002): 547 et seq.; F.G. Jacobs, 'Effective judicial protection of individuals in the European Union, now and in the future', *Dir. Un. eur.* (2002): 203 et seq.; L. Malferrari, 'The Functional Representation of the Individual's Interests Before the EC Courts: The Evolution of the Remedies System and the Pluralistic Deficit in the EC', *Indiana Journal of Global Legal Studies* (2005): 667 et seq.; E. Merlin, 'Sulla legittimazione dei private all'azione di annullamento degli atti normativi comunitari: evoluzioni e prospettive', *Riv. dir. proc.* (2011): 1098 et seq.
81. *See* the fundamental decision *Plaumann v. Commission*, CJ, 15 Jul. 1963, 25/62, ECR, 195 (which introduced the so-called Plaumann test). *See* other relevant decisions: CJ, 10 Jun. 1982, 246/81, *Lord Bethell v. Commission*, ECR, 2277; CJ, 17 Jan. 1985, 11/82, *Piraiki Patraiki v. Commission*, ECR, 247.
82. CJ, 16 May 1991, C-358/89, *Extramet v. Council*, ECR, I, 2501; CJ, 18 May 1994, C-309/89, *Codorniu v. Council*, ECR, I, 1853. *See* in literature A. Arnull, 'Private Applicants and the Action for Annulment since Codorniu', *Comm. M. L. Rev.* (2001): 7 et seq.

different point of view, each individual has the right to directly challenge a directive when it may be considered as a concealed decision, or it contains specific provisions appearing as individual decisions for the applicants. A directive having general application is also subject to be challenged if it concerns directly and individually the applicants.[83]

An interesting conflict between the CFI and the CJ took place a few years ago, about the wideness of the protection allowed to individuals. The CFI had distanced itself from the positions of the CJ, in the case *Jégo-Quéré*, stating, *inter alia*, that the need for an effective protection for individuals makes it necessary to consider whether, case by case, where an individual applicant is contesting the lawfulness of provisions of general application directly affecting its legal situation, the inadmissibility of the action for annulment would deprive the applicant of the right to an effective remedy. Should no effective remedy exist, other than the action for annulment, having regard to the fact that the treaties established a complete system of legal remedies and procedures designed to permit the EU judicature to review the legality of measures adopted by the institutions, the strict interpretation, applied until now, of the notion of a person individually concerned ought to be reconsidered. The CFI concluded that in the light of the foregoing, and in order to ensure effective judicial protection for individuals, a natural or legal person is to be regarded as individually concerned by an EU measure of general application that concerns him/her directly if the measure in question affects his/her legal position, in a manner which is both definite and immediate, by restricting his/her rights or by imposing obligations on him/her. The number and position of other persons who are likewise affected by the measure, or who may be so, are of no relevance in that regard.[84]

The CJ immediately overruled this statement of position in a subsequent decision,[85] pointing out that, according to the system for judicial review of legality established by the treaties, a natural or legal person can bring an action challenging a regulation only if it is concerned both directly and individually. Although this last condition must be interpreted in the light of the principle of effective judicial protection by taking account of the various circumstances that may distinguish an applicant individually, such an interpretation could not have the effect of setting aside the condition in question, expressly laid down in the treaties, without going beyond the jurisdiction conferred by the treaties on the EU courts. Moreover, the decision of the CFI in the *Jégo-Quéré* case has been subsequently quashed by the Court upon appeal.[86] The same CFI then confirmed that the alleged lack of an actual right of action is not an instrument to force the limits laid down by the treaties that represent a breakeven point between the jurisdiction of the Union and those of the Member States.[87]

The new text of Article 263 TFEU gives individuals most possibilities, which the EU case law had been denying, because of the elimination of the reference to the

83. GC, 27 Jun. 2000, joined cases T-172/98 and others, *Salamander v. Parliament and Council*, ECR, II, 2487.
84. GC, 3 May 2002, T-177/01, *Jégo-Quéré v. Commission*, ECR, II, 2365.
85. CJ, 25 Jul. 2002, C-50/00 P, *Unión de Pequeños Agricultores v. Council*, ECR, I, 6677.
86. CJ, 1 Apr. 2004, C-263/02 P, *Commission v. Jégo Quéré*, ECR, I, 3425.
87. GC, 16 Feb. 2005, ord., T-142/03, *Fost Plus v. Commission*, ECR, II, 589.

individual concern as a condition to bring an action for annulment against regulations. So, the position of the CFI, former defeated by the CJ, has been in part upheld by the Treaty of Lisbon.

III. Grounds for Annulment

60. The action to annul an Act implies a flaw of conformity with the system of a specific binding measure of the institution (or EU body, office or agency). For this kind of action, the merits and, therefore, the effective opportunity of any specific legislative (in case of regulations or directives) or administrative option is not included within the Union's jurisdiction.

As it has already been noted, an EU measure may be challenged on grounds of lack of competence, infringement of an essential procedural requirement, infringement of the treaties, or of any rule of law relating to their application or misuse of powers.[88]

61. The lack of competence exists when an institution issues an Act without having the necessary power for this. There is a potential distinction between a lack of territorial competence, when the Act is adopted outside the field of application under the legislative authority of the issuer; a lack of temporal competence, when exceeding the fixed time limits; a lack of competence on the matter, when the exercised power is not conferred to that institution by the treaties. In this regard, the Court tried to extend the powers of the institutions, considering as existing those powers that, even if not expressly provided by the treaties, result from European secondary sources.

62. The infringement of an essential procedural requirement consists of the failure by the EU institution which issued an Act, to comply with the basic formal and procedural conditions which prepare the decision. It is largely applied and it includes, for example, the lack of reasoning or the internal inconsistency of it or the lack of a factual basis for it (it should be recalled that the EU institutions shall state the reasons on which their measures are based); it also includes the violation of the right to be heard during the administrative proceedings or the lack of any required steps prior to the Act (e.g., the mandatory consultation of another institution or body or agency of the EU).

63. The violation of the treaties or of any rule of law relating to their application is perhaps the most common ground for the annulment of an Act. It includes all the cases where the challenged measure is in conflict with any provision of higher-ranking Union law. It is not by chance that this flaw is frequently called upon also when the claim is based on other grounds. Due to its wide definition, this flaw is

---

88. C. Curti Gialdino, *I vizi dell'atto nel giudizio davanti alla Corte di giustizia dell'Unione europea* (Milan: Giuffrè, 2008).

subject to be called upon in many different cases because it refers to a wide range of laws including the treaties and those Acts adopted for their enforcement, such as directives, regulations, and decisions.

64. Finally, misuse of powers is usually defined as the exercise of a power for a different purpose from the one declared in the measure or, in any event, for a purpose which is different from that for which the power was conferred.

IV. Consequences of the Decision of Annulment

65. The action for annulment (where, as mentioned, the EU courts exercise a legality review, without dealing with the merits of the administrative choices) is a quite fundamental remedy in the EU system. Indeed, it tends to expel certain Acts out of the system, depriving them of their legal existence. The decisions that upheld the claims for annulment declare the Act concerned to be null and void from the date on which that Act entered into force (*ab initio*). Once annulled, the Act is no longer effective, without any further action by the institution concerned.[89]

The decision of annulment has effects, first, in respect to the parties, but second, also in respect to any person in the EU system. In this regard, reference is made to the *erga omnes* effects. However, it has, at least, to be pointed out that in the case of measures affecting a specified person (e.g., a decision), the quashing is effective also in respect to third parties, in a historic sense and, possibly, as an indirect source of consequences. Whereas, if the measure has a general nature (e.g., a regulation), the annulment implies the termination of the effects in respect to any person to whom the measures were addressed (except for specific sectors, such as those regarding anti-dumping regulations).

In order to protect the rights of third parties and the certainty of law, the judge has the power to specify which effects of the Act which it has declared void (and no longer only of the regulations) have to be regarded as definitive. In this case, the judge has substantial discretionary power since its decision is not simply on the legality but also on the substance.[90]

However, where a judge annuls an Act, no provision may be found in the judgment, as far as it concerns how the Act ought to be substituted or how the matter ought to be ruled. The institution, body, office, or agency, whose Act has been declared void, is required to take the necessary measures to comply with the judgment. So, the judgment states the illegality of the Act and brings about its elimination from the system, but it never implies the condemnation of the institution to a specific conduct.[91]

---

89. Article 264(1) TFEU.
90. Article 264(2) TFEU.
91. Article 266 TFEU.

V. Claims in Matter of Intellectual Property Rights

66. EC Regulation No. 1001/17 (which took the place of Regulation No. 207/09 amended in 2015), relating to the EU trademarks, contains some relevant procedural provisions and gives some specific tasks to the EU jurisdiction.

Especially, the Regulation states that any party affected by a decision by the EU Intellectual Property Office (before, called Office for Harmonization in the Internal Market), which is an EU body and a legal person, may appeal before the Board of Appeal. It is not a jurisdictional claim, but an administrative remedy. Should the provision of the Board be unsuccessful, an action before the General Court may be brought, in order to get the annulment or the alteration of the decision.

Pursuant to Article 72 of Regulation No. 1001/17, the application has to be lodged within two months of the date of the notification of the decision of the Board of Appeal and should be based on the usual grounds for the annulment of an Act of the institutions, and so lack of competence, infringement of an essential procedural requirement, infringement of the treaty, the regulation or of any rule of law relating to their application and misuse of power.

The General Court has jurisdiction not only to annul but also to alter the decision. This is why the actions in the matter of EU trademark, even if having a structure like the actions for annulment, are partially different from them, as far as it concerns the kind of jurisdictional powers of the judges. It must be added that the same machinery is referred to in Article 61 of EC Regulation No. 6/02 on the EU designs and in Article 74 of EC Regulation No. 2100/94 on the EU plant variety rights.

The litigation before the Board of Appeal has features very similar to the judicial proceedings, although such Board may not be considered a judge.

VI. The Procedural Review of the Determination Pursuant to Article 7 EU

67. Article 269 TFEU establishes that the CJ shall have jurisdiction to decide on the legality of the Acts of the Council and the European Council, according to Article 7 EU, in respect solely of the procedural stipulations contained in the above-mentioned rule; it is not allowed to decide on the merits of the political decisions of the Council.

Pursuant to Article 7 EU, the European Council, after inviting the Member State in question to submit its observations, may determine the existence of a serious and persistent breach by a Member State of the values referred to in Article 2 EU, namely human dignity, freedom, democracy, equality, rule of law, human rights, and solidarity. This assessment supposes a qualified majority and may lead to very severe measures against the breaching State, like the suspension of some of the rights deriving from the treaties, included the voting of the representatives of the government of that State in the Council.

Few rules have been laid down on this matter: the State, made object of the contested measures, is the only possible applicant; the Council and the European Council are the only possible defendant; the action may be brought within one month from the date of the contested determination; and the Court has to decide the case within one month from the date of the request.

The jurisdiction of the Court in this very specific matter seems to be a jurisdiction of annulment. In fact, should the Court assess that the procedural requirements laid down by Article 7 EU have not been complied with and therefore there is a lack of legality, the procedure ought to be begun again and no effect would be produced with prejudice to the Member State concerned; that means that the determination would be annulled.

§5. Actions Against Failure to Act of the EU Institutions

68. The review on the conduct of the EU institutions has two faces. The first is the action for annulment, which controls the positive conduct of the institutions; the second consists in the action to establish the failure to act. The two remedies are somehow parallel and complementary; they form a complete protection of the EU persons.[92]

The action to have the failure to act of the EU institutions established, where such failure is an infringement of the EU law, is governed by Article 265 TFEU. The competence is shared between the CJ and the General Court, according to the criteria mentioned above.

Pursuant to Article 265 TFEU, should the European Parliament, the European Council, the Council, the Commission or the ECB, in infringement of the treaties, fail to act, the Member States and the other institutions of the Union may bring an action to have the infringement established. After the Treaty of Lisbon, this rule shall apply, under the same conditions, to bodies, offices, and agencies of the Union which fail to act.

The action shall be admissible only if the institution, body, office, or agency concerned has first been called upon to act. If, within two months of being so-called upon, the institution, body, office, or agency has not defined its position, the action may be brought within a further period of two months.

Any natural or legal person may, under the same conditions, complain to the EU courts that an EU institution (or body, office or agency) has failed to address to that person any Act other than a recommendation or an opinion. The case law of the CJ has interpreted these requirements in a wider sense: the standing to bring the action has been held also in an applicant, who is a potential addressee of a legal measure that the institution concerned is required to adopt.[93] Yet, this kind of application, where brought by individuals, is rarely successful and frequently inadmissible, because of the difficulty for the claimant to demonstrate the failing conduct of the institutions.

---

92. M. Dony & T. Ronse, 'Réflexions sur la spécificité du recours en carence', *Cah. dr. eur.* (2000): 595 et seq.; L. Prete, 'Infringement Proceedings in EU Law' (Alphen aan den Rijn: Wolters Kluwer, 2017), 289.
93. CJ, 10 Jun. 1982, 246/81, *Lord Bethell v. Commission*, ECR, 2277, quoted above.

69. It is necessary to define which cases of failure to act may be made subject matter of this kind of claim.

The failure to act may refer to any measure, and therefore also a recommendation or an opinion, where the applicant is a Member State or an EU institution.

On the contrary, where the action is brought by a natural or legal person, the failure to act should be referring to a measure which the institution concerned is obliged to enact, or which is apt to bring effects in the sphere of the applicant. Theoretically, individuals may also complain that a regulation has not been adopted.

The action against failure to act of the institutions is a typical merely declaratory action. There is no Act to be set aside, like in the actions for annulment, but only a situation, the illegality of which may be established. As far as it concerns the measures that the institutions are obliged to enact, it should be said that they must comply with the judgment, but they remain free in the choice of the best way to do it.[94]

§6. Declaration of Inapplicability of the EU Acts

70. Among the remedies against the lack of legality of the Acts of the EU institutions, the Treaties include the hypothesis of the declaration of the inapplicability of an Act.[95]

Pursuant to Article 277 TFEU, any party may, in proceedings in which an Act of general application adopted by an EU institution (or body, office, or agency) is at issue, plead the grounds for the annulment (and so, the well-known lack of competence, infringement of an essential procedural requirement, infringement of the treaties or of any rule of law relating to their application and misuse of powers) in order to invoke before the EU courts the inapplicability of that Act.[96]

71. The importance and the utility of this remedy consist in the possibility to use it notwithstanding the expiry of the short period of two months established for an action for annulment. It deals with a kind of declaratory jurisdiction, because the goal of the request (which may be better defined as an objection raised in proceedings begun by another party) is to obtain the inapplicability of a general Act with prejudice to a party, without delating such Act. The general Act, whose lack of legality is held, works here as a preliminary element to a following measure, or failure to act, against which the applicant seeks for protection before the EU courts. It should be noted that the general Act, the inapplicability of which is sought, has not been challenged or even might not be made object of review, according to the rules laid down relating to the actions for annulment or against the failure to act.

Moreover, the Treaty of Lisbon has adopted a wider wording (speaking of Acts of general application) than the former Article 241 EC. So, any general Act made by an EU institution, which is preliminary to that which the applicants seek to annul, may be declared inapplicable.

---

94. Article 266 TFEU.
95. Article 277 TFEU.
96. M. Vogt, 'Indirect Judicial Protection in EC Law: The Case of the Plea of Illegality', *Eur. L. Rev.* (2006): 364 et seq.

It should be clear from what has been said above that the declaration of the inapplicability of the EU Acts, even if it is considered by the Treaties as an autonomous remedy, with specific limits and effects, may not be sought by an application initiating a case, but only by means of an objection raised in a case already initiated. A necessary link exists between a main claim (which may have different content) and the request for the declaration of illegality and inapplicability of the contested measure, because the latter is admissible, only if it is ordered to the success of the claim (or the defence) of the same party in the former proceedings.

The request for the declaration of inapplicability of an EU Act is therefore quite different from the action for annulment, even if the grounds on which both are based are the same. From the point of view of the standing, individuals are entitled to get inapplicable in their respective Acts, which they might not challenge directly, by means of an action for annulment. On the other hand, here the Act is not deleted and keeps its efficacy in respect to other parties; of course, the finding of the illegality of an Act will bring the EU institution concerned to alter or annul it.

The remedy governed by Article 277 TFEU may be applied not only by individuals, but also by the Member States. Only the EU institutions are not entitled to request the declaration of inapplicability of an Act of another institution.

§7. Action for Non-contractual Liability of the EU

I. General Features

72. Pursuant to Article 268 TFEU, the European courts have jurisdiction in disputes relating to compensation for damages provided for in the second and third paragraphs of Article 340 TFEU. Such rule states that, as far as it concerns its non-contractual liability, the EU shall, in accordance with the general principles common to the laws of the Member States, make good damages caused by its institutions or by its servants, acting in the performance of their duties.[97]

The competence to decide this kind of actions in first instance is now assigned to the General Court (because of the combined effect of Article 256 TFEU and Article 51 of the Statute). Action for non-contractual liability is obviously a suit for damages and supposes that the form of order sought by the applicant is a condemnation of the EU institutions.

73. This action aims to punish the liability of the EU institutions, both when deriving from legislative Acts and when depending upon civil wrongs by the EU servants in the performance of their duties. Article 340 TFEU refers to the general principles common to the laws of the Member States as the rule of law to be applied by the judges (and this reference is quite a unique case in the treaties).

This reference has put the CJ (because of its former competence in this matter) in degree to elaborate the case law in this subject with remarkable freedom, exactly

97. Other hypotheses of non-contractual liability are established by Art. 340(3) TFEU with regard to the ECB and by many secondary sources (such as Art. 118 of the regulation on the EU trademark). *See also* Art. 188(2) EAEC.

because the laws of the Member States are very different and the work of comparison is hard and not very fruitful. In fact, the Court had to take care, in most cases, of the liability deriving from the administrative and lawmaking activity of the EU bodies, so having to face problems quite different from those usually existing before the national courts.

II. Liability of the EU for Legislative Acts

74. Lawmaking is the main and most relevant source of liability of the EU institutions, which very rarely carry out material activities but perform an enormous work concerning the production of legal Acts.[98]

The European case law has been defining the conditions, under which the non-contractual liability of the EU may be held. It may be remarked that a progressive attenuation of these conditions has been having place, with the effect of a wider judicial protection for the injured parties.

The ground for the non-contractual liability of the EU based on legislative measures is that a sufficiently serious and manifest breach of a superior rule of law for the protection of individuals may be found. When the EU institutions have no (or very small) discretionary power, the mere transgression of the rule of law may be sufficient to found the liability.[99]

75. According to the EU case law, the second paragraph of Article 340 TFEU bases the obligation which it imposes on the Union to make good any damage caused by its institutions on the 'general principles common to the laws of the Member States' and therefore does not restrict the ambit of those principles solely to the rules governing non-contractual EU liability for unlawful conduct of the institutions. National laws on non-contractual liability allow individuals, albeit to varying degrees, in specific fields and in accordance with differing rules, to obtain compensation in legal proceedings for certain kinds of damage, even in the absence of unlawful action by the perpetrator of the damage. When damage is caused by conduct of the EU institution not shown to be unlawful, the Union can incur non-contractual liability if the conditions as to sustaining actual damage, to the causal link between that damage and the conduct of the EU institution and to the unusual and special nature of the damage in question are all met.[100]

As far as it concerns the degree of blame to be attributed to the author of the measure, the case law has pointed out the necessity of a faulty conduct.[101]

---

98. F. Schockweiler, C. Wivenes & J.M. Godart, 'Le régime de la responsabilité extracontractuelle du fait d'actes juridiques dans la Communauté européenne', *Rev. trim. dr. eur.* (1990): 27 et seq.
99. CJ, 4 Jul. 2000, C-352/98 P, *Bergadern e Goupil v. Commission*, ECR, I, 5291; GC, 10 Feb. 2004, joined cases T-64/01 and T-65/01, *Afrikanische Frucht-Compagnie and others v. Council and Commission*, ECR, II, 521.
100. CJ, 15 Jun. 2000, C-237/98 P, *Dorsch Consult v. Council and Commission*, ECR, I, 4549; GC, 14 Dec. 2005, T-69/00, *FIAMM v. Council and Commission*, ECR II, 5393.
101. CJ, 28 Apr. 1971, 4/69, *Lütticke v. Commission*, ECR, I, 325; CJ, 9 Sep. 1999, C-257/98 P, *Lucaccioni* c. *Commissione*, ECR, I, 5251; GC, 12 Jul. 2001, T-2/99, *T. Port v. Council*, ECR, II, 2093.

The EU institutions are also liable for the wrongs committed by their servants, provided in the performance of their functions.[102] The servant should have acted in force of a direct and internal relation to the institution, so that his/her acting is a terminal of the tasks of the EU. Only in this case an action for damages may be brought before the EU courts. Should the agent commit the wrong out of the carrying out of its functions (in the strict meaning mentioned above), neither liability of the institution nor the EU court's jurisdiction exists; the claim should be brought by the injured person before the competent national judge, who shall apply the national law.

III. Other Aspects

76. The only condition to begin a suit for damages, as far as it concerns the applicant, is the held existence of an injury, which has a causal link with the activity of the EU institutions. The action should be brought against an EU institution. After the Treaty of Lisbon, it has been clarified that also the ECB may be held responsible for the damages caused by itself or by its agents, in the performance of their functions.[103]

Only actual and proved damages may obtain the grant of compensation. Damages may also be future, but imminent and foreseeable; merely hypothetic losses obtain no compensation and claims founded on them would be rejected. The economic operator who has suffered a prejudice, but then has transferred it upon his/her clients, may not claim damages. Also non-material damage may be object of compensation.[104]

At the same time, it should be noted that, according to consistent case law, it is first and foremost for the party seeking to establish the EU's liability to adduce conclusive proof as to the existence or extent of the damage he/she alleges and to establish the causal link between that damage and the conduct complained of on the part of the EU institutions.[105]

77. Proceedings against the Union in matters arising from non-contractual liability shall be barred after a period of five years from the occurrence of the event giving rise thereto.[106] Pursuant to the Statute, the period of limitation shall be interrupted if proceedings are instituted before the EU courts or if prior to such proceedings an application is made by the aggrieved party to the relevant EU institution.[107]

---

102. Article 340(2) TFEU.
103. Articles 268 and 340(3) TFEU.
104. GC, 21 Mar. 1996, T-230/94, *Farrugia v. Commission*, ECR, II, 197.
105. GC, 9 Jan. 1996, T-575/93, *Koelman v. Commission*, ECR, II, 5; GC, 16 Jan. 1996, T-108/94, *Candiotte v. Council*, ECR, II, 87; CJ, 7 May 1998, C-401/96 P, *Somaco v. Commission*, ECR, I, 2604; GC, 19 Oct. 2005, T-415/03, *Cofradía de pescadores and others v. Council*, ECR, II, 4355; GC, 30 Jun. 2009, T-444/07, *CPEM v. Commission*, ECR, II, 27.
106. Article 46 of the Statute.
107. M. Broberg, 'The Calculation of the Period of Limitation in Claims Against the European Community for Non-contractual Liability', *Eur. L. R.* (2001): 275 et seq.

Yet, the case law states that the involvement of such liability and the assertion of the right to compensation for damages suffered depend on the satisfaction of a number of requirements relating to the existence of an unlawful measure adopted by the EU institutions, actual damage, and a causal relationship between them. So, the period of limitation which applies to proceedings in such matters cannot begin before all the above-mentioned requirements are satisfied and in particular before the damage to be made good has materialized. Accordingly, since the situations concerned are those in which the liability of the EU has its origin in a legislative measure, the period of limitation cannot begin before the injurious effects of that measure have been produced.[108]

78. It remains to take into account the case of contractual liability of the EU, which may derive from a number of relationships between individuals and Member States. Save where liability is connected to the staff cases[109] and where the contract concerned contains an arbitration clause,[110] bringing the litigation before the EU judges, the controversies relating to such liability do not belong to the EU jurisdiction and are to be decided by the national courts. As a matter of fact, whenever jurisdiction is openly conferred on the EU courts by the Treaties, disputes to which the Union is a party are to be discussed before the national courts.[111] In fact, Article 340(1) TFEU states that the contractual liability of the Union shall be governed by the law applicable to the contract in question.

§8. Actions Relating to Controversies Between the Union and Its Servants

79. The EU courts shall have jurisdiction in any dispute between the Union and its servants, within the limits and under the conditions laid down in the Staff Regulations of Officials and the Conditions of Employment of other servants of the Union. So says Article 270 TFEU. The whole matter is now belonging to the General Court in first instance (but from 12 December 2005 to 31 August 2016 to the now dissolved CST).

In July 2016, with the transfer to the General Court of jurisdiction at first instance in disputes between the EU and its servants, the new Article 50a of the Statute provides that the General Court shall exercise jurisdiction at first instance in disputes between the Union and its servants as referred to in Article 270 TFEU, including disputes between any institutions, bodies, offices, or agencies, on the one hand, and their servants, on the other, in respect of which jurisdiction is conferred on the CJ of the EU. The Statute underlines that at all stages of the procedure, including the time when the application is filed, the General Court may examine the possibilities of an amicable settlement of the dispute and may try to facilitate such settlement.

108. CJ, 27 Jan. 1982, joined cases 256/80 and others, *Wührer Spa and others v. Council and Commission*, ECR, 85; CJ, 27 Jan. 1982, 5/81, *De Franceschi v. Council and Commission*, ECR, 117.
109. *See* Art. 340(4) TFEU.
110. Article 272 TFEU.
111. Article 274 TFEU.

In this matter, the EU jurisdiction goes out of the common scheme of litigation, consisting in the review of the conduct of the EU institutions and it affects the relationships arising from the tie of service between the EU and its servants. Usually, it deals with an unlimited jurisdiction on the merits and the proposable claims are quite different, since they include, for instance, applications for the payment of sums, requests for the annulment of measures relating to the servants' career or suits for damages. The staff cases include both the controversies which are directly relating to the employment relationship and those which are referring to it only indirectly. It should be recalled that the conditions of employment of the EU servants are laid down in the Staff Regulations,[112] which also contain procedural rules.

Even if usually the servants play the role of claimants, there may be actions brought by the EU institutions against their servants. For example, pursuant to Article 22 of the Staff Regulations of Officials, the General Court is granted the assessment (which is expressly defined as a case of unlimited jurisdiction) on the suits for damages brought by the Union against its Officials, when acting in service with a serious misconduct.

With regard to the claims brought by civil servants, the Staff Regulations state that they must submit their complaints to the appointing authority, before beginning a case before the General Court: only when the complaint has been rejected, the servant concerned can institute proceedings.[113]

§9. Actions Against Penalties

80. The EU institutions have the task to ensure the application of the rules about the functioning of the treaties, also by imposing penalties to natural or legal persons, when those rules are violated.[114]

Against any decision imposing penalties (which are an enforcing title in the Member States, when consisting in the delivery of goods or things or the payment of sums of money), a claim may be brought before the EU courts. Recently, with the amendments made by Regulation (EU, Euratom) No. 2019/62,[115] the Court has been given general jurisdiction to rule on actions for annulment relating to the payment of lump sums or penalty payments imposed on a State, pursuant to Article 260(2) or (3) TFEU.

Pursuant to Article 261 TFEU, regulations adopted jointly by the European Parliament and the Council, and by the Council, may give the EU courts jurisdiction with regard to the penalties provided for in such regulations. For example, that is the case of Article 31 of EC Regulation No. 1/03 in antitrust matter.

---

112. *See* the regulation of the Council No. 259/68, entered in force on 5 Mar. 1972, and afterwards many times amended.
113. Articles 90 and 91 of the Staff Regulations.
114. G. Tesauro, 'La sanction des infractions au droit communautaire', *Riv. dir. eur.* (1992): 477 et seq.; K. Lenaerts, 'Sanktionen der Gemeinschaftsorgane gegenüber natürlichen und juristischen Personen', *Eu. R.* (1997): 17 et seq.; D. Henry, 'Les amendes de la Commission en droit de la concurrence face à la censure du juge européen', *Cah. dr. eur.* (2006): 35 et seq.
115. Regulation (EU, Euratom) No. 2019/629, in O.J.E.U., L 111, 1, 25 Apr. 2019, amended the Art. 51 of the Statute.

The EU judges are entitled to decide not only on the legality of the measure but also on the merits of the decision; they may cancel, reduce, or even increase the amount of penalties payment imposed. In fact, in this matter, the EU jurisdiction is full and unlimited.[116]

§10. Arbitration Clauses

81. Near the mandatory jurisdiction of the EU courts, the treaties have established an optional jurisdiction. In fact, in some specific cases, arbitration clauses may confer on them the power to decide controversies, otherwise belonging to the jurisdiction of the national courts.[117]

The General Court has jurisdiction to give judgment pursuant to any arbitration clause contained in a contract concluded by or on behalf of the Union, whether that contract be governed by public or private law.[118] The CJ has jurisdiction in any dispute between Member States which relates to the subject matter of the Treaties, if the dispute is submitted to it under a special agreement between the parties.[119]

The EU courts exercise true jurisdictional powers and may not be considered as arbitrators. The reference to an arbitration clause or a special agreement has the only meaning to give the EU courts jurisdiction, in cases which are not under the mandatory jurisdiction. Moreover, when assessed in force of an arbitration clause, the Luxembourg judges have unlimited jurisdiction, even if referred only to the matter of the single agreement containing the clause.

It has to be said that the EU institutions frequently include arbitration clauses in contracts with private parties.

It has to be underlined that two important Treaties between groups of Member States give competence to the EU CJ according to Article 273 TFEU.

First of all, Article 8 of the so-called Fiscal Compact Treaty provides that if the European Commission, after having given the concerned Contracting Party (i.e., to say, the Member State) the opportunity to submit its observations, concludes in its report that such party has failed the balanced budget, the matter will be brought before the CJCJ. The same goes when a Member State considers that another State has failed the balanced budget. In both cases, the judgment of the CJ shall be binding on the parties to the proceedings. If the EU Court finds that the concerned State has not complied with its judgment, pursuant to Article 260 TFEU, it may impose on the unfulfilling State to pay a lump sum or a penalty appropriate to the circumstances.

---

116. *See also* Art. 144 EAEC.
117. A. Briguglio, 'L'art. 181 Tr. CE fra giurisdizione e arbitrato', *Rivista dell'arbitrato* (1996): 105 et seq.; C. Rasia, *Tutela giudiziale europea e arbitrato* (Bologna: Bononia University Press, 2010): 13 et seq.
118. Articles 272 and 256 TFEU. Former Arts 153 and 154 EAEC have been repealed and Arts 272 and 273 TFEU are now applicable.
119. Article 273 TFEU.

Second, a similar rule is in the European Stability Mechanism (ESM) Treaty: here Article 37(3) states a competence of the CJ according to Article 273 TFEU for the disputes arising between ESM Member and the ESM.[120]

120. CJ, 27 Nov. 2012, C-370/12, *Pringle*.

Chapter 2. Preliminary Rulings

§1. General Features of EU Preliminary Rulings

82. The EU law is usually and above all applied by the courts of each European legal order, since it is endowed with supremacy over national law. In order to avoid that, since most judges are called to apply the EU law, most different interpretations might come out, the European treaties introduced a special machinery, with the aim to separate the application, on the one hand, and the interpretation, on the other hand, of the EU rules.[121] So, while the application of the EU law belongs to national judges (except the claims that should be brought before the EU courts directly), the point of interpretation is reserved to the CJ (obviously, in the cases where such interpretation is really uncertain).

Pursuant to Article 267 TFEU, when in a case pending before a court or a tribunal of a Member State a reasonable doubt arises about the interpretation of an EU rule or the validity and interpretation of Acts of the institutions of the Union, the court or tribunal, before which the question is raised, may, if it considers that a decision on the question is necessary to enable it to give judgment, request the CJ to give a ruling thereon and put the Court a question, concerning the point of law involved in the case.[122] This possibility becomes a duty for those courts or tribunals of a Member State before which any such question is raised, against whose decisions there is no judicial remedy under national law. In this case, such courts and tribunals shall bring the matter before the Court.[123]

121. As recently stated, the preliminary ruling mechanism aims to secure uniformity in the interpretation of EU law, ensuring its consistency as well as its full effect and its autonomy; *see* CJ, 26 Mar. 2020, C-558/18 e C-563/18, *Miasto Łowicz,* ECR, 234.

122. *See* CJ, 6 Oct. 2021, C-561/19, *Consorzio Italian Management and Catania Multiservizi SpA v. Rete Ferroviaria Italiana,* ECR, 799. In accordance with the settled case law, the Court reaffirmed that the mechanism established by Art. 267 TFEU aims to ensure that EU law has the same effect in all Member States and thus to avoid any divergence in its interpretation.

123. A. Arnull, 'References to the European Court', *Eur. L. R.* (1990): 375 et seq.; A. Briguglio, *Pregiudiziale comunitaria e processo civile* (Padua: Cedam, 1996); P. Olivier, 'La recevabilité des questions préjudicielles: la jurisprudence des années 1990', *Cah. Dr. eur.* (2001): 15 et seq.; T. Andersson, 'Cleaning the Slate or Blasting the Past?', *Turku Law Journal* (2001): 5 et seq.; N. Trocker, 'Das Vorabentscheidungsverfahren aus italienischer Sicht: Erfahrungen, Probleme, Entwicklungstendenzen', *Rabels Zeitschrift* (2002): 417 et seq.; G. Raiti, 'Prima e dopo Nizza: il futuro della "pregiudiziale comunitaria" tra opposte istanze di conservazione e innovazione', *Riv. trim. dir. proc. civ.* (2002): 605 et seq.; G. Trisorio Liuzzi, 'Processo civile italiano e rinvio pregiudiziale alla Corte di giustizia della Comunità europea', *Riv. dir. proc.* (2003): 727 et seq.; A. Briguglio, 'I limiti soggettivi e oggettivi dell'obbligo di rinvio pregiudiziale comunitario', *Int'l Lis* (2003): 119 et seq.; Santa Maria, 'Il rinvio pregiudiziale nella nuova disciplina a seguito del trattato di Nizza', *Dir. comm. internaz.* (2003): 367 et seq.; G. Raiti, *La collaborazione giudiziaria nell'esperienza del rinvio pregiudiziale comunitario* (Milan: Giuffrè, 2003); L. Malferrari, *Zurückweisung von Vorabentscheidungsersuchen durch den EuGH* (Baden-Baden: Nomos, 2003); A. Barav, 'Une anomalie préjudicielle', *Dir. Un. eur.* (2004): 235 et seq.; M. Bobek, 'Learning to Talk: Preliminary Rulings, the Courts of the New Member States and the Court of Justice', *Comm. M. L. Rev.* (2008): 1611; E. D'Alessandro, *Il procedimento pregiudiziale interpretativo dinanzi alla Corte di giustizia. Oggetto ed efficacia della pronuncia* (Turin: Giappichelli, 2012); F. Ferraro and C. Iannone (eds.), *Il rinvio pregiudiziale* (Turin: Giappichelli, 2020).

The interpretative decision of the CJCJ after the reference made by the national court is binding the national judge of the merits, who shall follow the Court's solution in deciding the specific case. Therefore, it is correct speaking of EU preliminary question jurisdiction.

83. It is probably superfluous underlining both the theoretical importance and the enormous practical success of the preliminary reference, through which the Luxembourg court has not only advised Member State courts on the true interpretation of the EU law but has also played a role of fulfilment and integration of the European legal order, building the living European law: not against, but surely beyond the wording of the rules. It should be remarked that some basic principles of the EU law, such as its supremacy and its direct application over national systems, have been drafted only in judgments of the Court, given on occasion of preliminary references.

At the same time, the enormous growth of the workload of the Luxembourg judges and the progressive formation of a rich body of judicial precedents have led to the introduction, by the Court itself, of many conditions for accepting a preliminary question. These conditions will be discussed in the following pages. Anyway, it is not useless advising that behind any such problem one may see a conflict between the claim for justice of the civil society, the effort of the European bureaucracy to maintain a strong control over the machinery of preliminary references, and the evergreen temptation of the Member States to defend or to recover pieces of sovereignty. Although the lawmaker has introduced conditions on the admissibility of the reference for a preliminary ruling, a settled case law highlights that a rule of national law cannot prevent a national court from using its discretion in referring a question to the CJ, because it represents an inherent part of the system of cooperation between the national courts and the Court established in Article 267 TFEU.[124]

124. CJ,19 Nov. 2019, C-585/18, C-624/18 and C-625/18, *A. K. and Others (Independence of the Disciplinary Chamber of the Supreme Court)*, ECR, 982. *See also* CJ, 26 Mar. 2020, C-558/18 e C-563/18, *Miasto Łowicz,* ECR, 234. In this case, the Court pointed out that being subject of a disciplinary proceeding as a result of making a reference to the CJ (or deciding to maintain that reference after it was made) is likely to undermine the effective exercise by the national judges of their discretionary power under Art. 267. In particular, in a previous case, the Advocate General stated that the fact that the national law allows for the possibility of disciplinary proceedings against national judges as a result of their referral to the CJ not only undermines the functioning of the preliminary ruling procedure, but is also likely to influence the decisions of other national judges in the future as to whether to make a reference, thus giving rise to a 'chilling effect'(CJ, 20 Jul. 2021, C-791/19, *Commission v. Poland*, ECR, 596). On this matter, M. Carta, 'La recente giurisprudenza della Corte di giustizia dell'Unione europea in merito all'inadempimento agli obblighi previsti dagli articoli 2 e 19 TUE: evolutionary or revolutionary road per la tutela dello Stato di diritto nell'Unione europea?', available on *rivista.eurojus.it.*, n. 1, 2020. In a recent case, the Court stated that the national court against whose decisions there is no judicial remedy is required, in principle, to refer a question for a preliminary ruling concerning the interpretation of EU law even if, in the course of the same national proceedings, the constitutional court of the concerned Member had assessed the constitutionality of national rules in the light of regulatory parameters with content similar to rules under EU law (*See* CJ, 20 Dec. 2017, C-322/16, *Global Starnet Ltd,* ECR, 985). On this matter, CJ, 5 Apr. 2016, C-689/13, *Puligienica Facility Esco Spa (PFE) v. Airgest Spa,* ECR, 199, the Court held that a provision of a national court cannot prevent a chamber of Court of final instance faced with a question concerning the interpretation of Directive No. 89/665 from referring the matter to the CJ under Art. 267 TFEU.

§2. The Preliminary Reference as Means for the Protection of the Rights of Individuals

84. The meaning of the EU preliminary reference may not be fully understood, unless it is adequately considered under the point of view of the global protection of the individual rights in the EU system.

Any European citizen is entitled to get a fair and correct application of the EU rules. The treaties and the secondary sources grant him/her some direct specific actions (which have been described before). But most cases, where such protection is necessary, happen in litigation before national courts, in a great and not foreseeable number of proceedings. The limitations to the possibility for private litigators (i.e., parties which are neither States or EU institutions) to bring actions of annulment of EU Acts make the area of individuals protection smaller, as far as it concerns the validity of the Acts of the Union; but such area spreads out again, when the lack of legality of the Acts becomes the object of a preliminary ruling of the Court, by means of the reference made by a national judge.

Therefore, the preliminary reference is a precious tool of fulfilment of the system of protection of rights, because it lets any citizen claim the application of the EU law in the proceedings where he/she is concerned, even in the doubt of the national judge.[125]

85. About the issue of protection, it is necessary to stay briefly on the nature of preliminary proceedings before the CJ and on the position of the litigators in the national case, with regard to the way of writing the reference.

The Court has always given the following answer to these questions. Preliminary proceedings (whose exit is the interpretation of a point of EU law) are not contentious. Strictly speaking, no litigators are involved in it, but only interested subjects; the decision to make the reference or not is an exclusive power of the national referring judge.[126]

This position (which clearly obeys to the strong political need for the Luxembourg judges to keep in their hands the control of the machinery) is not adequate to describe what really happens. The decision of the Court is not an aseptic law exercise, but is the binding premise for the regulation of relevant issues, exactly because of its preliminary nature and its effects on the national case. The battle between the litigators before the Court is often hard and speaks of a real conflict, which may not be included in a kind of non-contentious jurisdiction.

At the same time, it is certainly true that only a national court or tribunal may refer a preliminary question to the Court; but it should be observed that, in the absolute majority of the cases, the parties of the national proceedings, and not the judges themselves, raise the question and that referring the question is a need for (at least, one of) the parties, in order to get the success in the claim brought before the national judge.

---

125. On the point of the effective protection of rights, *see* CJ, 19 Jun. 1990, C-213/89, *Factortame*, ECR, I, 2433; CJ, 9 Feb. 1999, C-343/96, *Dilexport*, ECR, I, 579.

126. *See* the solution given in CJ, 6 Oct. 1982, 283/81, CILFIT, ECR, 3415.

This is why the preliminary proceedings are the European stage of a national contentious case, which does not change its own nature when it is brought at Luxemburg, with the further consequence that the right to be heard should be seriously granted and respected. Besides, it is not far from true defining the request of a party to get a specific interpretation of a point of the EU law as a proper claim (of course, being object of such claim not goods or substantial utilities, but a decision on matter of law). Any litigator in the EU has the right to bring its question of interpretation (or of validity of Act) on the table of the CJ, even if he/she should be obliged to cross all the stages of the internal proceedings and provided the court or tribunal at the last stage respects its duty to refer to the Court, pursuant to the rules of the treaty.

86. At the light of this premise, three issues are to be considered: the content of preliminary reference; the criteria to define what a court or tribunal of a Member State is, in order to be entitled to refer a question to the Court; how the question should be put and the place of the EU reference inside the national proceedings.

§3. The Content of Preliminary References

87. The matter of preliminary references is the EU law and, therefore, at the first place, the treaties and the secondary sources (regulations, directives, decisions, and so on) and, then, the general principles of the legal order,[127] as well as the cases where national rules have used the EU law to shape internal law. After the Treaty of Lisbon, the Court is called to decide on the validity and interpretation not only of Acts of the institutions but also of bodies, offices, or agencies of the Union.

Two points should be underlined concerning this issue. First of all, it should be borne in mind that the referred question must deal with the interpretation of one or more rules of the EU law (or the validity of one or more Acts), even if related with the matter of a specific national case. On the contrary, it is not correct for the national judge (and, before, for the lawyers of the litigators) putting a question about the compliance of any national rule with the EU law (even if this confrontation will come out from the decision of the Court). One must never forget that the CJ makes a judgment, which defines the living rule of law, with effect over all legal orders of the Member States.

At the second place, it should be observed that the prevailing case law of the CJ has extended the admissibility of preliminary references also about national rules, when they copy EU rules.[128] The right care of the Luxembourg judges is to avoid that in any legal order a wrong interpretation of rules (national rules as for the source, but in the substance European rules, because often drafted strictly copying

127. That led the Court to state many times on the existence and the relevance of the human fundamental rights in the EU legal order (since CJ, 17 Dec. 1970, 11/70, *Internationale Handelsgesellschaft*, ECR, 1125).
128. S. Lefevre, 'The Interpretation of Community Law by the Court of Justice in Areas of National Competence', *Eur. L. R.* (2004): 501 et seq.

EU rules) may take place, in conflict with the proper European interpretation of such rules, in their original wording and collocation.[129]

§4. The National Bodies Enabled to Preliminary Reference

88. The notion of 'court or tribunal of a Member State', enabled to request the CJ the preliminary ruling, is a typical question of EU law. By means of its integrative case law, in a number of judgments the Court has defined the features and the criteria, which let a (usually but not always judicial) body to be considered as a 'court or tribunal' for purposes of Article 267 TFEU.[130]

These features, which may be now held established, are the following ones: it is settled case law that, in order to determine whether a body making a reference for a preliminary ruling is a court or tribunal within the meaning of Article 267 TFEU, which is a question governed by EU law alone, the Court takes account of a number of factors, such as whether the body is established by law, whether it is permanent, whether its jurisdiction is compulsory, whether its procedure is *inter partes*, whether it applies rules of law, and whether it is independent.[131]

The interpretation of the Court has therefore shaped a notion of 'court or tribunal', which is at the same time wider and narrower than the corresponding notion in the national legal orders. In many cases, the Court has admitted references coming from administrative bodies, even if endowed with deciding functions.[132] On the other hand, the private arbitral tribunals have always been excluded from cooperation with the Court, even if they do apply the EU law and their awards shall be acknowledged and enforced in their Member State.[133] Also judicial bodies have been excluded, when the reference has been raised in not contentious proceedings.[134] The position of the Court is also negative (even if, perhaps, a bit softer)

129. *See* the following judgments: CJ, 18 Oct. 1990, joined cases C-297/88 and C-197/89, *Dzodzi*, ECR, I, 3763; CJ, 17 Jul. 1997, C-130/95, *Giloy*, ECR, I, 4291; CJ, 15 Jan. 2002, C-43/00, *Andersen og Jensen*, ECR, I, 379. Somehow different, but never repeated, is the solution given by the Court of Justice in the case *Kleinwort-Benson* (28 Mar. 1995, C-346/93, ECR, I, 615). Recently, CJ, 6 Oct. 2021, C-561/19, *Consorzio Italian Management and Catania Multiservizi SpA v. Rete Ferroviaria Italiana,* ECR, 799.

130. A. Barone, 'Rinvio pregiudiziale e giudici di ultima isnza', *Foro it.* (2002): IV, 381 et seq.; L. Raimondi, 'La nozione di giurisdizione nazionale ex Art. 234 TCE alla luce della recente giurisprudenza comunitaria', *Dir. Un. eur.* (2006): 369 et seq.; M. Condinanzi, 'I giudici italiani "avverso le cui decisioni non possa porsi un ricorso giurisdizionale di diritto interno" e il rinvio pregiudiziale', *Dir. Un. eur.* (2010): 295 et seq.

131. *See* CJ, 17 Sep. 1997, C-54/96, *Dorsch Consult*, ECR, I, 4961; CJ, 18 Jun. 2002, C-92/00, *HI*, ECR, I, 5553, CJ, 17 Jul. 2014, ord., C-427/13, *Emmeci*; CJ, 16 Jul. 2020, C-658/18, *UX v. Italy*, where the Court held that the 'Giudice di Pace' (magistrate, Italy) is part of the public sector of activity so it falls within the notion of 'court or tribunal of a Member State', even though it is not expressly mentioned in the examples referred to in Art. 2(1) of Directive No. 89/39.

132. *See* CJ, 4 Feb. 1999, C-103/97, *Köllensperger and Atzwanger*, ECR, I, 551; CJ, 6 Jul. 2000, C-407/98, *Abrahamsson and Andersson*, ECR, I, 5539.

133. CJ, 23 Mar. 1982, 102/81, *Nordsee*, ECR, 1095; CJ, 27 Apr. 1994, C-393/92, *Almelo*, ECR, I, 1477; CJ, 27 Jan. 2005, C-125/04, *Denuit and Cordenier*, ECR, I, 923.

134. *See, inter alia*, CJ, 19 Oct. 1995, C-111/94, *Job Centre I*, ECR, I, 3361; CJ, 15 Jan. 2002, C-182/00, *Lutz*, ECR, I, 547.

about the independent national authorities.[135] Here, the Court plays a political role, which causes critical opinions and perplexities.[136] On the ground of the independence and impartiality of the referring body required in order to be categorized as a 'court or a tribunal' for the purposes of Article 267 TFEU, the Grand Chamber has recently stated that the independence of national courts and tribunals is essential to the proper working of the judicial cooperation system embodied by the preliminary ruling mechanism established by Article 267 TFEU.[137] Moreover, the mechanism works only if the body responsible for applying EU law satisfies the criterion of independence. The referring body can be considered independent when it works wholly autonomously, without being subject to any hierarchical constraint or subordinated to any other body and as long as it does not have any interest in the outcome of the proceedings apart from the correct application of the EU law.

Facing a different problem, the Court has held that the obligation to refer the question, pursuant to Article 267(3) TFEU, concerns those judicial bodies against whose decisions no judicial remedy is given, looking at the concrete case. A judicial body, against whose decisions appeals are usually possible, is nevertheless obliged to refer the question if, in given proceedings, its judgments are the last instance of protection. This interpretation is to be shared, for it makes preliminary references easier and more effective.[138]

§5. Preliminary References under the Perspective of the National Judge

89. Any national judge, who has stated to refer the case to the CJ, suspends its proceedings and notifies his/her decision to the Court. National laws rule about the procedural ways to do it.

Such decision may be a judgment, an order or any other kind of decision, pursuant to national laws. Surely, it is not a decision which closes the proceedings,

135. CJ, 31 May 2005, C-53/03, *Syfait*, ECR, I, 4690. *See* the commentary of B. Buttazzi, 'La Corte di giustizia esclude l'autorità garante per la concorrenza dal rinvio pregiudiziale', *Riv. trim. dir. proc. civ.* (2006): 1017 et seq.; A. Colavecchio, 'Colpirne uno per educarne cento? Problemi della legittimazione al rinvio pregiudiziale delle autorità indipendenti', *Riv. it. dir. pubbl. com.* (2005): 1867 et seq.; H. Tagaras & M. Waelbroeck, 'Les autorités nationales de la concurrence et l'article 234 du traité. Un étrange arrêt de la Cour de justice', *Cah. dr eur.* (2005): 465 et seq.

136. Critical opinion in Italian literature in P. Biavati, 'Pregiudiziale comunitaria e arbitrato', *Rivista dell'arbitrato* (1995): 421 et seq.; C. Rasia, 'Pregiudiziale comunitaria e giudizio arbitrale: nuovo confronto tra gabbie ideologiche, funzionalità degli scambi, esigenze di tutela effettiva', *Int'l Lis* (2006): 21 et seq.

137. *See* CJ, 21 Jan. 2020, C-274/14, *Banco de Santander*, ECR, 17. The Court pointed out that the Spanish Tribunal Económico-Administrativo Central (Central Tax Tribunal) cannot be considered independent because the above-mentioned requirements are not fulfilled in the present case. *See also* CJ, 16 Feb. 2017, C-503/15, *Margarit Panicello*, ECR, 126, where the Court stated that it has no jurisdiction to rule on the request for a preliminary ruling submitted by the Secretario Judicial del Juzgado de Violencia sobre la Mujer Único de Terrassa (Registrar of the Single-Member Court dealing with matters involving violence against women) because it does not meet the criterion of independence.

138. *See* CJ, 4 Jun. 2002, C-99/00, *Lyckeskog*, ECR, I, 4839.

because the case will be continued after the judgment of the Court about the question of interpretation or validity. Should the decision be affected by any kind of vice, illegality, and so on, the interested party would be allowed to apply for the national remedies against it; nevertheless, the CJ would not be prohibited to take the question into consideration and to state on it.

The national decision which refers the question to the Court may be withdrawn; for instance, because it is revoked by the judge himself/herself or it is reviewed or annulled by an upper judge. At the same way, it may happen that the proceedings, where the question has been raised, are closed because the parties reached a settlement of their dispute or because of other grounds of discontinuance. In this case, the CJ is entitled to make the preliminary ruling, until the referring national courts notify to it a new national decision annulling the effects of the first one.

Once again, the problem to establish at which stage of the proceedings the decision to refer to the Court should be taken is to be faced and solved under the point of view of the national Rules of Procedure. Anyway, it is not necessary that the judge has already ascertained facts completely.

90. The way of wording the question is remarkably important. It should be recalled that the question has to concern the EU law, and not the national law, or a generic comparison between the two. Specially, in the references for interpretation, national judges shall request the Court to explain the meaning of an EU rule, and not to establish, whether a national rule complies with the EU law or not. This task belongs to national courts, which will be able to fulfil it, as soon as they will be made certain about the correct interpretation of the EU law.

Since 1993, the CJ has held to be obliged to answer to the preliminary references, only where they are endowed with the requirement of clearness. A question is clear, according to the Court, when it puts in light well the issue of fact and law, where the relevance of one or more EU rules in the single concrete case comes out, and therefore makes the Luxembourg judges able to give a useful answer to the national judge and the parties involved at the proceedings to submit their statements or observations to the Court, with full awareness.[139]

Behind this choice of the case law of the Court (which any practical lawyer shall bring to account), many reasons may be pointed out. On the one hand, the widespread knowledge of the EU law and the need to reduce its workload compel the Court to discourage confused or exploratory questions. On the other hand, the Luxembourg judges have created an extraordinary tool of selecting cases, not rarely used just to avoid to answer questions in politically sensible matters.

Strictly speaking, national judges ought to transfer to the CJ not only the order, containing the referred question, but also a complete copy of the dossier of national proceedings. Yet, in practice, the long times required for translations of any statement to each single judge of the Court suggest to write a well-organized and reasoned order, with reference to the main points of fact and law, essential to

139. The first judgments on this line are: CJ, 26 Jan. 1993, joined cases C-320-322/90, *Telemarsicabruzzo*, ECR, I, 393 and CJ, 19 Mar. 1993, ord., C-157/92, *Banchero*, ECR, I, 1085. Some more recent examples: CJ, 8 Oct. 2002, ord., C-190/02, *Viacom*, ECR, I, 8287; CJ, 7 Jun. 2012, ord., C-21/11, *Volturno Trasporti*; CJ, 3 Jul. 2014, ord., C-19/14, *Talasca*.

understand the case and its connection with the interpretation question, so that the Court may be put in degree to answer, only by reading the few pages written by the national judge.[140]

Besides, it should be noted that pursuant to Article 101(1) Rules of Procedure (hereinafter RP) CJ, the Court may, after hearing the Advocate-General, request clarification from the national court, within a time limit prescribed by the Court, just to obtain the failing elements. Yet, this is a fully discretionary activity and the national judges are not free from the effort to write a question, which the Court may consider clear.

When the CJ has made its decision, the dossier shall come back to the table of the national judge. The decision is notified to all parties, pursuant to the general rules of the EU proceedings; one more copy is then notified to the national referring court, to which the original dossier is immediately given back.

Being aware of the difficulties Member State courts and tribunals face when trying to apply the preliminary reference properly, the CJ periodically updates and sends out a message called 'Recommendations to national courts and tribunals, in relation to the initiation of preliminary ruling proceedings'.[141] This text, though explicitly declared to be devoid of any regulatory or even merely interpretation power, is an interesting summary of the latest case law of the Court concerning preliminary reference. The above-mentioned summary represents a reminder of the fundamental characteristics of the preliminary ruling procedure. It also provides practical recommendations as to the form and content of requests for a preliminary ruling to the CJ in order to ensure that the mechanism is fully effective.

§6. The Requirements of Admissibility of the Preliminary Reference

91. Three kinds of abuse affect the correct development of the preliminary references: first, the abuses from the judges and the parties to the national proceedings, who exceed in using the tool of preliminary reference; then, those of the national courts judging at the highest national instance, which omit fair references and therefore violate the machinery by way of non-application; lastly, those made by the CJ itself, which somehow builds a tool different from what has been drawn by the treaties.[142]

92. Beginning with the first point, it should be observed that, year by year, the CJ has built a complex system of requirements of admissibility of the preliminary interpretation questions, around the neutral wording of Article 267 TFEU. The principal ones are to be stressed here.

First, the requirement of the clearness of the question, which has already been recalled.

---

140. *See* Art. 98(1) CJ RP.

141. The latest version is dated 8 Nov. 2019, in O.J.E.C, C 380, 1, 8 Nov. 2019.

142. L. Malferrari, *Zurückweisung von Vorabentscheidungsersuchen durch den EuGH* (Baden-Baden: Nomos, 2003); N. Wahl and L. Prete, 'The Gatekeepers of Article 267 TFEU: On Jurisdiction and Admissibility of Reference for Preliminary Rulings', *Comm. M. L. Rev.* (2018): 511 et seq.

Then, the Court has held that the preliminary question should be put with reference to a real, and not spurious, controversy. This position is to be shared; moreover, it should be observed that it is coherent with the notion of preliminary proceedings as a place of a contentious conflict, which the Luxembourg judges, on the contrary, formally deny.[143]

It is a task of the national referring courts to ascertain the relevance of the preliminary question in the internal case. Yet, the Court maintains the power to point out that no relevance exists, between the question and the controversy (which obviously means a hypothesis of abuse), and therefore to hold inadmissible preliminary references, which prima facie appear without any proper binding with the national case.[144] Nonetheless, the fact that a court or tribunal has already made a reference to the CJ for a preliminary ruling in the same national proceedings does not affect the obligation of reference. In fact, when a question concerning the interpretation of EU law is necessary for the resolution of the dispute, a court of last instance cannot be relieved of its duty.[145]

The increasing of these obstacles to the admissibility of preliminary references is surely necessary, in order to defeat the abuses which exceed the correct application of Article 267 TFEU; yet, it makes clear the existence of an attack, if not to the letter, at last to the spirit of the machinery of preliminary rulings.[146]

93. Among the aspects causing problems to the efficacy of the system, the one relating to the loyal application of the EU preliminary reference by the courts, against whose decisions no appeal is possible, is perhaps the most important. Should a national highest court omit to refer a question to the CJ, no internal judicial protection would be granted to the citizen.

Since many years, the CJ has made the obligation to refer questions to it less binding. This conduct has to be shared. The highest national courts may omit the reference when (and this is going to happen more and more frequently) no reasonable doubt arises about the interpretation of the EU rules and such interpretation could be shared by the highest courts of every Member State.[147] Recently, the Court stated that a national court must comply with its obligation to bring before the CJ a question concerning the interpretation of EU law, unless it finds that (a) the question is irrelevant or that the provision of EU law in question has already been interpreted by the Court or (b) the correct application of EU law is so obvious as to leave no scope for any reasonable doubt. Therefore, the national court may refrain from referring to the Court a question concerning the interpretation of EU law and take

---

143. The settled case law on this point started with the case CJ, 11 Mar. 1980, 104/79, *Foglia-Novello I*, ECR, 745.
144. *See* CJ, 16 Jun. 1981, C-126/80, *Salonia*, ECR, 1563, from which a settled case law has started.
145. *See* CJ, 6 Oct. 2021, C-561/19, *Consorzio Italian Management and Catania Multiservizi SpA v. Rete Ferroviaria Italiana,* ECR, 799.
146. *See* D. O' Keeffe, 'Is the Spirit of Article 177 under Attack? Preliminary References and Admissibility', *Eur. L. R.* (1998): 509 et seq.
147. Here the already-quoted case *CILFIT* (CJ, 6 Oct. 1982, 283/81, ECR, 3415) is fundamental. Yet, some recent cases show a bit different approach: *see* above all *X and van Dijk* (CJ, 9 Sep. 2015, 72/14 and 197/14) and Ferreira da Silva and Brito (CJ, 9 Sep.. 2015, 160/14). In literature, A. Kornezov, 'The New Format of the Acte Claire Doctrine', *Common M. L. Rev.* (2016): 1317 et seq.

upon itself the responsibility for resolving it where the correct application of EU law is so obvious as to leave no scope for any reasonable doubt. Nevertheless, before concluding that such is the case, the national court or tribunal of last instance must be convinced that the matter would be equally obvious to the other courts or tribunals of last instance of the Member States and to the CJ.[148]

It has to be pointed out that vis-à-vis an abusive refuse to refer, protection for citizens gets very difficult. The CJ has held that a State is failing to fulfil its obligations under the treaties when its Supreme Court uses to interpret some national rules in such a way that it objectively is an obstacle vis-à-vis the full exercise of the rights deriving from the EU law. As individuals are entitled to bring actions against Member States to recover damages deriving from the infringement of the EU law, even if by fact of a judicial independent body, a way of protection comes out from this perspective, although indirect and incomplete.[149]

§7. The Preliminary Rulings Proceedings

94. Preliminary proceedings are ruled by the special provisions contained in Article 23 of the Statute and by the whole title III of the Rules of Procedure of the CJ, which emphasizes the specialties that distinguish them from direct actions. There is not yet a specific discipline for cases where preliminary rulings proceeding will be (eventually) brought before the General Court.

They are shaped on the pattern of the ordinary EU proceedings, with an important difference concerning the beginning of the written stage.

In fact, pursuant to the Statute, the decision of the court or tribunal of a Member State which suspends its proceedings and refers a case to the Court shall be notified to the Court by the judiciary body concerned.[150]

Then, the decision shall be notified by the Registrar of the Court to the parties at national proceedings, to all Member States, and to the Commission, and also to the institution, body, office, or agency which adopted the Act the validity or interpretation of which is in dispute.[151] Within two months of this notification, all these subjects shall be entitled to submit statements of case or written observations to the Court. This means, first, that the number of potential parties at the preliminary proceedings is determined; then, that not all of them will take an active position, but only those ones whose political and economic interests might be sensibly affected by the decision; lastly, that each statement is submitted separately, so that no party may read the others' observations and no reply is allowed in the written stage.

---

148. *See* CJ, 6 Oct. 2021, C-561/19, *Consorzio Italian Management and Catania Multiservizi SpA v. Rete Ferroviaria Italiana,* ECR, 799 (already quoted).
149. The reference is made to cases: CJ, 30 Sep. 2003, C-224/01, *Köbler*, ECR, I, 10239; CJ, 9 Dec. 2003, C-129/00, *Commissione v. Italia*, ECR, I, 14637 (already quoted); and, more recently, CJ, 13 Jun. 2006, C-173/03, *Traghetti del Mediterraneo*, ECR, I, 5177.
150. As stated in CJ, 6 Oct. 2021, C-561/19, *Consorzio Italian Management and Catania Multiservizi SpA v. Rete Ferroviaria Italiana,* ECR, 799 (already quoted).
151. Article 23(1) of the Statute.

The order for reference must be succinct but sufficiently complete and contain all the relevant information to give the Court and the parties entitled to submit observations a clear understanding of the factual and legal context of the proceedings. In particular, according to Article 94 RP CJ, the order for reference must contain: (a) a summary of the subject matter of the dispute and the relevant findings of fact as determined by the referring court or tribunal or, at least, an account of the facts on which the questions are based; (b) the tenor of any national provisions applicable in the case and, where appropriate, the relevant national case law; (c) a statement of the reasons which prompted the referring court or tribunal to inquire about the interpretation or validity of certain provisions of EU law and the relationship between those provisions and the national legislation applicable to the main proceedings.

The CJ Rules of Procedure establish that the proceeding is regulated by the common rules described in title II and the special rules described in title III. This clearly outlines the specificity of preliminary ruling proceedings.

The adversarial debate will take place at the oral hearing, the performance of which is not absolutely ensured, since the Court might omit it. It has to be noted that Article 76 RP CJ is applied to preliminary rulings proceedings; it states that the oral part takes place upon request from the parties and, in any case, after the Court has assessed its suitability. Due to a tendency to compress oral procedures, any reasoned request for a hearing shall be submitted within three weeks after notification of the closing of the written part of the procedure. On the proposal from the Judge-Rapporteur and after hearing the Advocate-General, the Court may decide that no oral hearing is needed where it considers that it has sufficient information based on the pleadings or observations submitted during the written part of the procedure.[152] However, the Court is bound by a reasoned request when it has been submitted by an interested person referred to in Article 23 of the Statute who did not participate in the written part of the procedure.[153] The goal to involve States or institutions which, for various reasons, could not take part in the written phase is evident.

It is possible to add that an oral hearing is more necessary when the content of the observations is innovative, with reference to the issues discussed in national proceedings (for instance, by the Commission). It must be said that the Court usually takes care not to forbid the possibility of an open, large confrontation between the parties.

95. The need for simplification and reduction of the workload have led to insert in the Rules of Procedure some specific rules which make the Court able not only to decide by reasoned order referring to its previous judgments, but also to state the inadmissibility of the reference, without hearing the interested parties, with a hard limitation of the right to be heard.

In fact, where a question referred to the Court for a preliminary ruling is identical to a question on which the Court has already ruled, where the reply to such a question may be clearly deduced from existing case law or where the answer to the question referred for a preliminary ruling admits of no reasonable doubt, the Court may at any time, on a proposal from the Judge-Rapporteur and after hearing the

152. Article 76(2) RP CJ.
153. Article 76(3) RP CJ.

Advocate-General decide to rule by reasoned order.[154] This result is achieved (the point has to be underlined) without any obligation to hear the interested parties before deciding. Such orders may not be appealed and close the preliminary proceedings.

96. The CJ Rules of Procedure apply all the provisions of not only the first but also the second title of the Rules to the preliminary ruling proceedings. Therefore, except for the introductory phase, the other differences tend to lose momentum. First, the language of the case is the same of the national case, from which the reference has come.[155] Then, if the party before the national court was advised by a counsel, who is not a lawyer, the same counsel is entitled to represent the party before the CJ too.[156] Lastly, no intervention by third parties is admitted and only the subjects mentioned in Article 23 of the Statute are allowed to submit statements or observations.[157]

As for the rest, the common EU procedure rules are applied. It should be added that searching evidence is possible also in the preliminary proceedings.

97. Except when it decides by reasoned order, the CJ usually decides preliminary questions by judgment. All judgments are published on the European Court Report (ECR) in digital form and may be easily read on the website of the European judiciary. Unfortunately, preliminary proceedings are not quick. On average, decisions are taken about sixteen months after the beginning of the case; however, the length of the preliminary proceeding is significantly reduced in case of urgent preliminary ruling procedures (about four months).[158]

The consideration of the excessive duration of proceedings has recently led to the introduction of two different kinds of simplification: on the one hand, an accelerate procedure for preliminary rulings and, on the other hand, an urgent procedure.[159]

98. First, the common scheme of the accelerated procedure has been adapted to the preliminary proceedings. At the request of the national referring court or, exceptionally, of his own motion, the President of the Court may, where the nature of the case requires that it be dealt with within a short time, after hearing the Judge-Rapporteur and the Advocate-General, decide that a reference for a preliminary ruling is to be determined pursuant to an expedited procedure derogating from the provisions of common Rules.[160]

---

154. Article 99 RP CJ.
155. According to Art. 38(4) RP CJ, notwithstanding the foregoing provisions, a Member State shall be entitled to use its official language when taking part in preliminary ruling proceedings, when intervening in a case before the Court or when bringing a matter before the Court pursuant to Art. 259 TFEU.
156. Article 97(3) RP CJ.
157. Article 97(2) RP CJ.
158. *See The Year in Review, Annual Report 2021*, available on http://www.curia.europa.eu.
159. J. Inghelram, 'Quelques réflexions relatives à l'utilisation de la procédure préjudicielle simplifiée par la Cour de Justice des CE', *Dir. Un. eur.* (2007): 285 et seq.; P. Biavati, 'Profili critici del contraddittorio nel procedimento pregiudiziale europeo', *Studi in onore di Carmine Punzi*, vol. V, (Turin: Giappichelli, 2008), 379 et seq.
160. Article 105 RP CJ.

The requirements for the application of the accelerated procedure are therefore, on the one hand, the request of the national judge and, on the other hand, a discretionary evaluation from the Court, about the opportunity of speed decision of the proceedings (and a reference to the existence of an exceptional urgency is no longer present, unlike the previous text of the rules). In that event, the President immediately fixes the date for the hearing; parties, institutions, and Member States may lodge statements or written observations within a short period prescribed by the President, which shall not be less than fifteen days. Nevertheless, having regard to the nature and importance of the questions referred, according to Article 53(3) of the Rule of Procedure of the CJ,[161] the President may, in special circumstances, decide that a case be given priority over others. Article 53(3) enables the CJ to comply with the principle of procedural economy by guaranteeing the principle of a reasonable duration of proceedings.[162]

It is to be remarked that the President may request the parties and other interested person to restrict the matters addressed in their observations to the essential points of law raised by the question referred. The statements of case or written observations shall be notified to each party to the proceedings prior to the hearing (by widespread use of electronic data transmission).[163] Then, the Court shall rule after hearing the Advocate-General.

99. Second, the extension of preliminary reference to issues, which are characterized by the need of a very quick answer to the question, and above all to those belonging to the space of freedom, security, and justice, has led to the introduction to a kind of urgency preliminary procedure.[164] It should be observed that here it does not deal with an application of interim protection, but only with a very accelerated form of the preliminary proceedings. The urgent preliminary procedure may be applied only in controversies referring to the police and judicial cooperation in criminal matter and to the area of freedom, security, and justice in civil matter. The request for the urgent procedure usually comes from the national judge, which shall not only set out, in its order, the matters of fact and law which establish the urgency and justify the application of that exceptional procedure, but also, insofar as possible, shall indicate the answer it proposes to the question referred. In the first case admitted to the urgent procedure, the referring court relied on the need to protect a child against any possible harm coming from the litigation between her parents and on the ground that any delay would have been very unfavourable to the relationship

161. *See* Art. 53(3) RP CJ; Art. 67 RP GC.
162. In CJ, 21 Dec. 2021, C-497/20, *Randstad Italia SpA*, ECR, 1037, the Court, even though the requirements of Art. 105 RP are not fulfilled, finds that case should be given a priority treatment in accordance with Art. 53(3) of the Rules of Procedure.
163. Article 106 RP CJ.
164. Article 23a of the Statute; Arts 107–114 RP CJ. C. Barnard, 'The PPU: Is It Worth the Candle? An Early Assessment', *Eu. L. Rev.* (2009): 281 et seq.; L. Clément-Wilz, 'Special Procedure at the Court of Justice: A Focus on the PPU', in E. Guinchard & M-P. Granger (eds), *The New EU Judiciary* (Alphen aan den Rjn: Wolters Kluwer 2018), p. 307 et seq.

between the child and the parent with whom she did not live.[165] Yet, the President of the Court too, if the application of such procedure appears, prima facie, to be required, may ask the designated Chamber (composed by five judges) to consider whether it is necessary to deal with the reference under that procedure. It is to this Chamber to decide both on the procedure to be applied and, where the urgency exists, to answer the question.

As it concerns this special procedure, all subjects considered by Article 23 of the Statute are divided into two groups: the qualified subjects and all the others.[166] The first group includes the parties to the national case, the single Member State from which the reference is made, on the European Commission and on the institution which adopted the act the validity or interpretation of which is in dispute. The Member States other than that from which the reference is made and the other institutions belong to the second group. Only the qualified subjects are entitled to lodge statements of the case or written observations (within a very short period prescribed in the decision). Besides, the decision may specify the matters of law to which such statements or observations must relate and may specify the maximum length of those documents, pursuant to the usual care for sobriety in the pleadings by the Luxembourg courts.

Only later, the other interested persons referred to in Article 23 of the Statute shall receive the notifications of the decision to manage the case under the urgent preliminary procedure and of the observations of the qualified persons.

In cases of extreme urgency, the Chamber may even decide to omit the written part of the procedure, described above.[167]

Anyway, the oral hearing shall never be omitted. All interested persons (and not only the qualified ones) may take part in it. The Court hears the Advocate-General, but no written submissions are foreseen.

In the declaration annexed to the modification to the Statute, which has introduced Article 23a, the Council has invited the CJ to apply the new urgency procedure to cases involving the deprivation of personal freedom (and so above all in criminal matters), to grant to the interested persons time limits not shorter than ten working days to prepare the written statements and the oral hearing, and to care to close the proceedings within three months from the beginning.

§8. The Effects of the Preliminary Decisions

100. At the end of the preliminary proceedings, the CJ, unless it has held the question inadmissible, rules the case by a judgment or an order, explaining (expressly or with a reference to its prior case law) the correct interpretation of the point of EU law in discussion or establishing the validity or the invalidity of the Act

165. CJ, 11 Jul. 2008, C-105/08 PPU, *Rinau*. *See also* CJ, 12 Aug. 2008, C-296/08 PPU, *Santesteban Goicoechea*; CJ, 23 Dec. 2009, C-403/09 PPU, *Deticek*; CJ, 1 Jul. 2010, C-211/10 PPU, *Povse*; CJ, 5 Oct. 2010, C-400/10 PPU, *McB c. E.*; CJ, 27 Oct. 2016, C-439/16 PPU, *Milev*.
166. Article 109 RP CJ.
167. Article 111 RP CJ.

of the institutions which it has considered.[168] It is useful, therefore, to study the stability and the effects of the preliminary rulings. The preliminary decisions of the CJ have no force of res judicata (of course, in the meaning of this concept in the civil law systems), because it does not state on the merits of the controversy, which will be decided later by the national judge, whose judgment will have such force. The Court takes a lot of care to conserve the continuity with its precedents, but, strictly speaking, the same question may be submitted again from another national judicial body and the Luxembourg Court might change its mind about the point.

101. The settled case law has assessed that a judgment in which the Court gives a preliminary ruling on the interpretation or validity of an Act of an EU institution conclusively determines the questions concerned and therefore is binding on the national court, for the purpose of the decision to be given by it in the main proceedings; nonetheless, the authority of a preliminary ruling does not preclude the national court to which it is addressed from properly taking the view that is necessary to make a further reference to the CJ, when it encounters difficulties in understanding or applying the judgment, when it refers a fresh question of law to the Court, or again when it submits new considerations which might lead the Court to give a different answer to a question submitted earlier. However, the right to refer further questions may not be used as a means of contesting the validity of the judgment delivered previously, as this would call in question the allocation of jurisdiction between national courts and the CJ under the treaties.[169]

The ruling of the Court is binding for the national judge who made the reference and shall be applied in the proceedings, which the preliminary question arose from.

The very essential point of the EU preliminary rulings consists in that: the CJ makes a part of the whole job – the one referring to the interpretation of the issue of the EU law – which then goes to form the unique judgment on the merits by the internal judge. Should the Court hold the invalidity of an Act, such Act is not set off the EU legal order (like in the case of the decisions of annulment), but it may not be applied in the decision of the controversy, from which the question referred came out. Yet, in practice, a decision of the CJ denying the validity of an Act brings about the elimination of the Act by the institutions concerned.

But the effects of the preliminary rulings are not limited to the impact on the single national cases; on the contrary, their main importance consists in the definition of a point of the EU law, which has the consequence to clarify the living law for any person or institution in the Union. Also where the judgment writes the last word in a complex dispute in law, it must be held that no longer good faith exists for those who had considered true the opposite and losing interpretation. Under this perspective, the preliminary rulings have effect not only for the parties to the national proceedings but also for the third persons.

---

168. According to settled case law, the Court has to provide the national court with an answer which will be of use to it and will enable the national court to determine the case before it. Consequently, if necessary, the Court can reformulate the questions referred to it. CJ, 21 Dec. 2021, C-497/20, *Randstad Italia SpA*, ECR, 1037; CJ, 15 Jul. 2021, C-709/20, *The Department for Communities in Northern Ireland*, ECR, 602.
169. CJ, 5 Mar. 1986, ord., 69/85, *Wünsche*, ECR, 947.

Since the preliminary rulings interpret the EU law correctly, their effects go back in the time, up to the first moment in which the interpreted rule was introduced.[170] Of course, they do not affect those cases where the relations between the persons are already defined, because of the prescription or the res judicata. But their impact is sometimes so strong and involves so many relevant situations (where some relations had been managed for a long time in a different way from the EU law, as it has afterwards been interpreted) that the CJ has stated to have the power (which does not come from the wording of the treaties) to rule the effects of its decision in the time, with a balance between the principle of the efficacity since beginning (so-called efficacity *ex tunc*) with that of legal certainty and that of protection of good faith.[171]

§9. Expansions and Limitations of the Preliminary Rulings

102. The common structure of the preliminary references has been made object of some changes, in order to extend or to limit its application.

103. First, the CJ has received a task of interpretation by many conventions, operating outside the EU legal order, strictly considered. The most important of them has been the Brussels convention of 1968, on the jurisdictional competence, and the enforcement of decisions in civil and commercial matter, whose application is now very reduced, because of the introduction of the EU Regulation n° 44/2001 (today replaced by EU Regulation No. 1215/12).[172]

104. A very important limitation had been introduced by Article 68 EC, in the matter of the European space of freedom, justice, and security. Such rule forbade the national courts, other than the Supreme Courts, against whose decisions there is no judicial remedy under national law, to refer a case in this matter to the CJ. Therefore, the whole matter of cooperation in the field of civil justice could be brought before the CJ only by the supreme national courts. The effects of this limitation may be correctly weighted, if one thinks that about 80% of the preliminary references are made by judges acting in first or second instance. This rule has been discussed and criticized in literature.[173]

---

170. *See* CJ, 27 Mar. 1980, 61/79, *Denkavit*, ECR, 1205; CJ, 6 Jul. 1995, C-62/93, *BP Soupergaz*, ECR, I, 1883.

171. *See* in literature J. Kokott & L. Malferrari, 'La giurisprudenza della Corte di giustizia delle Comunità europee in materia fiscale: le limitazioni degli effetti nel tempo delle sentenze', *Giurisprudenza italiana* (2006): 1787 et seq.

172. *See*, *inter alia*, Collins, *The Civil Jurisdiction and Judgment Act 1982* (London: Butterworths, 1983); Droz, *Compétence judiciaire et effets des jugements dans le marché commun* (Paris: Dalloz, 1972); Gothot & Holleaux, *La convention de Bruxelles du 27 septembre 1968* (Paris: Jupiter, 1985); Hartley, *Civil Jurisdiction and Judgments* (London: Sweet & Maxwell, 1984); Kaye, *Civil Jurisdiction and Enforcement of Foreign Judgments* (Abingdon: Professional Books, 1987).

173. *See* P. Girerd, 'L'article 68 CE: un renvoi préjudiciel d'interprétation et d'application incertaines', *Rev. trim. dr. eur.* (1999): 239 et seq.; L. Garofalo, 'Sulla competenza a titolo pregiudiziale della Corte di giustizia secondo l'art. 68 del Trattato CE', *Dir. Un. eur.* (2000): 85 et seq.; P. Biavati, 'La Corte di giustizia delle Comunità europee e le questioni pregiudiziali in materia di giustizia e

The Treaty of Lisbon changes this scenario basically. The CJ has a general power in the interpretation of the EU law, without any distinction between the former three pillars of the Maastricht architecture.[174] Only some exceptions are possible; this is the case of the matter of the CFSP.[175] Article 267 TFEU brings back under the judicial control of the CJ most of the matter once included in the third pillar of the EU. The EU courts shall have no jurisdiction only to review the validity or proportionality of operations carried out by the police or other law-enforcement services of a Member State or the exercise of the responsibilities incumbent upon Member States with regard to the maintenance of law and order and the safeguarding of internal security. So, the common form of preliminary rulings is now applied in the field of civil justice cooperation and every court or tribunal, before which the question is raised, may refer the case to the CJ. The former Article 68 EC is abolished and no correspondent provision takes its place.

105. It has to be remembered the most important variation brought to the matter by the Treaty of Nice and conserved after the Treaty of Lisbon. Pursuant to Article 256(3) TFEU,[176] the Statute may lay down specific areas where the General Court shall have jurisdiction to hear and determine questions referred for a preliminary ruling. Where the General Court considers that the case requires a decision of principle, likely to affect the unity or consistency of the EU law, it may refer the case to the CJ for a ruling. Besides, decisions given by the General Court on questions referred for a preliminary ruling may be exceptionally reviewed by the CJ, where there is a serious risk of the unity and consistency of the EU law being affected.

This provision has not yet been enacted and the debate on its utility is still fervent. Surely, the workload of the CJ might be diminished and many very technical cases might be entrusted to the General Court. But some doubts remain, as far as it concerns a possible breach in the unity of the system of preliminary rulings; such unity, as everybody knows, has been up to now the strong point of the preliminary references machinery.[177]

Article 267 TFEU introduces a new paragraph in the former text of the rule. If a preliminary question is raised in a case with regard to a person in custody (which is possible, as a consequence of the new wider EU jurisdiction in criminal matters), the CJ shall act with the minimum of delay. The urgent preliminary procedure, already mentioned above, is the first application of this principle.

---

sicurezza: verso un modello alternativo?', in F. Carpi & M.A. Lupoi (eds), *Essays on Transnational and Comparative Civil Procedure* (Turin: Giappichelli, 2001), 201 et seq.; C. Cheneviere, 'L'article 68 CE – Rapide survol d'un renvoi préjudiciel mal compris', *Cah. dr. eur.* (2004): 567 et seq.

174. Article 19 EU.
175. *See* Art. 275 TFEU.
176. Former Art. 225 EC.
177. *See* the criticism by D. Ruiz-Jarabo, 'La reforme de la Cour de justice opérée par le traité de Nice et sa mise en œuvre future', *Rev. trim. dr. eur.* (2001): 705 et seq.

§10. PROBLEMS AND PERSPECTIVES

106. The machinery of preliminary reference has succeeded in having an enormous success, with great effects on the dynamics and the evolution of the EU legal order. Despite this, many problems are arising around it.[178]

First, it must be said that the increase in the workload of the Plateau Kirchberg judges has been remarkable and will probably further grow up, because of the enlargement of the EU law, both on the substantial and on the geographical field. Therefore, the delivery of judgments takes too much time and the Court is obliged to take care of very different questions, many of which are really not too important.

It should not be forgotten that preliminary rulings often play an important role in the progress of the EU legal order, even in such fields on which a full agreement among the Member States does not exist. Such an effect of anticipation brings about a conduct of the governments, not always in favour, but sometimes also openly hostile vis-à-vis the EU judiciary.

So, on the one hand, some reforms are proposed by the States, with the aim to limit the workload, but also the powers of the CJ; this is the case of the so-called limited preliminary reference and of the transfer of competences to the General Court. On the other hand, the Court tries to introduce reforms, which also are limiting its workload, but giving to it the discretionary power on the choice of the cases to be decided. The judiciary reforms maintain the power of the Court, but they often pay the price of a less effective protection of the parties; and this is not a small vice, taking into account the strategic role of the preliminary interpretation to enforce the EU law in the Member States.

It is not easy to find proper solutions; probably, the idea of pre-determined and not discretionary limitations to the admissibility of the preliminary references, applied by the Court itself, might better take into account the different and somehow opposite needs, giving back to the preliminary rulings their full effectiveness and preserving, at the same time, their authoritativeness.

178. C. Barnard & E. Sharpston, 'The Changing Face of Article 177 References', *Comm. M. L. Rev.* (1997): 1113 et seq.; G. Vandersanden, 'La procédure préjudicielle: à la recherche d'une identité perdue', in *Mélanges en hommage à M. Waelbroeck* (Brussels: Bruylant, 1999), 619 et seq.; A. Barav, 'Une anomalie prejudicielle', in *Dir. Un. eur.* (2004): 235 et seq.

Part II. Judges and Parties

Chapter 1. The Judges

§1. Number and Requirements of the Judges

107. The number of judges composing the EU courts, once fixed, is now variable, above all for what concerns the progressive enlargement of the Union. The CJ consists of one judge for each Member State (i.e., twenty-seven judges).[179] The General Court shall consist of at least one judge for each Member State; the number is fixed by the Statute, which envisages a progressive increase in the number of judges in the next few years, in order to have two judges per Member State (fifty-four judges in office as of 6 July 2022).[180] The consistency of the specialized courts is laid down by the regulation establishing each of them.[181]

108. The treaties establish the requirements to be appointed as a judge, with different, even if similar, wordings. The judges of the CJ shall be chosen from persons whose independence is beyond doubt and who possess the qualifications required for appointment to the highest judicial offices in their respective countries or who are jurisconsults of recognized competence.[182] For the appointment as a judge of the General Court, the rule about independence is repeated and the requirement about the ability for a simply high judicial office is laid down.[183] The wording used for the specialized courts is even a bit lighter.[184] However, the EU judges are chosen among very qualified jurists, above all university professors and magistrates.

The EU judges are appointed by common accord of the governments of the Member States (but in practice on the basis of a recommendation by the government of the State of each judge), for a term of six years and, after the Treaty of Lisbon, after consultation of a specific panel. The membership shall be partially renewed every

179. Article 19(2) EU.
180. *See* Art. 19(2) EU, Art. 254 TFEU, Art. 48 of the Statute, which provides that the General Court shall consist of: (a) forty Judges as from 25 Dec. 2015; (b) forty-seven Judges as from 1 Sep. 2016; (c) two Judges per Member State as from 1 Sep. 2019.
181. Article 257 TFEU. It must be noted that the UK withdrawal from the European Union had the effect of bringing to an end the terms of office of the UK Members of both courts with effect as of 31 Jan. 2020. The number of judges at the Court of Justice and the General Court was thus reduced with immediate effect as the UK left the European Union.
182. Article 253(1) TFEU.
183. Article 254(2) TFEU.
184. Article 257(4) TFEU.

three years and retiring members are eligible for reappointment.[185] When, every three years, the judges are partially replaced, one-half of the number of judges shall be replaced.[186] The members of the specialized courts are appointed by the Council, acting unanimously.[187]

109. Before any appointment of a judge of the CJ and the General Court, a special panel should be consulted. In fact, a panel is set up in order to give an opinion on candidates' suitability to perform the duties of judge in the EU courts. The panel comprises seven persons, chosen from among former members of the CJ and the General Court, members of national Supreme Courts, and lawyers of recognized competence, one of whom proposed by the European Parliament. The Council shall adopt a decision establishing the panel's operating rules and a decision appointing its members.[188]

The new rules try to enrich the weight of the considerations on the merit of the candidates in the appointment procedure. It is clear that the governments (and above all, the one proposing a candidate of its own nationality) are not bound by the opinion of the panel, but there is no doubt that such opinion will be taken into account.

110. A similar, though not identical, advisory panel existed in relation to the CST.[189]

111. The nationality of the judges of the CJ and the General Court is settled; they must be citizen of a Member State, at the rate of one or at least one for each State and, from 1 September 2019, there will be two Judges per Member State at the General Court.

However, the EU judges may be never considered as representatives of their Member States; when they take up their duties, the judges have only the task to ensure the application of the EU law, also in the event where a judgment would be delivered, condemning the State, which they are nationals of.

§2. Status of Judges

112. The high function assigned to the judges by the treaties brings about that a legal status is conferred on them, fit to guarantee their independence and impartiality and requires, at the same time, an exclusive dedication to the hard engagements, falling on them. The provisions concerning this point are laid down above all by the Statute and then more detailed by the Rules of Procedure.

---

185. Article 19(2) EU; Arts 253(2), 253(4), and 254(2) TFEU. *See* in literature H. de Waele, 'Belonging to a Club That Accepts You as One of Its Members: Some Further Thoughts on the Modern Procedure for Selection and Appointment as Judge or Advocate General', in E. Guinchard & M-P. Granger (eds), *The New EU Judiciary* (Alphen aan den Rjn: Wolters Kluwer 2018), p. 197 et seq.
186. Articles 9 and 47 of the Statute.
187. Article 257(4) TFEU.
188. Article 255 TFEU; *see also* the Council decision, 25 Feb. 2010, in O.J.E.U., L 50, 27 Feb. 2010.
189. *See* the Council decision, 18 Jan. 2005, in O.J.E.U., L 21, 25 Jan. 2005.

First of all, before taking up his/her duties each judge shall, before the CJ sitting in open court, take an oath to perform his/her duties impartially and conscientiously and to preserve the secrecy of the deliberations of the court. Then, they shall be immune from legal proceedings; that is stated in order to grant them an effective independence.[190]

The independence of the EU judges is also protected under the point of view of possible external pressures, which might affect their job. So, they may not hold any political or administrative office (and that is absolutely forbidden) and they may not engage in any occupation, whether gainful or not (but in this case, exemption is exceptionally granted by the Council).

Besides, the procedural rules take care to avoid that independence and impartiality of the judges be spoiled by any benefit, which they might obtain after their retiring, because of their high position. So, the Statute states that the judges, when taking up their duties, shall give a solemn undertaking that, both during and after their term of office, they will respect the obligations arising therefrom, in particular the duty to behave with integrity and discretion as regards the acceptance, after they have ceased to hold office, of certain appointments or benefits. Any doubt on this point shall be settled by decision of the CJ.[191]

The deliberations of the EU courts shall be and shall remain secret; this rule is another useful tool, in order to preserve the full independence of the judges.[192]

It is important to recall that the EU judges (as well as the Advocates-General) are helped in their work by a team of highly prepared jurists, called referendars, whose task is to assist them in the study of the cases, and above all of those assigned to each of them.

Two hypotheses of abstention of the judges are considered by the Statute. First, no judge may take part in the disposal of any case in which he/she has previously taken part as agent or adviser or has acted for one of the parties, or in which he/she has been called upon to pronounce as a member of a court or tribunal, of a commission of inquiry or in any other capacity. Then, if, for some special reason, any judge considers that he/she should not take part in the judgment of a particular case, he/she shall so inform the President; likewise, if, for some special reason, the President considers that any judge should not sit in a particular case, he/she shall notify him/her accordingly. Any difficulty about these points shall be settled by a decision of the Court.[193]

The General Court Rules of Procedure have introduced a special rule. Where a judge considers that he/she should not take part in the disposal of a case, he/she shall so inform the President who shall exempt him/her from sitting. In the event of any difficulty arising as to the application of this Article, the President shall refer the

190. Articles 2 and 3 of the Statute; Art. 4 RP CJ; Art. 5 RP GC.
191. Article 4, paras 3 and 4 of the Statute. Arts 5, 6, and 7 of the Statute deal with cases where judges design or are deprived of their office.
192. Article 35 of the Statute.
193. Article 18 of the Statute.

matters to the plenum. In that case, voting shall be by secret ballot in the absence of the Registrar after the Judge concerned has been heard; the latter shall not take part in the deliberations.[194]

The parties may apply for a change in the composition of the court, on the basis of the same grounds which lead a judge not to take part in a case; but such application is not admissible on the grounds of either the nationality of a judge or the absence from the court or the Chamber of a judge of the nationality of the applicant party.

Lastly, it must be said that the judges (like the Advocates-General and the Registrar) are required to reside at the place where the CJ has its seat, and therefore in Luxembourg.

§3. The Decisions

113. In the EU proceedings, the courts act by delivering decisions and giving opinions. Decisions have jurisdictional nature, while opinions have a consultative function. Two forms of decisions exist: judgments and orders.

114. The distinction between judgment and order is not very marked and it is going to become even less remarkable. Usually, judgments close the proceedings where the courts decide on the merits or even on a procedural question, after an adversarial procedure. The courts use orders to manage the case (such as to administrate evidence), or to decide it after a faster procedure, or to give interim provisions. Both judgments and orders may be appealed and the Statute uses the wording of final decision, just to include any form of judicial provision.

The European Rules of Procedure define the content of judgments and orders. Differences between judgments and orders are few. The judgments are delivered in open court, while the original of the order, signed by the President, shall be sealed and deposited at the Registry and then served on the parties and, if necessary, to the referring court or tribunal. Besides, sometimes orders, not subject to appeal, may not be reasoned.[195] All the EU decisions contain the grounds and a summary of the facts, the operative part, the signature of the judges, like the decisions in the national proceedings.

As a matter of fact, the Statute prescribes that judgments shall state the reasons on which they are based, shall contain the names of the judges who took part in the deliberations, shall be signed by the President and shall be read in open court.[196]

With more details, pursuant to the Rules of Procedure, the judgment shall contain: the name of the court which delivered it; the date of its delivery; the names of the President and of the judges taking part in it; the name, if any, of the Advocate-General; the name of the Registrar; the description of the parties, with the names of their representatives; a statement of the forms of order sought by the parties; a statement that the Advocate-General has been heard, if any; a summary of the facts; the

194. Article 16, paras 1 and 3 RP GC.
195. Article 89 RP CJ, Art. 119 RP GC.
196. Articles 36 and 37 of the Statute.

grounds for the decision; the operative part, including the decision as to costs.[197] The judgment shall be delivered in open court; the parties shall be given notice to attend to it. The original of the judgment is signed by the President, by the judges who took part in the deliberations, and by the Registrar and then is sealed and deposited at the Registry. The parties shall be informed of the date of delivery of a judgment.

115. As far as it concerns the way of writing them, the EU judgments are characterized by a remarkably long exposition of the grounds for the decision. They are divided into points, which may be easily quoted to find the exact part of the decision where the courts have made a certain statement in law or in fact. It must never be forgotten that one of the main tasks of the EU judiciary (and above all of the CJ) is that of affirming the principles of the EU legal order and to build the case law, with the goal to complete and integrate the rules of the treaties and of the secondary sources; besides, many a time the issues examined by the Luxembourg courts are very complex and require the description of complex economical and commercial questions.[198]

The reasoning of the courts is not only directed to the parties, but also to any person in the Union, since judgments have somehow a task of teaching the EU law: this is why they often contain references to the settled case law and show the continuity with the already delivered precedents.

116. The orders are usually reasoned (cases where they may be not reasoned are exceptional) and may usually be altered or revoked; sometimes, they may be enforced. Order is the typical management tool in the proceedings and is applied in the preparatory inquiry, in the joining of cases, in the suspension of the proceedings, in referring an action to another EU court because of the lack of competence.

Orders are also applied in deciding interim proceedings or where a case is closed in a faster way, without a complete finding on the merits (e.g., because the action is manifestly inadmissible or lacking any foundation in law). In other cases, order plays the role of a more simple judgment, without any relevant difference.

197. Article 87 RP CJ; Art. 117 RP GC.

198. U. Everling, 'Zur Begründung der Urteile des Gerichtshofs der Europäischen Gemeinschaften', *Eu. R.* (1994): 127 et seq.

Chapter 2. The Advocates-General

§1. General Features

117. The role of the Advocates-General is directly considered by the treaties. The CJ shall be assisted by eight Advocates-General. Should the CJ so request, the Council, acting unanimously, may increase the number of Advocates-General.[199] Until 1 July 2013 there were only eight Advocates-General at the CJ. Pursuant to Decision 2013/336/EU of 25 June 2013 this number was increased to nine on 1 July 2013 and further to eleven by 7 October 2015. The General Court is not assisted now by Advocates-General, but it might be assisted by them, under a future possible provision by the Statute.[200] Despite the UK's withdrawal from the EU, the number of Advocates-General of the CJ has not changed. In fact, unlike the number of judges, according to the Declaration of the conference of the representatives of the governments of the Member States of 29 January 2020, the number of Advocates-General was not affected by the UK withdrawal.[201]

The main duty of the Advocates-General is to make, in open court, acting with complete impartiality and independence, reasoned submissions on cases which, in accordance with the Statute, require his/her involvement, in order to advise the European courts in the fulfilment of their task to ensure the respect of the law in the interpretation and application of the treaties.

Each single case pending before the CJ is assigned to an Advocate-General, who follows with the judges every stage of it, up to the presentation to the Court of autonomous submissions, which consist in a global answer to the solution of the case in discussion. The submissions are a kind of 'parallel judgment'; they contain a description of the issue and of the questions of law, the examination of evidence, and the proposal for a solution. The Court uses them as a possible pattern for the judgment, with regard to its logical reasoning. The judges are not bound to the submissions of the Advocate-General, and not even to explain the reasons why they do not follow them. Yet, the submissions are really helpful and, above all in the first years of the functioning of the European justice, have given a relevant contribution to the decisions of the Court.

Under the point of view of the law, the submissions contain careful references to the pre-existing case law, and, when necessary, a comparative analysis on the legal orders of the Member States. Sometimes, the submissions suggest an original solution, which the Court may take account of.

---

199. Article 252(1) TFEU.

200. Article 254(1) TFEU.

201. It is the 'Declaration of the conference of the representatives of the governments of the Member States of 29 Jan. 2020 on the consequences of the withdrawal of the United Kingdom from the European Union for the Advocates-General of the Court of Justice of the European Union'. The declaration stated that 'the permanent post of Advocate-General which was assigned to the United Kingdom by Declaration No. 38 annexed to the Final Act of the Intergovernmental Conference which adopted the Treaty of Lisbon will therefore be integrated in the rotation system among the Member States for the appointment of Advocates-General. The rotation system will therefore involve the rotation of six Advocates-General. The Conference notes that, in accordance with the protocol order, the next eligible Member State is the Hellenic Republic ('Greece')'.

118. Nevertheless, the increasing of a relevant body of precedents make now possible to the Court deciding without the submissions of the Advocate-General, if the case does not raise new questions of law. Therefore, submissions by the Advocate-General are no longer mandatory; where it considers that the case raises no new points of law, the Court may now decide, even if after hearing the Advocate-General himself/herself, that the case shall be determined without any submission.[202]

Historically, the Advocates-General have played a very important role in the development of the European case law. Their work of assessment consisted of a true preparation of the case, by furnishing the elements of fact, but above all of law, useful to the decision; so, it may be easily understood how the propulsory role of the CJ in building the European legal order has been made possible, thanks to the cooperation of the Advocates-General.

As time is passing by, the function of the Advocates-General is going to lose some of its weight. The more and more adequate qualification of the judges, the progressive formation of an organic body of case law, the increasing of the workload of the Court: all of these lead to a less and less important role of this figure, as it may be clearly deduced from many factors: the modification of the Statute, which allows the Court to decide that a case shall be determined without a submission from the Advocate-General, as it has been stated above; the usual lack of the Advocates-General before the General Court (where, if it occurs, any judge may be called upon to perform the task of an Advocate-General); and, lastly, the absolute lack of the Advocate-General before the specialized courts.[203]

The Advocate-General is a quite typical figure of the EU proceedings, and it is very hard to find a reasonable comparison with other institutes in the procedural law of the Member States. It is better perhaps to define it stressing what he/she is not: he/she is neither a judge, nor an assistant of the judge, nor a representative of the EU institutions, nor a party. He/she is a person acting in the proceedings, with the task to be helpful to the court, by making his/her submissions and so somehow drafting a project of judgment, with which the judges may confront their own opinion and by which may be helped in the choice of the most correct solution. The latest evolution of the EU system clearly shows that this task is declining and still has a meaning only in the questions of law, while it is going to disappear with regard to the issues of fact.

---

202. Article 20(5) of the Statute. *See* J. Inghelram, 'Les arrêts sans conclusions de l'avocat général: aperçu de l'application, depuis le traité de Nice, de l'article 20, dernier alinéa, du statut de la Cour', *Dir. Un. eur.* (2007): 183 et seq.

203. T. Tridimas, 'The Role of the Advocate General in the Development of Community Law: Some Reflections', *Comm. M. L. Rev.* (1997): 1349 et seq.; D. Simon, 'Rôle de l'avocat générale et principe du contradictoire', *Europe* (2000): n. 4, 8 et seq.; F. Benoit-Rohmer, 'L'affaire Emesa Sugar: l'institution de l'Avocat général de la Cour de justice des Communautés européennes à l'épreuve de la jurisprudence Vermeulen de la Cour européenne des droits de l'homme', *Cah. dr. eur.* (2001): 403 et seq.; F. Benoit-Rohmer, 'Le commissarie du gouvernement auprès du Conseil d'Etat, l'avocat général auprès de la CJCE et le droit à un procès équitable', *Rev. trim. dr. eur.* (2001): 727 et seq.; C. Iannone,'L'avvocato generale della Corte di giustizia delle Comunità europee', *Dir. Un. eur.* (2002): 123 et seq.

§2. The Status of the Advocates-General

119. The Advocates-General assisting the CJ are now eleven. This number might be increased by the Council acting unanimously, should the Court so request.[204]

Like the judges of the CJ, also the Advocates-General are chosen from persons whose independence is beyond doubt and who possess the qualification required for appointment to the highest judicial offices in their countries or who are jurisconsults of recognized competence.[205]

The Advocates-General are appointed, like the judges of the CJ, by common accord of the governments of the Member States for a term of six years, after consultation of the panel mentioned above. Every three years a partial replacement is made and one-half of the number of Advocates-General shall be replaced. Yet, they may be re-elected.[206]

The common Declaration signed on 1 January 1995 has stated that five States (France, Germany, Italy, Spain, and United Kingdom) have always an Advocate-General appointed among persons of their respective nationality. With regard to the other three places, turnover among the other Member States is established. Should the number of the Advocates-General be brought up to eleven, according to the Declaration No. 38, also Poland would have an Advocate-General of its nationality and the rotatory system shall affect five Advocates-General. Nowadays, according to Declaration No. 38, annexed to the Treaty of Lisbon and Council Decision 2013/336/EU, increasing the number of Advocates-general, is provided that Poland would have a permanent Advocate-general and the turnover system among the Member States does not concern three but five Advocates-General.

The provisions of the Statute referred to the judges and above described, about duties, oath, immunity, resignation and depriving of the office, are applied to the Advocates-General.[207]

Every year, the CJ appoints the First Advocate-General, among the Advocates-General.[208] He/she has the task to assign each case to an Advocate-General and to adopt the necessary provisions, when an Advocate-General is absent or prevented from acting.[209] He/she has neither supremacy nor control on the other Advocates-General, nor powers of calling cases to himself/herself. Simply, he/she shall manage the distribution of the cases. He/she has also the task of proposing that the CJ reviews the decisions of the General Court, given in the appeal against the decisions of the specialized courts or in the preliminary rulings.[210]

204. Article 252 TFEU.
205. Article 253(1) TFEU.
206. Article 253 TFEU; Art. 9 of the Statute.
207. Article 8 of the Statute.
208. Article 14 RP CJ.
209. Article 16 RP CJ.
210. Article 62 of the Statute.

§3. Advocates-General and General Court

120. The rules relating to the General Court confirm the trend which has been pointed out above: the Advocates-General play now a role only when an important question of law is discussed.

As it has been said, no established body of Advocates-General assists the General Court. On the contrary, each judge may be called upon to perform the task of an Advocate-General. Of course, a member of the General Court called upon to this job in a case may not take part in the judgment of the case.[211] The function of Advocate-General may be performed by every judge, with the exception of the President and the Presidents of Chambers of the General Court.[212] The conditions about the calling upon of a judge to assist the General Court as an Advocate-General are laid down in the Rules of Procedure, and exactly the General Court may be assisted by an Advocate-General if it is considered that the legal difficulty or the factual complexity of the case so requires.[213] The decision to designate an Advocate-General in a particular case shall be taken by the plenum at the request of the Chamber to which the case has been assigned or referred. The President of the General Court shall designate the Judge called upon to perform the function of Advocate-General in that case. The Rules provide when the Advocate-General, after being so designated, shall be heard before the decisions are taken.[214]

Pursuant to the treaties, the Statute might provide, in the future, for the General Court to be assisted by Advocates-General, here intended as an autonomous body of persons.[215] This provision has not yet been enacted and it seems to be connected with the task of the General Court to give preliminary rulings. Should the General Court exercise such power, so the need of a help of submissions in law by an Advocate-General might become stronger. Anyway, before the General Court the function of the Advocate-General would never become necessary, but it would be limited to certain cases.[216]

The task of the Advocate-General before the General Court is the same as before the CJ. Moreover, his/her reasoned submissions may be made in writing, instead of being presented at the oral hearing.[217]

211. Article 49 of the Statute.
212. Article 3 RP GC.
213. Article 30 RP GC.
214. Article 31 RP GC.
215. Article 254(1) TFEU.
216. Article 49(2) and (3) of the Statute.
217. Article 53(3) of the Statute; Art. 112 RP GC.

Chapter 3. The Organization of the EU Courts

§1. The Court of Justice

I. The President

121. The President directs the judicial business and the administration of the Court; at the same time, he/she presides at hearings and deliberations (working in strict cooperation with the Registrar).[218] He/she is elected by the judges of the Court from among their number, immediately after the partial replacement of the judges, for a term of three years and may be re-elected.[219]

Therefore, two kinds of powers are assigned to the President. On the one hand, the powers dealing with the decisions in special cases (such as interim measures); such powers will be examined in the following pages of this book. On the other hand, the powers of organization which he/she exercises as the head of the CJ as an office.

Under this second point of view, the President, *inter alia*, directs the judicial business of the Court; he/she presides at general meetings of the Members of the Court and at hearings before and deliberations of the full Court and the Grand Chamber; he/she designates a judge to act as Rapporteur; he/she controls the work of the Registry and the other departments of the Court; he/she may convene the judges and the Advocates-General during the vacations. In few words, he/she has the role of the highest authority in the EU judiciary.[220]

II. The Vice-President

122. The modification of the Statute with Rule No. 741/2012 of 11 August 2012 introduced the role of the Vice-President into the European judicial system. He/she has to assist the President in the performance of his/her duties and takes the place of the President when the latter is prevented from attending or when his/her office is vacant. As President, he/she is elected by the judges of the Court from their number for a term of three years and may be re-elected. The Rules underline the Vice-President takes the President's place, at his/her request, representing the Court and ensuring the proper functioning of the services of the Court.[221]

The conditions under which the Vice-President takes the place of the President in the performance of his/her duties are fixed by Decision of the CJ No. 671 of 23 October 2012.[222]

---

218. Article 9 RP CJ.
219. Article 253(3) TFEU.
220. *See* Arts 9, 15(1), 20, 24(3), RP CJ.
221. Article 10 RP CJ. *See* K. Lenaerts, 'Les nouvelles fonctions de vice-président de la Cour de justice de l'Union européenne', *Rec. Dalloz* (2012): 2880 et seq.
222. In O.J.E.U., L 300, 47, 30 Oct. 2012.

III. The Chambers and the Validity of the Decisions

123. The CJ at the very beginning of its activity used to judge as a full Court, composed of all the judges. On the contrary, now it uses to sit in Chambers.[223]

The Court shall sit in three possible formations: the full Court, composed of all the judges; the Grand Chamber, composed of fifteen judges; Chambers composed of five or three judges. This organization has the goal to better distribute the energies of the Court, to face its workload. The treaties state that the CJ shall sit in Chambers or in a Grand Chamber and lets the Statute to provide on the matter (and so, to specify when in the former and when in the latter formation) and to establish if and when it should sit as a full Court.

The Chambers may consist of three or five judges. In each Chamber, a President is elected by the judges from among their number. The Presidents of the Chambers of five judges are elected for three years and they may be re-elected once.

The Grand Chamber consists now of fifteen judges. It shall be presided over by the President of the Court. There form part of it the Vice-President and three of the Presidents of the Chambers of five judges and other judges appointed in accordance with the conditions laid down in the Rules of Procedure. The Rules state that the panels are complemented by Judge-Rapporteur and the number of Judges required to attain the number of five and three Judges, respectively.[224]

The Court shall sit as a full Court (i.e., twenty-seven judges) in very few cases.[225] But the full Court may also decide cases of exceptional importance.

124. As soon as an application initiating proceedings has been lodged, the President designates a Judge to act as Rapporteur in the case. The Court assigns to the Chambers of five and of three Judges any case brought before it insofar as the difficulty or importance of the case or particular circumstances are not such as to require that it should be assigned to the Grand Chamber. The Court sits in a Grand Chamber when a Member State or an institution of the EU that is party to the proceedings so requests (and this is one of the privileges which distinguish Member States and EU institutions from the individuals). Other cases are referred to the Grand Chamber, according to flexible criteria, such as the difficulty or importance of the case or the presence of particular circumstances, which so require.[226]

The formation designed to decide is chosen taking into account the peculiar features of each case, which is an interesting example of flexibility. In fact, the formation to which a case has been assigned may, at any stage of the proceedings, request the Court to assign the case to a formation composed of a greater number of judges.[227]

---

223. Article 251 TFEU; Art. 16 of the Statute. *See* in literature, D. Edward, 'How the Court of Justice Works', *Eur. L. R.* (1995): 539 et seq.
224. Article 27 RP CJ.
225. Exactly, Arts 228(2), 245(2), 247, and 286(6) TFEU.
226. Articles 60(1) and (2) RP CJ; Art. 16(5) of the Statute.
227. Article 60(3) RP CJ.

The final decision, as to which formation the case ought to be assigned, is taken by order in a well-defined moment; exactly, after the closing of the written stage of the proceedings, on the basis of the preliminary report of the Judge-Rapporteur, after hearing the Advocate-General.

The Presidents of the Chambers are elected by the judges: for a term of three years the Presidents of the Chambers of five judges and for a term of one year the Presidents of the Chambers of three judges. The President of the Chamber exercises the powers of the President of the Court, insofar it refers to the work of that Chamber.[228]

125. Lastly, the quorum required as to the validity of the decisions of the Court has to be recalled. Since decisions shall be valid where an uneven number of judges is sitting in the deliberations, pursuant to Article 17 of the Statute, decisions shall be valid: (a) for the full Court, only if seventeen judges are sitting; (b) for the Grand Chamber, only if eleven judges are sitting; (c) for the Chambers, if they are taken by three judges. In the event of one of the judges of a Chamber being prevented from attending, a judge of another Chamber may be called upon to sit in accordance with conditions laid down in the Rules of Procedure.[229]

As it will be better described later, the EU procedural system, like most national legal orders, gives the task of managing the cases to a single judge, the Judge-Rapporteur.

IV. General Meeting

126. The ECJ Rules provide the figure of the general meeting. This is a meeting in which all Judges and Advocates-General take part and have a vote. In the general meeting, the Court does not judge but it takes decisions concerning administrative issues or the action to be taken upon the proposals contained in the preliminary report of the Judge-Rapporteur.[230]

V. The Seat of the CJ

127. The CJ has its seat in Luxembourg, at Plateau Kirchberg.

Nowadays, the offices of the EU judiciary are occupying many different buildings. The Court works in the Thomas More Building, the General Court in the near Erasmus Building. The offices of administration and the translating service are located in separate buildings.

228. *See* Arts 9, 10, and 11 RP CJ.
229. Article 17 of the Statute, Arts 34 and 35 RP CJ.
230. Article 25 RP CJ.

§2. THE GENERAL COURT

128. The organizational structure of the General Court is very similar to that of the CJ.

The President of the General Court is elected by the judges from among their number for a term of three years and he/she may be re-elected. If his/her office falls vacant before the normal date of expiry thereof, the General Court elects a successor for the remainder of the term. The way of the election is like the one of the CJ.

The President, in cooperation with the Registrar, directs the judicial business and the administration of the General Court and presides at the plenum, over the Grand Chamber and over the Chamber, to which he/she is attached, if any. As in the CJ, also in the General Court there is a Vice-President.

The General Court sits in Chambers of three or five judges. It may also sit in plenary session, or in a Grand Chamber, or even be constituted by a single judge, in cases and under the conditions specified by the Rules of Procedure. The flexibility of the composition of the deciding formations arrives here at the top.[231] The internal organization of the Chambers is the same as by the CJ.

The cases are usually decided by the Chambers of three or five judges; the General Court may sit in a formation with a greater number of judges only when the legal difficulty or the importance of the case or special circumstances so justify.[232]

The plenum is the full court composition in which all the Judges shall take part and have a vote and the Registrar is usually present. Its competence is specific on its decisions concerning administrative issues (i.e., constitution of Chambers, designation of an Advocate-General).[233]

As soon as the application initiating proceedings has been lodged, the President of the General Court assigns the case to one of the Chambers. The Chamber seised of the case, the Vice-President of the General Court, or the President of the General Court may, at any stage in the proceedings, either of its or his/her own motion or at the request of a main party, propose to the plenum that the case be referred to the Grand Chamber or to a Chamber composed of a different number of judges, if the legal difficulty or the importance of the case or special circumstances so justify.[234] The Advocate-General, if designated, shall be heard by the plenum before the decision.

The case shall be decided by a Chamber composed of at least five judges, where a Member State or an EU institution, which is party to the proceedings, so requests. Each case is then assigned to a Judge-Rapporteur.

The sittings of the General Court are valid, pursuant to the following quorum; seventeen judges for the plenum, three judges for the Chambers, and eleven judges for the Grand Chamber.

---

231. Article 50 of the Statute.
232. Articles 14 and 28(1) RP GC.
233. Article 42 RP GC.
234. Articles 26, 28 RP GC.

129. As it has already been noted, the General Court, differently from the CJ, may be constituted by a single judge.[235]

The single judge has been introduced by the decision of the Council n° 291/99, as usual with the aim to face as best as possible the workload of the General Court. It does not deal with a new judicial body, but only with the provision of a new way of deciding, in addition to the existing ones, in order to ensure to the General Court a great flexibility in its composition, having regard to the peculiar features of each case. Yet, the very restrictive rules about the application of the single judge formation have not let this innovation have the expected efficacy.

130. Some cases may be assigned to a single judge, pursuant to three criteria of predetermination relating to the subject matter, which are combined with the common criterion of the lack of difficulty or the limited importance of the case. Therefore, (a) cases relating to intellectual property rights; (b) actions of annulment or for failure to act or a suit for damages, brought by individuals, and staff cases that raise only questions already clarified by established case law or that form part of a series of cases in which the same relief is sought and of which one has already been finally decided; (c) cases relating to an arbitration clause. It is also necessary that the case, even if belonging to the above-mentioned groups, is relating to a not too delicate subject matter. Then, delegation to a single judge shall not be possible: (a) in an action for annulment against an act of general application or in cases in which a plea of illegality is expressly raised against an act of general application; (b) in staff cases in which a plea of illegality is expressly raised against an act of general application, unless the CJ or the General Court has already given a ruling on the issues raised by that plea; (c) in cases concerning the implementation of rules on competition and on control of concentrations, relating to aid granted by States, relating to measures to protect trade, relating to the common organization of the agricultural markets, with the exception of cases that form part of a series of cases in which the same relief is sought and of which one has already been finally decided.[236]

Lastly, where all those requirements are found, the case has to be fit to be determined by the Judge-Rapporteur alone, sitting as a single judge, having regard to the lack of difficulty of the questions of law or fact raised, to the limited importance of those cases and to the absence of other special circumstances.[237]

It is easy to note that this wording is too careful and is quite far from the experience of the national legal orders, which usually give the single judges (even if under the possibility of challenge before an upper body, consisting of a formation of three or more judges) the task to determine also difficult and complex cases.

The procedural ways of referring the case to the single judge are governed by the Rules of Procedure. It should be stressed, above all, that the decision to delegate a case to a single judge shall be taken, after the main parties have been heard, unanimously by the Chamber sitting with three judges, before which the case is pending. Where a Member State or an EU institution which is a party to the proceedings

235. Article 50 of the Statute.
236. Article 29 RP GC.
237. Article 29(1) RP GC.

objects to the case being heard and determined by a single judge, the case shall be maintained before to the Chamber to which the Judge-Rapporteur belongs.[238]

§3. The Registrar and the Services of the EU Courts

131. The role played by the Registrar in the organization of the EU courts is more important than that of the Registrar in most national procedural systems. In fact, the Registrar has not only the usual tasks of assisting the courts and the judges in their official functions and ensuring all the activities in support of the fair management of the proceedings, but he/she is also the head of the administration of the courts, with remarkable powers in matter of organization of the departments and of financial management.

The EU courts appoint their own Registrar and lay down the rules governing his/her service.[239] More detailed provisions with regard to the tasks of the Registrar are contained in the Rules of Procedure of each court and in the Instructions to the Registrar, established by each court. The Registrar has important procedural tasks too, as it will be better described in the following pages.

Pursuant to the Statute, the Registrar shall take an oath before its court to perform his/her duties impartially and conscientiously and to preserve the secrecy of the deliberations, to which he/she assists.[240]

As far as it concerns the role of the head of the EU courts administration, it has to be said that officials and other servants shall be attached to the CJ to enable its functions: they shall be responsible to the Registrar, even if under the authority of the President. The Presidents of the CJ and of the General Court determine, by common accord, the conditions under which officials and other servants attached to the CJ shall render their services to the General Court, being responsible to the Registrar of the General Court.[241]

132. Among the services of the EU courts, the translating service deserves a special consideration. It has the task, which is absolutely fundamental, to translate the statements in the proceedings, the decisions of the courts, the submissions of the Advocates-General. The enlargement of the Union and the multiplication of the procedural languages have made this service more complicated and difficult.

The Registrar has also the duty to arrange for the publication of report of cases before the EU courts and ensures the processing of personal data of the parties. A very useful source of information consists now in the already-quoted EU courts' website, which contains the text of the Rules applied to the proceedings, documents, the decisions of the courts, the calendar of hearings, and many other useful pieces of news.

---

238. Article 29(3) RP GC. Different rules on the delegation of cases to the single judge are established with regard to the procedures of exceptional review and to the control relating to judgments and orders (*see* Art. 162(2), RP GC).
239. Articles 253 and 254 TFEU.
240. Article 10 of the Statute.
241. Articles 12 and 52 of the Statute.

Chapter 4. The Parties

133. A party is he/she who acts or resists in the proceedings. Every natural or legal person who makes an application with regard to any means of judicial protection established by the EU legal order is a party, as well as those who defend or intervene in the case. The applicant becomes a party, because of the mere lodging of the application, notwithstanding the lack of admissibility of the claim, if such is the case. Therefore, any person who has complied with the procedural requirements to begin or to defend in the case is a party; and so, the Member States, the EU institutions, bodies, offices, or agencies, natural and legal persons.

In the EU proceedings two kinds of parties exist: their respective position is not perfectly equal. On the one hand, one must refer to the EU institutions and the Member States; on the other hand, one must refer to every other party which may be defined as private parties or individuals.

134. The EU institutions include the European Council, the Council, the Commission, the Parliament, the Court of Auditors, the ECB, the Committee of the Regions and, with regard to the cases brought by its servants, the CJ of the EU itself. As far as it concerns the Rules of Procedure, they include also any other body, office, or agency of the Union, whose acts may affect third parties, such as the EIB and the Economic and Social Committee.

135. The concept of private parties (or individuals) includes not only any natural or legal persons, governed by the private law, but also any legal person governed by public law, which is not a Member State. For instance, a German Land or an Italian Region (which are institutions endowed with public and even legislative powers under the constitutional laws of these States) is to be considered as a private party. It is not rare that applicants at Luxembourg are not nationals of a Member State (included private legal persons and undertakings, whose seat is out of the EU); their standing comes down from any link between them and the territory or the market of the Union.[242]

136. These two groups play different roles in the EU litigation; their respective powers and rights of protection are not equal, as well as their powers in the proceedings. That depends upon the international origin of the Union; the original contractors of the treaties, the Member States, and the institutions which they have created are not on the same level as the European citizens. The inequality of the parties is one of the main features of the EU procedural system.

One may speak of procedural differences, laid down by the written rules, between parties belonging to the two groups, and substantive differences. The procedural differences are described along the pages of this book: the reader has already met some

242. C. Harding, 'Who Goes to Court in Europe? An Analysis of Litigation Against the European Community', Eur. L. R. (1992): 105 et seq.

of them and will meet others. For instance, while the Member States or the EU institutions may always intervene in cases pending before the EU courts, the private parties have to establish an interest in the result of the case;[243] the Member States and the EU institutions are represented by their agents[244] and may request changes in the formation of the courts; an appeal to the CJ may be brought by Member States and EU institutions which were not parties to the proceedings before the General Court (while no equal power is granted to private parties).[245] The bill might go on.

The substantive differences, not founded on the Rules, are perhaps even more important. The Member States and above all the EU institutions have more information, a better know-how, more facility to get evidence, may be represented by very qualified agents (one may think to the legal service of the Commission), and they are therefore in degree to manage litigation before the EU courts, better than the private parties. This consideration is important, above all if the view is accepted, according to which the EU proceedings are essentially party-proceedings, not only with regard to the initiating of the case, but also on the ground of evidence.

243. Article 40 of the Statute.
244. Article 19 of the Statute.
245. Article 56(3) of the Statute.

Chapter 5. Agents, Advisers, and Lawyers

137. Pursuant to the European procedural law, the parties at the proceedings are obliged to be represented by an expert, which may be able to censure their technical defence before the courts of Luxembourg.[246]

Yet, this rule has different features, if one deals with a private party, or a Member State or an institution of the Union.[247]

138. The private party (in the wide notion aforesaid) shall be represented and advised by a lawyer, authorized to practise before a court of a Member State (or of an other State which is a party to the European Economic Area (EEA) Agreement). It is not necessary that the lawyer belongs to the same State of the party which he/she represents, provided he/she is a citizen of a country of the Union; therefore, for instance, a Belgian party may be represented by an Italian or a French lawyer, but not by an American or a Swiss lawyer.

The condition of the authorization to practise before a court belonging to the European judicial space, as above defined, makes any European lawyer able to represent a party before the judges of Luxembourg. The lawyer shall only be obliged to prove such authorization, lodging at the Registry a specific certificate.

An exception to these rules is given in the matter of preliminary rulings: as the proceedings on preliminary references are to be considered a stage of the corresponding national cases, the EU Rules of Procedure establish that as regards the representation and assistance of the parties to the main national proceedings, it shall be taken account of the Rules of Procedure of the national court or tribunal which made the reference. The goal is to make the representation of such parties easier. As a consequence, a party, if it is enabled to be represented to the proceedings without the mandatory presence of a lawyer under its national law, may act personally before the CJ too;[248] in the same way, the parties may be represented and assisted before the European courts also by experts, which are not lawyers, but are authorized to practise before that specific referring national court or tribunal (which, under the case law of the Court, may be sometimes a non-judiciary body). Other exception (which may be easily explained) is the application for legal aid, which need not be made through a lawyer.

The lawyer representing the party cannot be an officer of the applicant. The requirement to use a 'third party' as one's lawyer is based on a conception of the

246. U. Everling, 'Niederlassungsrecht und Dienstleistungsfreiheit der Rechtsanwälte in der Europäischen Gemeinschaften', *Eu. R.* (1989): 338 et seq.; G. Corso, 'Dalla disciplina comunitaria delle professioni alla libertà di circolazione del professionista. Il caso degli avvocati', *Riv. it. dir. pubbl. com.* (1992): 71 et seq.; Z. Jaqub, 'Lawyers in the European Community Courts', *The Legal Professions in Europe* (Oxford: 1993), 36 et seq.; V. Skouris, 'Common Lawyers and Their Influence on the EU Court of Justice', *Dir. Un. eur.* (2014): 685 et seq.; B. Wägenbaur, 'The Parties' Lawyers', in E. Guinchard & M-P. Granger (eds), *The New EU Judiciary* (Alphen aan den Rjn: Wolters Kluwer 2018), p. 255 et seq.

247. *See* Art. 19 of the Statute.

248. Article 47(2) RP CJ.

lawyer's role as collaborating in the administration of justice and as being required to provide, in full independence and in the overriding interests of justice, such legal assistance as his client needs.[249]

139. Rules about the representation of the States and the EU institutions are quite different. These parties shall be represented before the EU courts by an agent (usually, an employee) appointed for each case; the agent may be assisted (for what concerns the technical activity in the proceedings) by an adviser or a lawyer, also in this case authorized to practise before a court of a Member State or of a non-EU EEA State.

The choice of adding a private lawyer to the agent is obviously discretionary and depends upon the features of the case. The private lawyer may be chosen because of his/her specific qualification in a specific subject involved in the case. The States are usually advised by the members of their bodies of State lawyers. The Council and the Commission are represented, as agents, by the members of their legal services, which are a remarkable body of lawyers, with a great experience in the matter of the EU law.

It should be added that university professors being nationals of a Member State whose law accords them a right of audience shall have the same rights before the Court as are accorded to lawyers.

140. Pursuant to the Statute, agents, advisers, and lawyers, when they appear before the EU courts, enjoy the rights and the immunities necessary to the independent exercise of their duties,[250] above all for what concerns immunity in respect of words spoken or written by them concerning the case or the parties. The Rules of Procedure grant to agents, advisers, university professors, and lawyers (including those who are nationals of EEA States) some privileges and facilities; at the same time, they submit agents and lawyers to some controls, which give the judges a disciplinary power.[251]

The rules about control and punishment concern agents of the States and the institutions, advisers, or lawyers. Their conduct may be punished in three cases: when it is incompatible with the dignity of the court, or with the requirements of the proper administration of justice, or when such agent, adviser, or lawyer is using his/her rights for purposes other than those for which they were granted. In this case, the EU courts shall inform the concerned agent, the lawyer, or the adviser and the competent authorities to whom the concerned person is answerable.

On the same grounds, the courts may at any time, having heard the person concerned and the Advocate-General, exclude the agent, adviser, or lawyer from the

249. CJ, 29 Sep. 2010, ord., C-74/10 P and C-75/10 P, *European Renewable Energies Federation c.Commission;* GC, 6 Sep. 2011, ord., T-452/10, *ClientEarth c. Council.*

250. *See* CJ, 4 Feb. 2020, C-515/17 P e C-561/17 P, *Uniwersytet Wrocławski and Poland v. Research Executive Agency (REA),* ECR, 73. The Court stated that the existence of a civil law contract relating to teaching assignments between the University of Wrocław and the legal adviser representing it does not affect the independence of that advisor. The Court set aside the order under appeal and referred the case back to the General Court because it held that there was no risk that the defendant's professional opinion had been influenced by his/her professional environment.

251. *See* Art. 19 of the Statute and Art. 43 RP CJ.

proceedings by reasoned order, which shall have immediate effect.[252] As the incorrect conduct of the agent, adviser, or lawyer must not give prejudice to the reasons of the party, the order of exclusion brings about the suspension of the proceedings for a period fixed by the President of the court, just to allow the party concerned to appoint a new agent, adviser, or lawyer. Should the party fail to appoint another agent, adviser, or lawyer within such period, the proceedings would go on automatically.

The punishments described above may strike also the lawyers or advisers, appointed by a State or an institution. The exclusion from the proceedings may cause consequences in the national legal orders too, because it may bring about the beginning of punishment proceedings against the liable lawyer.

252. *See* Art. 46 RP CJ and Art. 55 RP GC.

Chapter 6. Costs of Proceedings

§1. Costs

141. The EU proceedings are not basically different from the rules which generally are applied in national proceedings; while pending the case, parties shall bear the costs of proceedings (except if legal aid is granted), but in the final judgment or in the order which closes the proceedings, the unsuccessful party shall be ordered to pay the costs, in favour of the successful party, if such party has applied for it in its pleadings.[253]

If there are several unsuccessful parties, the judge shall decide how the costs are to be shared. Where the party succeeds on some and fails on other heads, or if it appears justified in the circumstances of the case, the judge may order that the costs be shared or that the parties bear their own costs (which happens rather frequently). It is also foreseen that the judge may order a party, even if successful, to pay costs which it considers that party to have unreasonably or vexatiously caused the opposite party to incur.[254]

The recoverable costs include:

(a) the avoidable costs which a party has caused the court to incur (on specific order of the court, after hearing the Advocate-General, if present at the case);
(b) the costs for any copying or translation work, carried out at the request of a party, insofar as the Registrar considers them excessive;
(c) the sums payable to witnesses and experts;
(d) the expenses necessarily incurred by the parties for the purpose of the proceedings, in particular the travel and subsistence expenses and the remuneration of agents, advisers, or lawyers.[255] Yet, the modern communication media allow the partics to save travels and that must be considered with regard to the costs.[256]

It may be easily understood that any party saves most expenses (such as court or registrar charges), but it must pay its lawyers and experts, which is the heavier part of the costs. These costs are recoverable: they are the total amount, which shall be paid for by the unsuccessful party in favour of the successful one.

142. Usually, the Kirchberg judges decide which party shall pay the costs of the case, but they do not establish the amount, with the consequence that the successful party is not under control about the amount of the sum, which it claims for recovery.[257] Nevertheless, if there is dispute concerning the costs to be recovered, the interested party (and therefore the unsuccessful one) may apply to get an order

253. *See* Art. 38 of the Statute.
254. Articles 137 and 138 RP CJ, Arts 133, and 134 RP GC.
255. Articles 143 and 144 RP CJ, Arts 139 and 140 RP GC.
256. GC, 13 Jan.. 2006, ord., T-331/94 DEP, *IPK-München v. Commission*, ECR, II, 51.
257. M. Bierry & A. Dal Ferro, 'The Practicc Followed by the Court of Justice with Regard to Costs', *Comm. M. L. Rev.* (1987): 509.

about the issue. The court makes such order, after hearing the opposite party and the Advocate-General. The order may not be appealed and may be enforced.[258]

The Luxembourg courts may establish the amount of the costs for the remuneration of the lawyers which the unsuccessful party owes to the opposite party, but not the sum that the party owes to its lawyer. There is no European scale of charges concerning the lawyers and national scales, if available, are not applicable. So, the costs are fixed in the discretion of the judge, taking into account such aspects as the subjects of the case, its importance, the level of difficulty, the entity of the work carried out by the lawyers, the economic relevance of the case. The importance of the case under the point of view of the EU law, because of the novelty of the questions of law and the complexity of the issues of fact, may justify high fees and the presence of more lawyers on representation of the party.[259]

The Rules of Procedure take care of some particular cases. A party who discontinues or withdraws from proceedings shall be ordered to pay the costs if they have been applied for in the other party's observations on the discontinuance. Yet, upon application by the party who discontinues or withdraws from proceedings, the costs shall be borne by the other party if this appears justified by the conduct of that party. As one may notice, the Luxembourg judges try to avoid any form of vexatious litigation.

Where a case does not proceed to judgment, because there is no need to adjudicate, the costs shall be in the discretion of the court.[260]

143. For what concerns intervention, the Member States and the institutions which intervene in the proceedings shall bear their own costs (and the same happens for States which are parties of the EEA Agreement and the EFTA Surveillance Authority). The judge may order a private intervener to bear his/her own costs.

The Rules of Procedure of the General Court confirm the general rule; the unsuccessful party shall be ordered to pay the costs if they have been applied for by the successful party, but gives the General Court (e.g., in staff cases) the possibility to decide in a different way if equity so requires and even to order the successful party to pay some or all of the costs, if this appears justified by the conduct of that party. So, without any pre-established rule, the judge may decide on the costs, in a flexible way, pursuant to the features of each single case.[261]

258. Article 145 RP CJ; Art. 170 RP GC. Such sums shall be paid in Euro (Art. 146 RP CJ; Art. 141 RP GC).
259. Some examples: CJ, 30 Nov. 1994, ord., C-294/90, *British Aerospace v. Commission*, ECR, I, 5423; GC, 15 Jul. 1998, ord., T-115/94, *Opel Austria v. Council*, ECR, II, 2739; GC, 22 Mar. 1999, ord., T-97/75, *Sinochem v. Council*, ECR, II, 743; GC, 18 Mar. 2005, ord., T-234/01 DEP, *Sony v. Commission*, ECR, II, 1121; GC, 17 Jul. 2007, ord., T-8/03 DEP, *El Corte Inglés v. OHIM and Emilio Pucci*; GC 12 Sep. 2012, C-5/10, *Klosterbrauerei Weissenohe c. Torresan.*
260. Article 142 RP CJ and Art. 137 RP GC.
261. Article 135 RP GC.

§2. LEGAL AID

144. Also in the European proceedings it must be faced the need to grant the access to justice to those people who are in difficult financial situation. The venue for the cases brought by individuals (so, those who may need an economic aid) belongs to the General Court. This is why above all, the Rules of Procedure of this court are to be considered.[262]

Legal aid shall cover, in whole or in part, the costs involved in legal assistance and representation by a lawyer; pursuant to the Rules of Procedure, the cashier of the court shall be responsible for those costs.

145. There are two conditions to admit a party (not only a natural person) to legal aid: the party, because of his financial situation, is wholly or partly unable to meet the costs relating to the case and the action, in respect of which the application for legal aid is made, and it does not appear clear that the General Court has no jurisdiction to hear and determine the action in respect of which the application for legal aid is made, or if that action appears not to be manifestly inadmissible or manifestly lacking any foundation in law. Both conditions are assessed under a certain discretion and without reference to the criteria which are applied in the legal orders of the Member States.

The financial situation of the applicant shall be assessed taking into account objective factors such as income, capital and the family situation. Obviously, the party must give all information and supporting documents, such as (but not only) a certificate issued by the competent national authority attesting to his/her financial situation.

146. It is important to stress that the application for legal aid, which may be made before or after the action has been brought, need not be made through a lawyer (as it has already been remarked). The General Court has provided for the compulsory use of a form in making the application.

The introduction of an application for legal aid has the effect to suspend the period prescribed for the bringing of the action (and the time limit prescribed for the bringing of the appeal) until the notification of the order making a decision on that application or designating the lawyer instructed to represent the applicant. If the application is made before the action has been brought, the applicant must briefly state the subject of the proposed action, the facts of the case, and the arguments in support of the action, with the supporting documents; the judge has to be put in degree to assess whether the action is clearly inadmissible or unfounded.

Before giving its decision on the application for legal aid, the General Court shall invite the other party to submit its written observations, unless it is already apparent that there are no conditions to grant legal aid. The choice of the EU rules deserves to be stressed; the interest of the opposite party, to avoid that the managing of a case without the proper conditions may be financed, is correctly taken into consideration.

262. Articles 146, 147, 148, 149, 150 RP GC. *See also* Arts 185, 186, 187, 188, 189 RP CJ.

The decision on legal aid is an order. The order shall state the reasons on which it is based, only when the judge refuses the granting of legal aid (in whole or in part). Such order may not be appealed, but may be withdrawn at any time, if the circumstances which led to the grant of legal aid should alter during the proceedings. Of course, an order withdrawing legal aid shall contain a statement of reasons.

In any order granting legal aid, the court shall designate a lawyer to represent the person concerned. The applicant may indicate his/her choice of lawyer; if the person has not indicated his/her choice or if this choice is unacceptable, the Registrar sends a copy of the order to the competent authority of the Member State. In this case, the lawyer instructed to represent the applicant shall be designated having regard to the suggestions made by that authority. The courts may also decide, on application by the lawyer, that an amount by way of advance shall be paid.

147. Should the recipient of the aid win the case, the costs shall be usually paid by the opposite party, pursuant to the rules examined above.

Yet, despite any previous assessment, it may happen that the party, whom the legal aid has been granted to, be unsuccessful (or, however, be kept to bear its own costs). In such case, the courts fix the global amount of the disbursements and fees which are to be paid to the lawyer by the cashier of the court. Obviously, the problem of protecting the opposite party is to be faced; the successful litigator has to recover its costs vis-à-vis a natural person, who – as for definition – is unable to bear its ones. The court, in ruling as to costs in the decision closing the proceedings, if equity so requires, may also order that those costs be borne, in whole or in part, by the cashier of the court, by way of legal aid.

Part III. The Ordinary Proceedings

Chapter 1. General Features

§1. Introduction

I. The Ordinary Pattern in the EU Proceedings

148. Until 1989, the Rules of Procedure of the CJ were the only form of the European proceedings. Afterwards, the introduction of the CFI, and that of the Civil Servants Tribunal, the perspective of new specialized tribunals, and the enlargement of the tasks of the EU courts have strongly changed this situation. Nevertheless, the European legislator has the aim to maintain the unity of the procedural rules as far as possible.

Nowadays, the situation is the following. Before the CJ, there are common provisional provisions which then differentiate depending on the specificity of the procedure in direct actions where the Court works as a single instance judge in the references for preliminary ruling in the appeal proceedings. Specific rules exist for special proceedings. There are also direct actions before the General Court as judge in the first instance.

The rules in matter of appeal shall be studied later and here we shall take into account those referred to the proceedings in single or first instance.

The rules before the CJ and the General Court are quite similar; moreover, both judiciary bodies apply the rules of the Statute, originally drawn for what concerned the CJ and then extended to the General Court.[263] The wording of the articles of the rules is often the same and most differences may be explained because of the unequal situations to be ruled.

149. Therefore, the presentation of the EU rules shall pick up those features which are common to the different judiciary bodies, so defining an ordinary pattern in the EU proceedings. Of course, the differences of the rules, if any, will be underlined in the proper place.

Moreover, it should be stressed that in the EU proceedings the same rules are applied in controversies, concerning very different matters. An action for annulment or an action for infringement of the treaties or a claim for damages are managed in

263. *See* Arts 47 and 53 of the Statute.

the same way. After the Treaty of Nice, only one Statute has been applied to the controversies under the EC, the EAEC, the EU Treaty, and the further unification, consequent to the Treaty of Lisbon, makes this trend even stronger.

150. As it will be underlined, in this scenario of uniformity a relevant role is played by flexibility; the rules are bent to the peculiar features, not of a single judiciary body or of a determined subject, but of the specific cases managed by the courts. This flexibility is helped by the peculiar form of organization of the EU courts and could hardly be transferred, in the same way, in the mass management of the national proceedings. Yet, some of this may be considered as a possible reference for the procedural national rules of the Member States, in the view of the harmonization foreseen by Article 81 TFEU.[264]

The good practice of flexibility brings about other problems. The risk consists now in the excessive facility in the modification of the procedural rules and in the tendency of the courts to apply discretionary measures in the cases (e.g., in the name of the 'proper administration of justice'). Flexibility and discretion are quite different notions, even if in the concrete application the border is sometimes faint. The cultural basic statement is the protection of the right of the defence, in the light of which the concrete conduct of the courts should be made object of evaluation.

II. Outline

151. Till the introduction of the CFI, the concept of the European proceedings might be identified with the proceedings before the CJ, before which the whole of the European jurisdiction was concentrated. Now, the word 'EU proceedings' defines the proceedings before the two bodies of the EU judiciary (the CJ and the General Court). In our opinion, it is not correct to define EU proceedings as the ones before the national courts, even if they apply the EU law.

It is not possible to speak of jurisdictional proceedings where EU bodies, which are not the EU courts, have the power to decide controversies, with the respect of the right of the defence of the concerned persons. This is the case of the pre-contentious stages in the proceedings relating to intellectual property rights or of the proceedings before the EU Commission in antitrust matter, ruled by the EU Regulation No. 1/03. Even if it has to be said that one must go towards the perspective of overcoming old and obsolete patterns, and globally study the protection of the rights at any decision level, the true jurisdictional proceedings must be distinguished from other proceedings that have some elements in common with them.

152. The EU jurisdictional proceedings should ensure the full respect of the essential requirements now established by Article 47 of the Charter of the Fundamental Rights, which had already been generally acknowledged by the European case law. So, the following rights shall be granted:

264. P. Biavati, 'Il processo a struttura elastica nell'esperienza comunitaria', *Riv. trim. dir. proc. civ.* (1994): 113 et seq.

(a) the right to an effective remedy to the protections of rights and freedom guarantees by the EU law;
(b) the right to a fair and public hearing, within a reasonable time, by an independent and impartial tribunal previously established by law;[265]
(c) the possibility for every person of being advised, defended, and represented;
(d) legal aid to those who lack sufficient resources, insofar as such aid is necessary to ensure effective access to justice.

153. The main features of the EU proceedings are the following ones.

First, the proceedings before the Kirchberg courts are above all written. The procedure before the EU courts consists of two parts, written and oral, but it is sufficient to look at the list of the activities included in each of them to perceive a clear prevalence of the written ones.

The written procedure – in the wording of the Statute – shall consist of communication to the parties and to the EU institutions whose decisions are in dispute, of applications, statements of case, defences and observations, and of replies, if any, as well as of all papers and documents in support or of certified copies of them.

The oral procedure shall consist of the hearing by the Court of agents, advisers, lawyers, and of the submissions of the Advocate-General, as well as the hearing, if any, of witnesses and experts.[266]

Also a preparatory inquiry may find place; and here a remarkable prevailing of the written elements is to be stressed. Then, the oral measures of inquiry are usually undertaken by the Judge-Rapporteur and not by the deciding composition of the judiciary body. Therefore, the force of oral measures gets weaker, because the court shall decide the case later, taking into account what the witness or the expert said, not directly, but only reading the records relating such declarations.

The oral stage is getting less and less important. As it will be recalled, the CJ is generally entitled to omit the oral stage, which may be sometimes omitted also before the General Court.

The EU proceedings are adversary. Every statement and document is lodged and communicated, in order to make possible a full confrontation of the positions of the parties.[267] The right to be heard happens to be limited only in exceptional cases and, in such cases, proper remedies are established.

The main problem does not consist in the lack of rules stating the formal equality of the parties (even if the States and the EU institutions are sometimes put in conditions of privilege in comparison with the individuals), but above all consists in the substantial inequality between them. The legal specialized services, the facility to reach the sources of evidence, the direct knowledge of the EU administrative machineries give the EU institutions a remarkably greater force in the management of the cases.

---

265. CJ, 17 Dec. 2009, C-197/09 RX-II, *M. v. Emea.*
266. Article 20 of the Statute.
267. Articles 123, 124, 126, 127, 62, 64 65, 171, and 175 RP CJ; Arts 201, 206 RP GC. *See also* cases CJ, 10 Dec.. 1998, C-221/97, *Schröder and others v. Commission*, ECR, I, 8255; CJ, 10 Jan. 2002, C-480/99 P, *Plant and others v. Commission and South Wales Small Mines Association.*

The most ancient literature has often marked the inquisitorial feature of the EU proceedings as far as it concerns the activity of fact-finding.[268] The EU courts may certainly administrate any measure of inquiry of their own motion. But the concrete conduct of the courts – to which the rule of the burden of the proof and the parties' powers in the preparatory enquiries are to be added – shows that they rarely organize a preparatory inquiry (save the request for information or documents) and, if they do, they limit it to the measures of inquiry which the parties themselves have requested. This is why it seems better to define the EU proceedings as adversary (or more adversary than inquisitorial) ones.

Generally, the role of the parties in the EU proceedings should be more appreciated. The decision as whether to begin a case belongs to the parties only, and the parties are free to fix the subject matter of any case; no power in this being given to the courts, which may neither begin proceedings of their own motion nor decide further questions not stated by the parties.

With regard to duration, unfortunately the EU proceedings are not very fast. In 2021, proceedings before the CJ lasted on average about sixteen months; before the General Court, approximately seventeen months (but it increased to thirty months in cases relating to State aid).[269]

III. The Development of the Proceedings

154. The EU proceedings in first or single instance begin with a written application lodged at the Registry and served on the opposite party. This opens the written stage of the case, which includes a pre-determined number of statements: the defence by the defendant and, usually, the reply and the rejoinder. The statements in intervention by third parties should be added, where the courts have held the intervention admissible.

155. The written stage has the task of fixing the subject matter of the case. Only the parties may establish what has to be decided and no power is given to the courts on this point (even if the courts may raise objections to their own motion, but only within the questions brought by the parties). The parties may discontinue the proceedings and/or reach a settlement of their dispute; if so happens, the courts are no longer entitled to decide the case. Therefore, the principle of the party control over the EU proceedings may be stated.

When the written stage goes to the end, the Judge-Rapporteur presents to the court his/her report about the situation of the case and the steps which should be undertaken. The courts may prescribe a preparatory inquiry or any other measure of organization of the proceedings or begin the oral stage immediately.

156. The oral procedure – which consists basically in the debate in the public hearing, save where new measures of inquiry are instituted or completed – is no

268. *See* M. Brealey, 'The Burden of Proof Before the European Court', *Eur. L. R.* (1985): 250 et seq.
269. *Judicial Activity, 2021*, available on http://www.curia.europa.eu.

longer a necessary stage in the EU proceedings; since 1991, many amendments have made possible to omit such stage, in different cases.

157. The courts are endowed with a remarkable power of direction of the proceedings, made stronger by the measures of organization of procedure. It is correct to say that a case may arrive at the final decision also where the applicant remains inactive and that the management of the case belongs to the courts, but nevertheless the parties may play an active role; one may think, for instance, to their contribution in the choice, as whether to omit the oral stage or not.

The EU courts have a wide power in the preparatory inquiry: they may administrate all the measures of inquiry foreseen by the Rules of Procedure of their own motion. Yet, such power is referred only to those facts which the parties have alleged in their statements and pleadings, and the parties themselves are in degree to be active in fact-finding, which is coherent with their duty to bear the burden of the proof of the facts that they state in the proceedings.

158. Moreover, it is very important to stress that the EU proceedings are getting more and more flexible; in other words, some differences are possible, according to the features of the different cases. Where the circumstances of the case make it proper, the courts are entitled to decide the controversy in the merits with more simple and expedite procedures. It should be noted that the cases always begin following the ordinary rules and only afterwards the courts, taking into account the features of the case, may opt to follow a different procedural path.

A remarkable example of such flexibility is the possibility for the EU courts to issue practice rules relating, in particular, to the preparations for and conduct of hearings before them and to the lodging of written pleadings or observations. Both EU judiciary bodies have used such possibility and the practice directions are getting an important tool in the case management.[270]

The practice rules deal with many arguments: the way of using the technical means of communication, the way of redacting and the length itself of the statements, the oral hearings, with the specification of how much time is given to any lawyer in the debate. They are an interesting form of modern proceedings, consisting of transparency, information to the lawyers and the citizens, more simple rules. The procedural rules are not considered as obstacles or traps, but as means in order to get a better and more adequate management of the case. At the same time, consulting the practice rules is an essential duty for the lawyers, to ensure a correct redaction of the pleadings, and a fruitful use of the oral debate. Besides, in some cases, the rules may be brought up to the level of the admissibility of some procedural activities, because of the powers given to the Registrar to order the parties to comply with them.

In recent years, practice rules have become increasingly more important, up to the point that they sometimes are the juridical basis for inadmissibility of claims. In this respect, the expression 'procedural soft law' appears to be legitimate.[271]

---

270. *See* Art. 208 RP CJ; Art. 224 RP GC.
271. *See* CJ, 22 Sep. 2011, C-426/10, *Bell & Ross v. UAMI.*

§2. Service

159. In the EU proceedings, all communications are made by the Registrar.[272]

For service, the new Rules provide telefax and, above all, electronic means. In the Rules of the CJ, electronic service is only possible where the addressee (i.e., to say, a lawyer or an agent during a proceeding) has agreed; before the General Court, it is also possible to serve documents on lawyers and agents in this way, where they agree by stating it in the application or in the defence.[273]

By decision of 11 July 2018, the General Court has determined that, for the lodging and service of procedural documents in proceedings before it, it is mandatory to use electronic means, in particular, the information technology application known as 'e-Curia'. Procedural documents, including judgments and orders, shall be served by e-Curia on the holders of access accounts in the cases which concern them.

Where, for technical reasons or on account of the nature or length of the document, transmission by telefax or any other technical means of communication is impossible or impracticable, the document shall be served at that person's address for service or, if the addressee has not specified an address for service, at his/her address by the dispatch of a copy of the document by registered post with a form for acknowledgement of receipt. The addressee shall be so informed by telefax or any other technical means of communication. Service shall then be deemed to have been effected on the addressee by registered post on the tenth day following the lodging of the registered letter at the post office of the place in which the Court has its seat, unless it is shown by the acknowledgement of receipt that the letter was received on a different date or the addressee informs the Registrar, within three weeks of being informed by telefax or any other technical means of communication, that the document to be served has not reached him.[274]

In the European order, services are effected when the document is received by the addressee.

When a document is served by the dispatch of a copy of the document by registered post, service shall then be deemed to be duly effected by the lodging of the registered letter at the post office of the place in which the Court has its seat.

§3. Time Limits and Preclusions

160. Two kinds of time limits exist in the EU proceedings: periods of time to bring the claim and periods of time for the taking of any step in the proceedings. Only the latter are to be considered as procedural time limits *sensu stricto*.

It is useful to underline that the rules about these two kinds of time limits are the same, save some exceptions. Yet, the time limits to bring the claim are bound to the substantive structure of each single kind of remedy; the rules about them may not be altered by the judge; any breach about them may be raised by the judge of its own motion.

---

272. Article 20(3) of the Statute; Art. 48(1) RP CJ; Art. 57(1) RP GC.
273. Article 121 RP CJ; Arts 77, 81, 177, 180, 194, 199 RP GC.
274. Article 48 RP CJ; Art. 57 RP GC.

So, while the procedural time limits may be extended by whoever prescribed them, the time limits to bring the claim are always peremptory, save the general rule, pursuant to which no right shall be prejudiced in consequence of the expiry of a time limit if the party concerned proves the existence of unforeseeable circumstances or of force majeure.[275]

The procedural rules which permit the extension of some time limits entitle the courts, their President, or their Registrar to modify the periods of time for the taking of any procedural step.[276]

The time limits are calculated according to the traditional rules *dies a quo non computatur* and *dies ad quem computatur in termino*.

In fact, when a period expressed in days, weeks, or months is to be calculated from the moment at which an event occurs or an action takes place, the day during which that event occurs or that action takes place shall not be counted as falling within the period in question.

Then, a period expressed in weeks, months, or in years shall end with the expiry of whichever day in the last week, month, or year is the same day of the week, or falls on the same date, as the day during which the event or action from which the period is calculated occurred or took place. If, in a period expressed in months or in years the day on which it should expire does not occur in the last month, the period shall end with the expiry of the last day of that month. When a period is expressed in months and days, it shall first be reckoned in whole months, then in days.[277]

A very peculiar EU procedural rule is that any prescribed time limit shall be extended on account of distance from Luxembourg by a single period of ten days, no importance being given to the place in the territory of the Union the party concerned has its seat.[278] The pre-existing rule, which distinguished the extension of the time limits according to the greater or smaller distance of each EU country from Luxembourg, has no longer reason to be kept in life, because of the nowadays facility of the communications. Moreover, any document or pleading may be received at the Registry of the courts by telefax, e-mail or any other technical means available.

Any period considered above includes official holidays, Sundays, and Saturdays. If the period would otherwise end on a Saturday, Sunday, or an official holiday, it shall be automatically extended until the end of the first following working day. It should be noted that the list of official holidays is drawn up by the CJ in a specific decision. The list includes the most important Christian feasts, such as Christmas and the Ascension Day (Easter being always included as a Sunday). Lastly, it must be said that period shall not be suspended during the judicial vacations, including Summer.

161. It is very important determining the moment at which a period of time begins to be calculated, above all for what concerns the time limits to bring actions.

---

275. *See* Art. 45 of the Statute. *See* GC, 28 Jan. 2009, T-125/06, *Centro Manieri v. Council.*
276. Article 52 RP CJ; Art. 61 RP GC.
277. Article 49 RP CJ; Art. 58 RP GC.
278. Article 45 of the Statute; Art. 57 RP CJ; Art. 72 RP GC.

The main distinction is between those EU measures which have effectiveness by the publication and those ones which shall be communicated to the concerned person. The time limits fixed for challenging a measure adopted by an institution run from the end of the fourteenth day after publication thereof on the Official Journal of the European Union (OJEU), where the publication is necessary; on the contrary, they run from the day after the concerned person has received the communication of the measure, pursuant to the common rules on time limits.

For what deals with the measures which are individually communicated, should the communication be not fully regular or effective, the time limits for commencing proceedings against them run from the moment of the real knowledge of them by the concerned persons. The burden of the proof of the date of knowledge is on the resisting institution.

162. The time limits to bring an appeal against a judiciary decision are fixed in two months running from the service of the judgment. Such time limits are peremptory, may not be extended, and their running may be raised by the courts of their own motion.[279]

As the time limits to bring actions may not be extended and sometimes the parties state to have been mistaken in calculating them despite their good faith, the EU case law has elaborated a restrictive notion of excusable mistake. It has been held that such a mistake is possible only in exceptional cases, where the conduct of the institution has caused, or strongly concurred to cause, a confusion admissible in an applicant acting in good faith, with the due diligence of a careful operator. It may not be excused the mistake of a party who has miscalculated the time limits, because a wrong information given by an employee of the Registry; neither it may be excused the mistake made by a party which is not adequately informed about the procedural rules.[280]

The Rules of the General Court underline that a procedural document lodged at the Registry after expiry of the time limit set by the President or by the Registrar pursuant to these Rules may be accepted only pursuant to a decision of the President to that effect.[281]

We have already said that no right shall be prejudiced in consequence of the expiry of a time limit if that depends upon the existence of unforeseeable circumstances or of force majeure. This rule should be interpreted stressing that no prejudice may derive to the person concerned, all the time long the referred circumstances have been existing.

The case law has tried to give a definition of unforeseeable circumstances or force majeure, which might avoid abuses. Therefore, it has been held that force majeure consists in facts which make the conduct referred (e.g., lodging an application within a date) impossible. An absolute impossibility is not held as necessary; yet,

279. *See* Art. 56 of the Statute.

280. GC, 15 Mar. 1995, T-514/93, *Cobrecaf and others v. Commission*, ECR, II, 621; GC, 1 Sep. 2011, ord., T-109-09, *Maftah v. Commission*; CJ, 15 May 2003, C-193/01, *Pitsiorlas v. Council and ECB*, ECR, I, 4837; GC, 24 Feb. 2000, ord., T-104/99, *Bolderaja and others v. Council*, ECR, II, 451; CJ, 27 Nov. 2007, ord., C-163/07, *Diy-Mar Insaat v. Commission*, ECR, I, 10125.

281. Article 62 RP GC.

the invoked circumstances should be quite unusual, independent from the will of the concerned person and unavoidable, despite the adoption of any reasonable precaution.[282]

§4. LANGUAGES

163. The chapter of the language of cases, often a secondary one in the study of the national civil procedural laws, is absolutely important for what concerns the EU proceedings. It is a part of the wider and more complex question of the multilingual organization of the EU.[283]

Two options are possible in this subject: or permitting any party to use its own language or adopting only one language for each case. The EU procedural law follows the latter solution (at last, as a trend, because the Member States have the privilege to be entitled to use their official language), by this way ensuring more unity to proceedings, but being obliged to face the question of the protection of the right of defence of the parties.

In fact, it frequently happens that the parties to proceedings are natural or legal persons of different language. The EU system has therefore to ensure to any party the possibility to state its defence at the best level, with the conscience that using a language which is not its own is a concrete obstacle to the full exercise of the party's right of defence.

In itself, the multilingual system is a knot without solution, above all for persons belonging to the smallest Member States. The parties will be compelled to present their pleas and arguments at the oral hearing and to take evidence before judges, who may understand them only by a translation, even if a very well done one. The impact of language barriers has not a small weight as far as it concerns the tendency to use written and documentary evidence, instead of oral evidence, and to concentrate the best efforts in written pleadings. The enlargements of the Union to the new east countries have surely made the question more complicate.

164. The rules about language may be parted into two groups: rules concerning the choice of the language of the case, on the one hand, and rules which try to overcome the language barriers, as far as it is possible.

---

282. GC, 14 May 1996, ord., T-194/95 INT, *Area Cova and others v. Council*, ECR, II, 343; GC, 24 Feb. 2000, ord., T-37/98, *FTA v. Council*, ECR, II, 373; GC, 16 Mar. 2006, T-322/03, *Telefon & Buch v. OHIM*, ECR, II, 835; GC, 28 Jan. 2009, T-125/06, *Centro Studi Antonio Manieri v. Council.*

283. L. Sevòn, 'Languages in the Court of Justice of the European Communities', *Riv. dir. eur.* (1997): 533 et seq., and in *Scritti in onore di G.F. Mancini*, vol. 2, (Milan: Giuffrè, 1998), 933 et seq.; M.P. Heusse, 'Le multilinguisme ou le défi caché de l'Union européenne', *Revue du Marché commun* (1999): 202 et seq.; N. Yasue, 'Le multilinguisme dans l'Union européenne et la politique linguistique des États membres', *Revue du Marché commun* (1999): 277 et seq.; M.Derlén, 'Multilingualism and the European Court of Justice: Challenges, Reforms and the Position of English after Brexit', in E. Guinchard & M-P. Granger (eds), *The New EU Judiciary* (Alphen aan den Rjn: Wolters Kluwer 2018), p. 341 et seq.

The language of the case shall be (in alphabetic order) Bulgarian, Croatian, Czech, Danish, Dutch, English, Estonian, Finnish, French, German, Greek, Hungarian, Irish, Italian, Latvian, Lithuanian, Maltese, Polish, Portuguese, Romanian, Slovak, Slovene, Spanish, and Swedish: so, twenty-four languages.[284] There is no possibility to use other languages, even if belonging to language or race minorities, such as Basque, Catalan, or Arab. The EU institutions and courts are obliged to know and use every language, among the twenty-four taken in consideration by the Rules of Procedure.

As it has been stressed, only a language is used in each case. The chosen language shall be used in the written and oral pleadings of the parties and in supporting documents, and also in the minutes and decisions of the courts.

As a general rule, the language of the case shall be chosen by the applicant. Such solution may be understood, if one thinks that the applicant (not rarely, an individual) is a person prejudiced by an unlawful conduct, to which he/she has to resist by opposing the judicial protection, often within very short time limits. Should one or more pre-determined languages (such as English or French might be) be imposed, the equality of position of the single Member States would be broken and a serious obstacle to the access to justice, above all for private parties, would be introduced.

Yet, this rule has many exceptions.

Where the defendant is a Member State or a natural or legal person having the nationality of a Member State, the language of the case shall be the official language of that State; where that State has more than one official language (such as French and Dutch for Belgium), the applicant may choose between them. This specific rule has the effect to limit the general one to the sole case of an action brought against one of the EU institutions. The consequence is that the language of the case is usually the language of the defendant, save it is a multilingual defendant, where the language is the applicant's once again.

Besides, at the joint request of the parties, the use of another language for all or part of the proceedings may be authorized.

Lastly, at the request of one of the parties (except the EU institutions), and after the opposite party and the Advocate-General have been heard, the use of another language may be authorized, by way of derogation from the rules which have been already mentioned.

In the proceedings of appeal, the language of the case shall be the language of the decision against which the appeal is brought. Nevertheless, the parties may jointly request the use of a different language, or each of them may submit an application requesting the use of another language. The court deciding the appeal decides also on such request of authorization.

165. These are the rules which may be applied in the direct actions. In the preliminary rulings, the language of the case is automatically the language of the national judge who made the reference. Yet, on the reasoned application of one of the parties to the national proceedings, after hearing the other party to the national proceedings and the Advocate-General, the use of a different language for the oral

284. Article 36 RP CJ; Art. 44 RP GC.

stage only may be allowed. Where granted, such authorization shall apply in respect of all the interested persons referred of the preliminary ruling proceeding.

166. The Member States, when intervening in a case before the EU courts, when taking part to proceedings about preliminary or when bringing a matter before the Court with an action for failure to fulfil obligations are not compelled to accept the language of the case, but are entitled to use their official languages. This provision shall apply both to written documents and to oral statements. In each instance, the Registrar shall arrange for translation into the language of the case.

167. Whichever may be the language of the case, the Rules of Procedure try to face the problem of the language barriers and to put all the parties in equal condition in the proceedings. Therefore, any supporting documents expressed in another language must be accompanied by a translation into the language of the case. In the case of lengthy documents, translations may be confined to extracts; however, the courts may at any time call for a complete or fuller translation of their own motion or at the request of a party.

All this brings about a remarkable effort for the translators and interpreters of the EU judiciary. The possible language crosses are now 529; even the budget of the EU judiciary is hardly involved in this point. In practice, the courts organize the service of translation around five pivot-languages. A very good service of simultaneous translation in the hearings is ensured.

168. Up to now, we have dealt with the public stage of the proceedings. When the judges work in closed session, no interpreter is admitted and the debate is made in whatever language may let them communicate better: usually, French or English.

The texts of documents drawn up in the language of the case or in any other language authorized by the court shall be authentic. Texts in other languages (e.g., the texts of the judgments) are mere translations.

The case law of the EU courts has stated that the rules about language may not be considered as public order provisions. This does not mean that they may be violated with prejudice to the parties. For example, a decision where the rules about language have been violated may be appealed on the ground of a breach of procedure which adversely affects the interests of the party concerned.

Chapter 2. The Written Stage

§1. The Application of the Claimant

I. The Application

169. In the European proceedings in first or unique instance, the written procedure begins with the lodging of an application, whose formal requirements are controlled by the Registrar and the court and that shall afterwards be served to the opposite party.

An application shall state the name and the address of the applicant, particulars of the status and address of the applicant's representative, the name of the main party against whom the action is brought, the subject matter of the proceedings, the pleas in law and arguments relied on, and a summary of those pleas in law, the form of order sought by the applicant, and, where appropriate, the nature of any evidence produced or offered.[285]

Should these requirements fail, so the application, in the EU procedural system, would become inadmissible.

Name and address of the applicant do not give rise to any peculiar question. Of course, the applicant has to be endowed with the law conditions to bring the action. At the same way, the designation of the party or the parties against whom the application is made usually brings about no problem. The adverse party may be however identified by reading the wording of the application and the order sought (e.g., the annulment of an Act from the Commission may be requested only against such institution); should the pleas in law or the form of order sought be absolutely uncertain, the application would be inadmissible, because of the failure of the other requirements.

In the statement which begins the case, the applicant shall explain the issues of fact and law, which identify the action, both under the point of view of the admissibility of the application and that one of the merits.

170. Also in the EU system some basic and general principles of procedural law are valid: the courts' power to decide a case only on a claim by a party; the prohibition for the courts to begin case of their own motion; the courts' duty to state about the whole subject matter brought by the parties, but not beyond it; the right of the parties to be heard. The issues of fact and law shall be sufficiently explained, taking into account that, on the one hand, the court is to be put in degree to judge and, on the other hand, the opposite party has to be put in condition to defend itself.

171. The case law of the Luxembourg courts holds that any application should clearly and precisely state the subject matter of the proceedings and the summary of the pleas in law, just to enable the opposing party to adopt a position on the case in light of it and the judge to exercise its power of review and decision. Especially, the

285. Articles 21 of the Statute, Art. 120 RP CJ; Art. 76 RP GC.

issues of fact and law on which the claim is based shall be well specified in the text of the application; it must be possible to understand them, even if they are concisely exposed.[286]

Facts should be described clearly enough to include all the constituent elements of the plea: the application has to set out the precise facts and circumstances relied on. It is not necessary for the applicant to identify the pleas properly, by reference to specific EU rules; yet, the claim should be classified in one of the kinds of action considered by the EU legal order.

The form of order, which defines the relief sought by the applicant, includes both kinds of decision requested (a judgment of annulment of an Act, the condemnation of the adverse party to pay a sum of money, and so on) and the specific subject of the claim (the specific Act the annulment of which is requested or the amount of the sum sought for damages).

II. Features of the Application

172. For the purpose of the proceedings before the CJ, the application shall state an address for service in the place where the court has its seat (now, in Luxembourg) and the name of the person who is authorized and has expressed willingness to accept service. In addition to, or instead of, specifying an address for service, the application may state that the lawyer or agent agrees that service is to be effected on him/her by telefax or any other technical means of communication.

The failure of such requirements does not bring about the inadmissibility of the application, but it has nevertheless a heavy consequence for the claimant: all service on the applicant shall be effected by a registered letter addressed to its agent or lawyer and service shall then be deemed to be duly effected by the lodging of the registered letter at the Luxembourg post office.

Before the General Court, the application shall state whether the method of service to which the applicant's representative agrees is by electronic means or by telefax. In its absence, the consequence is identical to that envisaged for the CJ.

The original of the application (like the original of every other pleading) must be signed by the party's agent or lawyer and shall bear a date.

173. The EU procedural rules do not detail any formal requirement for the appointment of the lawyer, which cannot fail. In particular, the General Court Rules provide that where the party represented by the lawyer is a legal person governed by private law, the lawyer must lodge at the Registry an authority to act given by

286. GC, 18 Sep. 1996, T-387/94, *Asia Motor and others v. Commission*, ECR, II, 961; GC, 29 Jan. 1998, T-113/96, *Dubois and sons v. Council and Commission*, ECR, II, 125; GC, 11 Jan. 2002, T-174/00, *Biret International v. Council*, ECR, II, 17; GC, 10 May 2006, T-279/03, *Galileo International v. Commission*, ECR, II, 1291; GC, 19 May 2008, T-144/04, *TF1 v. Commission*; GC, 20 Sep. 2011, T-267/10, *Land Wien v. Commission*; GC, 25 Oct. 2012, T-161/06, *Arbor v. Commission;* GC, 28 Jun. 2000, ord., T-338/99, *Scheurer v. Council*, ECR, II, 2571; GC, 20 Feb. 2004, ord., T-319/03, *French and others v. Council and Commission*, ECR, II, 769.

that person.[287] The ways of appointment ruled by each national system may be considered proper. The identification of the lawyer or agent will be found in text of the pleading, which has to be signed by him/her. The lawyer is not compelled to lodge an Act of appointment, but he/she shall demonstrate the existence of it, in case of contestation.

174. The methods to lodge are now strongly, though not exclusively, limited to electronic forms. Before the General Court it is mandatory to lodge electronically by means of the e-Curia application, unless it is impossible to do so with a certain information technology system. Instead, before the Court, the possibility of lodgement in paper form is still present. If the paper form is used, the original of the application (like any other pleading) shall be lodged together with five copies for the court (three copies for the General Court) and a copy for every other party to the proceedings. Copies shall be certified by the applicant. In this case, remote lodgement by telefax or by electronic means is by far the preferred ones. It should be remarked that, in the reckoning of time limits for taking steps in proceedings, the date of lodgement of the application (like any other pleading) is not only that of the physical delivery of it to the Registry, but also the date on which a copy of the signed original is received at the Registry by telefax or other technical means of communication available to the court. In this case, however, the signed original of the application, accompanied by the mandatory annexes and copies, shall be physically lodged at the Registry no later than ten days thereafter. The CJ and the General Court may, by decision (and the General Court has already done so), determine the criteria for a procedural document sent to the Registry by electronic means to be deemed to be the original of that document. This practice makes it superfluous to lodge a paper document.[288]

In some cases, when appropriate, the application shall be accompanied by specific documents. First, the lawyer acting for a party must lodge at the Registry a certificate that he/she is authorized to practice before a court of a Member State (or an EEA State). If the applicant is a legal person governed by private law, the application shall be accompanied by the instrument constituting or regulating that legal person or a recent extract from the register of companies, firms or associations, or any other proof of its existence in law. Such legal person shall also prove that the appointment of the lawyer has been properly made by someone authorized for the purpose.

The application shall be accompanied, where appropriate, by the measure the annulment of which is sought. If the application concerns an action for failure to act, documentary evidence of the date on which the defendant institution was requested to act shall be alleged. If the documents are not submitted with the application, the Registrar shall ask the party concerned to produce them within a reasonable period; but in that event the rights of the party shall not lapse even if such documents are produced after the time limit for bringing proceedings.

In a dispute between the Union and its servants, the application shall be accompanied, where appropriate, by the complaint within the meaning of Article 90(2) of

287. Article 51(3) RP GC.
288. Article 57 RP CJ; Art. 73 RP GC.

the Staff Regulations and the decision responding to the complaint, together with an indication of the dates on which the complaint was submitted and the decision notified.

When the application is brought under Articles 272 and 273 TFEU, a copy of the arbitration clause has to be produced.

175. The compliance of the application with the formal requirements set out in the Rules of Procedure is controlled at two stages. First, if some requirements fail, the Registrar shall prescribe a reasonable period within which the applicant is to comply with them, whether by putting the application itself in order or by producing any of the required documents. If the applicant goes on failing to do that, the court (after hearing, when appropriate, the Advocate-General) decides whether the non-compliance renders the application formally inadmissible. Of course, this control looks after the formal aspects of the application. Afterwards, the court shall decide about the substantial admissibility of the claim.

176. Parties begin the EU proceedings, but the courts manage them. After the lodging of the application, the claimant, strictly speaking, might forget the developments of the case, however, getting the judge decide on his/her claim.

As soon as the application has been lodged, the Registrar makes a note of it in the register and gives it a progressive number, in the order in which it has been lodged. The Registrar shall also give notice in the OJEU of the date of registration of an application initiating proceedings, the names and addresses of the parties, the subject matter of the proceedings, the form of order sought by the applicant and a summary of the pleas in law and the main supporting arguments.

The application is served by the Registrar on the defendant (of course, after the above-mentioned control) by new electronic means. Only in this moment the opposite party knows the existence of the case.[289]

§2. The Defence of the Defendant

I. General Outline

177. The defendant who wants to be actively present to the proceedings shall lodge a defence after service on him/her of the application. The defence contains the same statement as the application; so, the name and address of the defendant, particulars of the status and address of the applicant's representative, the pleas in law and arguments relied on, the form of order sought by him/her and any evidence produced or offered by him/her. The rules about the address for service in Luxembourg, the effecting of service by telefax or other technical means and the documents which should accompany the pleading are to be applied to the defence too.[290]

---

289. Article 123 RP CJ; Art. 80 RP GC.
290. Article 124 RP CJ; Art. 81 RP GC.

Before the CJ, the lodging of the defence shall be made within two months after the service of the application; this time limit may be extended by the President, in exceptional circumstances, at the defendant's reasoned request.

178. The content of the defence is somehow simpler than that of the application. Strictly speaking, the defendant might propose a generic contestation of the claim; the judge is obliged to review the admissibility and the lack of foundation in the merits of the application of his/her own motion, so that he/she could reject the claim (because of its inadmissibility or its lack of proof or of foundation in law), without any relevant cooperation by the defendant. Yet, it is clear that usually the defendant has interest to develop his/her arguments, suggesting a different point of view in law or about facts, just to obtain the rejection of the claim.

The question relating to the contestation of facts is particularly interesting. European courts apply the rule, which considers the facts not directly contested by the opposite party, if present to the proceedings, as proved. This point may often orient the strategy of the defendant, who is charged by the burden of proof of any fact, alleged in contrary to those set down by the claimant. Surely, the defendant should propose (in the first defence or in the following rejoinder) his/her objections, in the meaning of all arguments in fact and law, contrasting with the pleas on which the application is based. This is exactly what the Rules of Procedure mean, when they mention 'the pleas in law and arguments relied on'. Of course, these arguments may attack the application on its admissibility or its foundation in fact or in law.

At the same way, the form of order sought by the defendant may be limited to the simple request that the application should be rejected (besides the application to obtain the condemnation to pay the costs of the proceedings).

Yet, it seems to be better for the defendant to specify, whether he/she seeks a decision on the lack of competence of the court or on the inadmissibility of the application, or on the lack of foundation in the merits. As the judge is compelled to decide about any request of the parties, in this way the defendant obliges him/her to take a position on all the arguments of the defence.

179. Nothing is said in the EU Rules of Procedure about counterclaims. The defendant may certainly bring an action in the form of a counterclaim, in those proceedings where courts exercise a full substantive jurisdiction (e.g., when the courts decide in base of an arbitration clause, related to a private law contract). On the contrary, the structure of the typical declaration or annulment actions gives no space to this kind of defence. In these cases, which are obviously the most frequent ones, the most common strategy for a defendant, who wishes to bring an action against the claimant, is that of lodging an autonomous claim (with the possibility to join the cases later).

II. The Inadmissibility

180. It is useful to spend some lines about the notion of inadmissibility, because of its concrete importance in the EU proceedings.

The EU notion of inadmissibility is very wide; probably, it must be held a generic and residual notion. It includes any order which does not admit the claim, except those relating to the lack of competence of the court, on the one hand, and to the foundation of the claim in the substance, on the other hand.

An application may be held inadmissible because of vices of form, or because of a basic impossibility to bring that claim according to the law. In the first group, one can put the vices of form which make pleadings unvoid. The second group consists of cases where a claim is rejected, because it may not be collocated in any typical hypothesis of judicial protection of rights, established by the EU law. For instance, this is the case of a claim brought against a regulation by an individual who is not directly affected by it, or the case of a claim brought by an individual against another individual, or of a claim for annulment initiated after the expiring of the time limit to bring it.

The consequences are different and important. Should an application be held inadmissible because of a procedural reason, the claim may be brought once again (provided the general requirements of the action are still existing; for instance, time limits are not yet expired). On the contrary, when a claim is rejected because the EU courts have no jurisdiction on it or because no EU rule allows the claimant to bring it, the decision of the judge has the force of res judicata.

The claim is inadmissible where the applicant has no *locus standi* or no interest to bring it.

In their case law, the Luxembourg courts have carefully developed the notion of interest (to bring an action or to intervene) of the associations (above all, consumers or enterprises associations), having the aim to protect the interests of their members. The prevailing solution is the following one: associations are entitled to bring an action, even if not directly interested, where: (a) according to their Statutes, they have the right to represent the interest of their members; (b) they represent a relevant part, even if not the majority, of the operators in the referred market; (c) they are opposing an Act or a conduct of the institutions, which has the effect of give prejudice to such interests.[291]

181. The question of inadmissibility brings about an evaluation by the judge, which is quite independent from the ones on the competence or the substance of the case; therefore, it consists in a separate point of decision, which is usually (but not absolutely) prior to that relating to the foundation of the claim. In fact, when the applicant's claim may be easily dismissed as unfounded, it is unnecessary to consider the preliminary objection of inadmissibility raised by the defendant.[292] Especially, it has to be noted that, where the first application made by a party is not admissible because of the lack of compliance with procedural rules, a second application, meeting the proper requirements, is admissible.[293] The Court has also held

291. *See* cases GC, 24 Jan. 1995, T-114/92, *BEMIM v. Commission*, ECR, II, 147; GC, 6 Jul. 1995, joined cases T-447/93 and others, *AITEC and others v. Commission*, ECR, II, 1971.

292. CJ, 15 Dec. 1977, 95/76, *Bruns v. Commission*; ECR, 2401; CJ, 5 Apr. 1979, 157/77, *Gilbeau v. Commission*, ECR, 1505.

293. CJ, 18 Mar. 1980, joined cases 26 and 86/79, *Forges de Thy-Marcinelle and Monceau v. Commission*, ECR, 1083.

that the admissibility of an action must be judged by reference to the situation prevailing when the application is lodged and that, if at that time the conditions for an action to be brought are not fulfilled, the action is inadmissible, unless the defect is rectified within the period prescribed for proceedings to be instituted.[294]

The inadmissibility may be the matter of an objection raised by a plea in law of the defendant, or be object of a decision of the court of its own motion (even if in specific cases), or be decided as a preliminary issue, as disposed by Article 151 RP CJ.

In fact, as in the event where the court should hold the application inadmissible, no discussion on the substance of the case would be possible, and since the question of inadmissibility is an autonomous point of the decision, a party may request the court to give its decision on such question before examining the substance and not going to it.

The question of admissibility is a very important aspect of the EU proceedings. In fact, as actions may be brought only under some narrow requirements, the parties usually try to interpret the EU rules about protection of rights extensively, in order to let their claims be included in them; at the same time, it is a task of the courts to discuss in the substance only those actions, which may actually be brought according to law.[295]

The settled case law of the EU courts holds that a plea of illegality of an Act may be considered by the judges of their own motion, even if that plea is not accompanied by formal conclusions.[296] A number of questions may be considered by the EU courts of their own motion: among them, it is useful to quote the questions of res judicata,[297] of the lack of jurisdiction of the court,[298] of the lack of the necessary precision of an application,[299] of the breach of the principle of observance of the rights of defence,[300] of the conditions for admissibility of an action.[301] The EU courts may also state of their own motion that a claim brought after the beginning of the case is new[302] or that the applicant has no interest to have his/her claim granted.[303]

294. CJ, 27 Nov. 1984, 50/84, *Bensider v. Commission*, ECR, 3991.
295. F. Castillo De La Torre, 'Le relevé d'office par la juridiction communautaire', *Cah. dr. eur.* (2005): 395 et seq.
296. CJ, 18 Mar. 1980, joined cases 154/78 and others, *Valsabbia v. Commission*, ECR, 907; GC, 6 Dec. 1990, T-130/89, *B. v. Commission*, ECR, II, 761.
297. CJ, 1 Jun. 2006, joined cases C-442/03 P and C-471/03 P, *P&O European Ferries v. Commission*, ECR, I, 4845 (which is an example of a settled case law).
298. GC, 7 Jul. 2004, joined cases T-107/01 and T-175/01, *Société de mines de Sacilor v. Commission*, ECR, II, 2125.
299. GC, 6 May 1997, T-195/95, *Guérin Automobiles v. Commission*, ECR, II, 679.
300. GC, 10 May 2001, joined cases T-186/97 and others, *Kaufring and others v. Commission*, ECR, II, 1337.
301. CJ, 29 Apr. 2010, C- 160/08, *Commission v. Federal Republic of Germany*.
302. CJ, 28 Nov. 1985, ord., 19/85, *Grégoire-Faulon v. Parliament*, ECR, 3771.
303. CJ, 19 Oct. 1995, C-19/93 P, *Rendo and others v. Commission*, ECR, I, 3319.

§3. Reply and Rejoinder

182. After the first two pleadings, the parties may exchange a reply (from the applicant) and a rejoinder (from the defendant), which supplement the respective positions. The President of the court shall fix the time limits within which these new pleadings are to be lodged.[304]

The latest amendments to the Rules of Procedure have marked a strong simplification of this stage, with very flexible features. So, the General Court may exclude reply and rejoinder, stating that no new pleadings are required, where the documents before it are sufficiently comprehensive. However, the General Court may always authorize the parties to supplement the documents (but not the pleas) if the applicant presents a reasoned request to that effect within two weeks from the notification of that decision.

Moreover, the President may specify the matters to which the reply or the rejoinder should relate, in order to prescribe the time limits within which those procedural documents are to be produced.

It may be easily observed, therefore, that the parties are not given the full freedom to expose their pleas and arguments in an open number of statements, but, on the contrary, that the trend goes towards the limitation of the pleadings to the two introductory ones only.

§4. Amendments to Pleas

183. The reply and the rejoinder are the proper place, just to change or modify the strategy in the proceedings, by putting new elements on the table of the judge. In fact, in reply or rejoinder a party may offer further evidence, even if giving reasons for the delay in offering it.

Yet, it should be said that they are the usual, but not exclusive seat to introduce new elements in the case. The Luxembourg courts have interpreted the Rules of Procedure in a very open way. According to these rules, no new plea in law may be introduced in the course of proceedings, unless it is based on matters of law or of fact, which come to light during the procedure. The case law of the courts underlines that these rules do not prescribe any time limit or any specific pleading for introducing new pleas. Especially, the courts have held that the introduction of new pleas (of course, within the limits of admissibility fixed in the rules) should be made immediately or within a certain time limit from the coming to light of the new matters of law or fact, under condition of losing the faculty itself.[305]

Therefore, it is possible to conclude that the introduction of new pleas should comply only with substantial, but not with formal or time, requirements. An idea of

304. Article 126 RP CJ; Art. 83 RP GC.

305. GC, 29 Jun. 1995, cases T-31/91 and T-32/91, *Solvay v. Commission* e *Imperial Chemical Industries v. Commission*, ECR, II, 1821. Moreover, these conclusions should be re-read in the light of more recent legal modifications, like Art. 84(2) RP GC.

the proceedings so prevails, which above all takes care of the full right of the parties to bring any element useful to make their point of view prevail in the proceedings.

It should be added that the EU courts hold that the rules containing limitations as far as it concerns the admissibility of new pleas are binding for the parties and not for the judge. Therefore, the courts may always raise a question of their own motion which the parties have not introduced without being bound to the requirement that the matter of law has come to light in the course of the proceedings.[306]

It should be stressed that the question of determining which new pleas are admissible is not concerning any new argument of law, which a party holds helpful to its strategy.

184. So, after the application and the first defence, the parties may:[307]

(a) introduce new arguments in law and new matters of fact (if in the event, offering further evidence);
(b) introduce new pleas, only if they are based on matters of law or of fact which come to light in the course of the procedure;
(c) modify the request for the form of order sought, if so doing they bring no new action.

On the contrary, they may not:

(a) bring new actions;
(b) modify the request for the form of order sought, in a way to change the subject matter of the controversy.

185. New pleas are no new action, but only different aspects of the same action which has already been brought. For instance, if the party seeks the annulment of an Act of an institution, after having introduced a plea relating to a breach of the treaties, it may request the annulment also because of misuse of power.

As it has been remarked, the admissibility of a new plea requires a new fact (which, in order to be really new, should not exist or not be known by the applicant when he/she began the case) or the introduction of new matters of fact or of law, effected by the opposite party. The settled case law has better specified that no new plea in law may be introduced in the course of proceedings unless it is based on matters of law or of fact which come to light in the course of the procedure. The fact that the applicant became aware of a factual matter during the course of the procedure before the EU court does not mean that that element constitutes a matter of fact which came to light in the course of the procedure. A further requirement is that the applicant was not in a position to be aware of that matter previously.[308]

It should be added that a submission which expands upon a plea made earlier, directly or by implication, in the originating application, and which bears a close

---

306. CJ, 19 Nov. 1998, C-252/96 P, *Parliament v. Gutiérrez de Quijano*, ECR, I, 7421.
307. Article 127 RP CJ; Art. 84 RP GC.
308. GC, 8 Mar. 2007, T-340/04, *France Telecom v. Commission*, ECR, II, 573.

relationship to that earlier plea, must be held to be admissible; in these cases, the need not to limit the right of judicial protection of the parties is prevailing.[309]

If in the course of the procedure one of the parties puts forward a new plea in law, the President may, even after the expiry of the normal procedural time limits, acting on a report of the Judge-Rapporteur and after hearing the Advocate-General, allow the other party time to answer on that plea. The decision on the admissibility of the new plea shall be reserved for the final judgment.

186. As far as it concerns the modification of the request for the form of the order sought, the Rules of Procedure keep silence. It may therefore be held that such modification is possible, with reference to the new facts or issues of law, which come out during the proceedings. For instance, should the institution annul the Act challenged by the applicant, of its own motion, and decide on the matter by a new Act, which nevertheless seems to the applicant unfair and to be reviewed, the claimant may change the form of the order sought, pointing out the new Act. Obviously, it must not deal with a new action, but only with a specification of the action which has been already brought (in the example above, the annulment of the Act).

187. The difference between new pleas and modification of the form of the order sought is to be exactly underlined. When introducing a new plea, the party has not changed the final goal of its claim, but it has only set out a new, different ground supporting the success of the claim. This is why a plea, which makes clear a ground, that was already included in the application, is admissible. On the contrary, when the form of the order sought is modified, the goal itself changes; the party may reduce its claim, but not enlarge it, or add to the former claim a new one.

The EU case law has admitted true that in the interests of the proper administration of justice and of the requirement of procedural economy, heads of claim directed against a decision which is replaced, during the course of proceedings, by a decision with the same subject matter, may be regarded as being directed against the replacement decision because the latter decision constitutes a new factor which entitles the applicant to amend his/her heads of claim and pleas in law. Also in matters of non-contractual liability of the EU institutions, it has been held that the amount requested may be amended during the proceedings, where, at the moment of the application, it was not possible to specify the amount of the damage which the applicant claimed to have suffered.[310]

On this subject matter, the rules of the General Court introduced a specific rule: where a measure, the annulment of which is sought, is replaced or amended by another measure with the same subject matter, the applicant may, before the oral part of the procedure is closed, or before the decision of the General Court to rule without an oral part of the procedure, modify the application to take that new factor into account.

---

309. *See* GC, 27 Feb. 1997, T-106/95, *FFSA v. Commission*, ECR, II, 229; GC, 17 Jul. 1998, T-118/96, *Thai Bicycle v. Consiglio*, ECR, II, 2991; GC, 12 Jul. 2001, T-204/99, *Mattila v. Council and Commission*, ECR, II, 2265.

310. CJ, 10 Apr. 2003, C-217/01 P, *Hendrickx v. Cedefop*, ECR, I, 3701; CJ, 2 Jun. 1976, joined cases 56-60/74, *Kampffmeyer and others v. Commission and Council*, ECR, 711; CJ, 27 Jan. 2000, joined cases C-104/89 and C-37/90, *Mulder and others v. Council and Commission*, ECR, I, 203.

The modification of the application must be made by a separate document within the time limit of two months, which the annulment of the measure justifying the modification of the application may be sought. The statement of modification shall contain the modified form of order sought and, where appropriate, the modified pleas in law and arguments and, where appropriate, the evidence produced and offered in connection with the modification of the form of order sought. The statement of modification must be accompanied by the measure justifying the modification of the application. The President shall prescribe a time limit within which the defendant and any interveners may respond to the statement of modification. The proceeding then continues following its normal procedure.[311]

Lastly, the case law prohibiting new claims, brought while the proceedings are pending, is absolutely settled. A new claim means a new action, which changes the subject matter of the case.

§5. The Preliminary Report

188. Once lodged all the pleadings, the court is informed about the matter of the case and may therefore lead the proceedings to the oral stage, or the taking of evidence, or to hold it ready to be decided.

The passage between the written stage and the following ones is marked by the preliminary report by the Judge-Rapporteur. As far as it concerns this point, the Rules of Procedure of the EU courts put some differences into light.

189. Before the CJ, as soon as an application initiating proceedings has been lodged, a judge is designated by the President to act as Judge-Rapporteur. The Judge-Rapporteur takes care of any development of the case from beginning on and may refer to the Court about any decision to be taken. After the end of the exchange of pleadings, his/her role becomes more important.

Such end includes many cases: first, the normal event of the lodging of a rejoinder by the defendant; then, the events where reply or rejoinder have been lodged after the expiry of the fixed time limits, or where they have not been lodged at all.

At this moment, the President fixes a date on which the Judge-Rapporteur is to present his/her preliminary report.

In such report, the Judge-Rapporteur must not advise the solution of the case, but only inform the general meeting of the Court about it. The preliminary report shall contain recommendations as to whether a preparatory inquiry or any other preparatory step should be undertaken and so the formation to which the case should be assigned for the decision. It shall also contain the Judge-Rapporteur's recommendations, if any, as to whether fixing an oral hearing or dispensing with it and as to whether to dispense with an opinion of the Advocate-General. The Court shall decide, after hearing the Advocate-General, what action to take upon these recommendations.[312]

---

311. Article 86 GC RP. *See* GC, 12 Jul. 2016, ord., T-347/14, *Yanukovych v. Council*.
312. Article 59 RP CJ.

190. Before the General Court, the preliminary report is presented when the written part of the procedure is closed. It shall contain an analysis of the relevant issues of fact and of law raised by the action, proposals as to whether measures of organization of procedure or measures of inquiry should be undertaken, whether there should be an oral part of the procedure. It also takes position on whether the case should be referred to the Grand Chamber, or to a Chamber made up of a variable number of judges, or to a single judge sitting with a different number of Judges, and whether the case should be delegated to a single Judge.[313]

191. Once received the preliminary report and having the help, if necessary, of the measures of organization of procedure, the EU courts are in degree to lead the proceedings towards one of three possible directions.

First of all, the courts may decide, in its general meeting, to take evidence, undertaking such a measure of inquiry itself or entrusting the task of so doing to the Judge-Rapporteur.

Otherwise, the court may decide to go to the oral stage without taking any evidence. In this event, the President fixes the date for the hearing.

Lastly, on a proposal from the Judge-Rapporteur and after hearing the Advocate General, the CJ (but, substantially, also the General Court) may decide not to hold the oral hearing if it considers, on reading the written pleadings or observations lodged during the written part of the procedure, that it has sufficient information to give a ruling.

§6. Measures of Organization of Procedure

192. The concrete experience of the Luxembourg courts has shown the helpfulness of a continuous dialogue between the judge and the parties. The measures of organization of procedure, which are to solve many a problem in the management of the case, are the tools applied to this goal. Until 2012, in the Rules of the CJ the denomination was 'preparatory measures', but it has been changed into 'measure of organization of procedure', without any practical difference.

193. Before the CJ, in addition to the measures which may be prescribed in accordance with Article 24 of the Statute (which consist of the requirement the parties to produce all documents and to supply all information), the Court may invite the parties to answer certain questions in writing, within the time limit laid down by the Court, or at the hearing. Then, the Judge-Rapporteur and the Advocate-General may always request the parties to submit, within a specified period, all such information relating to the facts and all such documents or other particulars, as they may consider relevant. The replies and documents provided shall be communicated to the other parties. They may also send to the parties questions to be answered at the hearing.

The measures of organization of procedure have no fixed place in the development of the proceedings. Nevertheless, it is reasonable to think that they are placed

313. Article 87 RP GC.

between the written and the oral stage. The Judge-Rapporteur may deal with them in the preliminary report and, however, such measures will be helpful to better manage (or often to omit) the taking of evidence and to ascertain the existence of the conditions to omit the oral procedure.[314]

194. The discipline of the measures of organization of procedure before the General Court is a bit more complex.[315]

The purpose of measures of organization of procedure shall be to ensure that cases are prepared for hearing, procedures carried out, and dispute resolved under the best possible conditions. They are prescribed by the General Court and, in particular, they shall have as purpose: (a) to ensure the efficient conduct of the written and oral procedure and to facilitate the taking of evidence; (b) to determine the points on which the parties must present further argument or which call for measures of inquiry; (c) to clarify the forms of order sought by the parties, their pleas in law and arguments, and the points at issue between them; (d) to facilitate the amicable settlement of proceedings.

Measures of organization of procedure may, in particular, consist of: (a) putting questions to the parties; (b) inviting the parties to make written or oral submissions on certain aspects of the proceedings; (c) asking the parties or third parties for the information; (d) asking the parties to produce any material relating to the case; (e) summoning the parties to meetings.[316]

195. Despite some analogies, the measures of organization of procedure should be distinguished from the measures of inquiry as far as it concerns their content and their purpose. In fact, while the measures of inquiry have the aim to take evidence through the fact-finding, the measures of organization are placed on a prior and different field, because they tend to prepare the case and the measures of inquiry themselves.[317]

§7. Preliminary Issues

196. A short preamble about the way of deciding the subject matter of the case seems to be useful, before examining the rules on the preliminary issues.

The courts, before going to the substance of the case (therefore deciding about the right claimed by the applicant), have to ascertain their competence and the admissibility of the claim. So, they must examine those preliminary issues which

314. Articles 61 and 62 RP CJ.
315. Article 89 RP GC.
316. *See* CJ, 26 Mar. 2009, C-113/07 P, *Selex v. Commission and Eurocontrol*; CST, 14 Feb. 2008, F-74/07, *Meierhofer v. Commission.*
317. *See*, for instance, GC, 6 Apr. 1995, joined cases T-80/89 and others, *BASF and others v. Commission*, ECR, II, 729; GC, 29 Jan. 1995, T-31/91, *Solvay v. Commission*, ECR, II, 1821 (already quoted: points 14 and 16); GC, 5 Jun. 1996, T-162/94, *Nmb France v. Commission*, ECR, II, 427 (point 17); GC, 4 Dec. 2008, T-284/08, *PMOI v. Council* (points 13 and 17).

might bring about the closing of the proceedings, where the lack of any preliminary condition would prohibit them to decide on the merits (e.g., because the application is not admissible).[318]

Besides, the courts are requested to decide all the procedural questions, which do not bring about the closing of the proceedings, such as, any question relating to the validity of the Acts, the administration of the measures of inquiry, the applications on the confidentiality of any documents, the possibility for a judge to take part in the disposal of any case, and so on. All that is dealt with in the Rules of Procedure with the wording of 'decision on admissibility', or 'lack of competence', or 'declaration that the action has become devoid of purpose and that there is no longer any need to adjudicate on it or for a decision on another preliminary issue'.[319]

Now, the courts may decide the preliminary issue either at the end of the ordinary proceedings, since the subject matter of a case should always be considered as a whole, or, if it is proper, by means of an autonomous procedural path, which is a digression inside the ordinary proceedings, whenever the debate about the substance of the case is not requested.[320]

197. Taking into account this preamble, it may be remarked that the requirements for this autonomous procedure are the following ones:

(a) a preliminary issue which may be logically decided by the EU courts without necessarily going to the substance of the case. A mere objection about the lack of foundation of the claim or relating to the existence of circumstances which deny the facts alleged by the applicant gives no matter for an autonomous and separate decision, but is to be kept inside the ordinary proceedings;
(b) the application made by a party, which requests the judiciary body to give a decision on the raised issue, without going to the substance of the case, or the decision by the court itself to decide about the inadmissibility of the claim, on grounds of public order. No specific time limits exist as far as it concerns such application or decision;
(c) the discretionary decision by the court to deal with the issue separately from the substance of the case.

198. A party applying to the courts for a preliminary decision shall make the application by a separate document (so, a pleading different from the common statements, as the defence, the reply or the rejoinder). Such application must contain the pleas of fact and law relied on and the form of order sought by the applicant; any supporting documents must be annexed to it. It is quite frequent that the defendant requests the courts to decide about an objection of inadmissibility of the claim immediately, without managing the case in the ordinary way.

---

318. D. Louterman & M. Febvre, 'Les incidentes de procédure au sens de l'article 91 du règlement de procédure de la Cour de Justice des Communautés Européennes', *Gazette du Palais: Doctrine* (1989): 276 et seq.
319. Article 130 RP GC.
320. Article 151 RP CJ; Art. 130 RP GC.

As soon as the application has been lodged, the President of the court shall prescribe a period within which the opposite party may lodge a document containing the form of order sought and the arguments of fact and law relied on.

199. Unless the courts decide otherwise, the remainder of the autonomous proceedings shall be oral. But it should be noted that the EU courts often decide only on the basis of the written statements. This is what usually happens when the courts decide on the preliminary issue of their own motion.

It is clear that in these procedural steps the right of the parties to be heard is somehow limited. But the CJ has stressed that the Rules of Procedure do not always grant an oral debate and that a decision about the inadmissibility of the claim, even if taken only on the basis of the written pleadings, brings about no prejudice for the procedural rights of the applicant.[321]

200. The courts may decide on the preliminary issue in three different ways (after hearing the Advocate-General, if present): either reserving its decision for the final judgment, therefore omitting any separate decision, or deciding the issue, admitting, or rejecting the application.

If the court refuses the application or reserves its decision, the President shall prescribe new time limits for further steps in the proceedings. In fact, the autonomous procedure has stayed the usual development of the proceedings; for example, if the defendant has requested the decision on the preliminary issue before the reply, new time limits should be given for the reply and the rejoinder. In other cases, the preliminary inquiry shall be prescribed or the oral hearing on the merits shall be fixed.

On the contrary, where the application has been successful, two scenarios may be opened. The courts may have decided the preliminary issue, stating the inadmissibility of the claim, or the lack of competence; of course, in this event the proceedings are closed. On the other hand, the court might have decided on an issue, which is merely internal to the proceedings (e.g., a witness has been admitted or the invalidity of an Act has been stated); here, there is no closing of the proceedings and the court shall order the further steps.

It is not easy to establish the kind of decision of the EU courts, in the matter of the preliminary issues: where the proceedings are closed, it may be a judgment, as well as an order; where the proceedings shall go on and no decision on the substance of the case has been taken, it is usually an order, even if it might be also a judgment (and this is the case of those judgments which do not close the proceedings).

The grounds for the decision are always stated, even when the form chosen is an order.

321. CJ, 19 Jan. 2006, C-547/03 P, *AIT v. Commission*, ECR, I, 845; CJ, 2 May 2006, C-417/04 P, *Regione Siciliana v. Commission*, ECR, I, 3881. *See* in literature R. Bonatti, 'La Corte di giustizia fa il punto sulla nozione di irricevibilità «manifesta», *Riv. trim. dir. proc. civ.* (2008): 683 et seq.

§8. Fast Proceedings

201. As it has already been observed, one of the most important features of the EU proceedings is flexibility, which means the possibility to adapt the procedure to the different needs of any single case. The tendency is to introduce ways of faster management of the case, as far as it is possible.

So, where the decision of the controversy is easy, the Rules give the courts the chance to go to the closing of the proceeding in a faster way, without waiting for the complete exchange of pleadings and the oral hearing. It should be said that it is not a kind of special proceedings, but only an adaptation of the ordinary proceedings.

Such tendency comes out from different rules, which deal with different situations, but, at the same time, are consistent enough, to let us speak of fast proceedings as a general and common phenomenon in the EU procedural law.

The rules concerned are the following ones:

(a) where the court decides the case without going to the substance, rejecting the claim of its own motion for grounds of manifest inadmissibility or clear lack of competence;[322]
(b) where the court rejects the claim by reasoned order without taking further steps in the proceedings, where the action is manifestly lacking any foundation in law;[323]
(c) where the court at any time dismisses an appeal, in whole or in part clearly inadmissible or clearly unfounded;[324]
(d) where there is no need to adjudicate on an action.[325]

Some features are common to all these rules: the courts act of their own motion (should they act on application by a party, the above mentioned rules on the preliminary issues would apply); they are free to act and decide at any time, even if usually inside and before the end of the written stage; they decide by a reasoned order; the decision rejects the claim.

Fast proceedings are possible also in the preliminary rulings.[326]

§9. Intervention

I. General Outline

202. Third parties may intervene in the EU proceedings. A distinction has to be made, between Member States and EU institutions, on the one hand, and any other person, on the other hand. States and EU institutions may always intervene; on the

322. Articles 53 and 150 RP CJ; Art. 126 RP GC.
323. Article 126 RP GC.
324. Articles 181 RP CJ and 208 RP GC.
325. Articles 149 RP CJ, 131 RP GC.
326. Article 99 RP GC.

contrary, natural and legal persons (in a word, individuals) may intervene only when establishing an interest in the result of any case (and save in cases pending between Member States, EU institutions, or Member States and institutions). It has to be recalled that also the States, other than the Member States, which are parties to the EEA Agreement (as well as the EFTA Surveillance Authority) may intervene before the EU courts, where one of the fields of application of that Agreement is concerned.[327] Moreover, a specific case of intervention is the one granted to the European Data Protection Supervisor, with regard to the tasks conferred to it.[328]

203. Pursuant to the Statute, any intervention shall be limited to supporting the form of order sought by one of the parties (so, both the claimant and the defendant). No autonomous claim may be brought by the intervener in the case and no intervention may be ordered by the judge, not even on application of one of the parties.[329]

204. An important exception to the common rules on intervention has place in the matter of intellectual property rights. In fact, in the special proceedings in such matter, some interveners (those having been party in the pre-contentious stage before the Board of Appeal) may apply for a form of order and put forward pleas in law independently of those applied by the main parties. In these cases, intervention is not limited to supporting the claims of the main parties.[330]

205. As far as it concerns the preliminary rulings, some qualified persons, which had not been parties at the national proceedings, may be present and submit observations before the CJ (such as the Commission, the Member States, sometimes the EU Council, the Parliament, the ECB, the EFTA States, and the EFTA Authority);[331] but this participation is not an intervention, because the EU institutions and the Member States take part in the preliminary rulings at the same conditions of the parties at the national proceedings.

206. It must be said that any intervention brings about more complexity in the management of the case; for example, more communications, more statements, more translations. This is why the amendments to the Rules of Procedure have been trying to make the intervention less easier.

---

327. Article 40 of the Statute.
328. *See* Art. 47(1)(i) of Regulation (EC) No. 45/2001 of the European Parliament and of the Council of 18 Dec. 2000 on the protection of individuals with regard to the processing of personal data by the Community institutions and bodies and on the free movement of such data. *See also* CJ, 17 Mar. 2005, ord., C-318/04, *Parliament v. Commission*, ECR, I, 2467.
329. G.P. Manzella, 'L'intervento e le osservazioni degli Stati membri davanti alla Corte di giustizia delle Comunità europee: profili statistici', *Riv. it. dir. pubbl. com.* (1996): 903 et seq.; P. Biavati, 'Interessi e mercato nel processo comunitario', *Riv. trim. dir. proc. civ.* (1999): 794 et seq.; D. Adamo, *L'intervento di terzi nel processo dinanzi ai giudici dell'Unione europea* (Napoli: ESI, 2011).
330. Articles 40(4) and 53 of the Statute.
331. Article 23(3) of the Statute.

II. The Rules on Intervention

207. As it has already been underlined, the Registrar gives notice in the Official Journal of the date of registration of any application initiating proceedings, with every proper information relating to it.[332] A time limit of six weeks runs since the publication of this notice, within which any application to intervene should be correctly made.

The procedure for intervention is organized in two stages: the first one, with the goal to decide as whether the intervention may be admitted, and the second one, where the intervener, having become a party to the proceedings, is allowed to present its pleadings. Of course, there are some differences between the position of those persons who are obliged to prove their interest to intervene and those ones (Member States and EU institutions) who are free from this charge.

208. Any third person who aims to intervene shall make an application, whose structure depends upon the goal to get the leave to intervene. The application shall contain, *inter alia*, the form of order sought by one or more of the parties, in support of which the third person is applying for leave to intervene and a statement of the circumstances establishing the right to intervene (of course, if it deals with an individual).

The application to intervene contains neither offer of evidence, nor the pleas and the arguments in fact and law alleged by the third party; all that will be included in the statement in intervention, which the intervener shall lodge after the decision of the court, holding its intervention admissible.

Any intervention effected within the time limit of six weeks gives the intervener the full possibility (even if with some limits) to state its defences. Yet, the Rules of Procedure of the CJ take into account also the case of an intervention effected after the expiry of the above-mentioned time limit, but before the beginning of the oral stage. In this event (and if his/her intervention is allowed), the intervener may only, on the basis of the report for the hearing communicated to him/her, submit his/her observations during the oral procedure.[333] As the oral hearing may be omitted, the late intervener is never sure that his/her defence may reach the court.

The third person may intervene only if the court (and for it usually the President) previously allows his/her intervention. The application to intervene shall contain, *inter alia*, the description of the case and the main parties, the form of order sought, by one or more of the parties, in support of which the third person is applying for leave to intervene and a statement of the circumstances establishing the right to intervene (where the third person is not a Member State or an EU institution).

The application shall be served on the parties. After giving the main parties an opportunity to submit their written or oral observations about the request to intervene, the court decides, by order. In the Rules of the General Court, the problem of privacy of the documents is particularly relevant: the idea is to prevent anyone from

332. Article 21(4) RP CJ; Art. 79 RP GC; Art. 130(1) RP CJ; Art. 143(1) RP GC.
333. Article 129 RP CJ.

taking action in order to acquire information by abusing the procedure. Therefore, the main parties may require, if necessary, some reserved documents not to be shared with the intervener.

According to the Rules of Procedure of the General Court, if the application is submitted by Member States and EU institutions and the main parties have not identified information in the file in the case that is confidential, the intervention shall be allowed by decision of the President; in any other case, the President shall decide on the application to intervene by order and, where applicable, on the communication to the intervener of information which it is claimed is confidential.[334] Moreover, before the General Court, where the application is dismissed, the order shall be reasoned; this is why such orders may be appealed.

Before the CJ, the rules are easier: the intervention shall be allowed by decision of the President and the intervener shall receive a copy of every procedural document served on the parties, provided that those parties have not, within ten days after the service has been effected, put forward observations on the application to intervene or identified secret or confidential items or documents which, if communicated to the intervener, the parties claim would be prejudicial to them; in any other case, the President shall decide on the application to intervene by order or shall refer the application to the Court.[335]

209. The determination of the interest to intervene has given birth to a wide case law of the EU courts; both the substantial and the procedural perspective of the question are to be focused. Generally, it may be held that the interest to intervene should be direct, concrete, and relevant under the law with reference to the granting of the form of order sought by one of the main parties. In other words, the success itself of that party has to bring about a concrete benefit to the intervener (and not only a precedent, useful to be invoked in a quite different case).[336]

Representative associations whose object is to protect their members in cases raising questions of principle liable to affect those members are allowed to intervene. They should demonstrate that they represent the interests of their member and that the case directly raises questions, which are liable to affect the members.[337] Leave to intervene may not be granted to associations representing undertakings in

334. Article 44 RP GC.
335. Article 131 RP CJ.
336. GC, 24 Mar. 1997, ord., T-367/94, *British Coal v. Commission*, ECR, II, 469; CJ, 17 Jun. 1997, ord., joined cases C-151/97 P(I) and C-157/97 P(I), *National Power and PowerGen*, ECR, I, 3491; GC, 28 May 2001, ord., T-53/01 R, *Poste italiane v. Commission*, ECR, II, 1479; GC, 26 Jul. 2004, ord., T-201/04 R, *Microsoft v. Commission*, ECR, II, 2977.
337. GC, 26 Feb. 2007, ord., T-253/03, *Akzo Nobel and others v. Commission*, ECR, II, 479. In this case, intervention was admitted with regard to a lawyers' organization, which represented an appreciable number of operators active in the sector concerned in this case, whose objects included the protection of its members' interests, in a case raising fundamental issues concerning confidentiality of communications between a lawyer and his/her client.

competition with those affected by that decision, even if they are third-party complainants, where the interests of their members cannot, having regard to the nature of the contested measure, be affected to an appreciable extent by the judgment in that case.[338]

For example, the right to intervene for a public territorial body in support of the claim of some firms or economic groups supposes that the challenged measure strongly affects the economy of the whole zone; a mere risk of a lower prosperity or a future greater unemployment is not enough.[339]

210. The question about the admissibility of the intervention is to be faced also for the Member States and the EU institutions; they have not to demonstrate their interest to intervene, but, however, they must comply with the general rules on this matter; for example, what concerns the time limits and the form of order sought, which must be form of order sought by one of the parties and not an autonomous one.[340]

211. In the proceedings before the CJ, if the order refuses the intervention, the exclusion of the third person is to be considered a final decision. No appeal is possible and the application to intervene may not be made again, because of the expiry of the time limit of six weeks. Before the General Court, on the contrary, the order which refuses the intervention may be appealed before the upper judiciary body. It is never possible to appeal the orders which allow the intervention.

III. The Procedural Powers of the Intervener

212. If the intervention is allowed, the intervener becomes a party to the proceedings; if he/she has brought his/her application in the time limit of six weeks, he/she receives a copy of every document served on the parties (save that any document is omitted, because secret or confidential). The intervener must accept the case as he/she finds it at the time of his/her intervention.

The ancillary position of the intervener is underlined in special rules. The intervention is ancillary to the main proceedings, with the consequence that it becomes devoid of purpose if the case is removed from the register of the Court as a result of a party's discontinuance or where the application is declared inadmissible.[341] Besides, before the General Court, if the defendant lodges a plea of inadmissibility

338. GC, 18 Mar. 1997, ord., T-135/96, *UEAPME v. Council*, ECR, II, 373; GC, 23 Mar. 1998, ord., T-18/97, *Atlantic Container and others v. Commission*, ECR, II, 589.
339. GC, 3 Jun. 1999, ord., T-138/98, *ACAV and others v. Council*, ECR, II, 1797; GC, 10 Jul. 2000, ord., T-54/00 R, *Federación de Cofradías and others v. Council*, ECR, II, 2875; CJ, 6 Mar. 2003, ord., C-186/02 P, *Ramondín v. Commission*, ECR, I, 2415; GC, 10 Jan. 2006, ord., T-227/01, *Territorio Historico de Álava v. Commission*, ECR, II, 1.
340. For instance, GC, 14 May 1996, ord., T-194/95 INT, *Area Cova and others v. Council*, ECR, II, 343 (already quoted).
341. Article 129 RP CJ.

or of lack of competence, the decision on the application to intervene shall not be given until after the (preliminary) plea has been rejected or the decision on the plea reserved.[342]

Now the intervener may at last play an original role in the proceedings, even if his/her game is limited to supporting the claim of one of the parties, and he/she may present its position. In particular, he/she may submit a statement in intervention, which contains the form of order (sought by the intervener in support, in whole or in part, of the form of order sought by one of the parties), the pleas in law and arguments relied on and, where appropriate, any evidence produced or offered. Before the Court, the statement may be submitted within one month after communication of the procedural documents and that time limit may be extended by the President at the duly reasoned request of the intervener. Before the General Court, the President prescribed the time limit within which the intervener may submit a statement in intervention.[343]

As the right to be heard must always be protected, after the statement in intervention has been lodged, the President shall, where necessary, prescribe a time limit within which the main parties may reply to that statement.

The intervener may introduce neither new plea (in view of attacking the challenged measure) nor new claims; should he/she be entitled to do so, he/she ought to begin a new case (which might be joined to the first one later). Yet, he/she may introduce new pleas in law and arguments, even if different from the ones brought by the supported party, and may also allege new facts, in reference to which he/she may request measures of inquiry. According to the EU case law, the intervener may not arise a new objection of inadmissibility of the claim, if the defendant (whom he/she is supporting) did not do it; but the courts may arise of their own motion any objection of public order, within which also the objections suggested by the intervener are included.[344]

Since the time limit to intervene is quite short, in practice no problem comes out as far as it concerns the preparatory inquiry. The intervener may not request that any measure of inquiry be repeated, but such case never happens, because the intervention has place within the written stage, when no measure of inquiry has already been adopted.

The intervener who made his/her application to intervene after the expiry of the time limit of six weeks has even less possibilities to play an effective role in the proceedings. Not only he/she may not lodge any statement, but no document of the case is communicated to him/her, except the report for the oral hearing.

It is perhaps superfluous to add that the judgment has full effect also towards the intervener; such effect is different, according to the kind of action, in which the intervention was made.

---

342. Article 144 RP GC.
343. Article 132 RP CJ; Art. 145 RG GC.
344. CJ, 24 Mar. 1993, C-313/90, *CIRFS and others v. Commission*, ECR, I, 1125; CJ, 15 Jun. 1993, C-225/91, *Matra v. Commission*, ECR, I, 3203; CJ, 30 Jan. 2002, C-107/99, *Italy v. Commission*, ECR, I, 1091; GC, 24 Oct. 1997, T-243/94, *British Steel v. Commission*, ECR, II, 1887; GC, 14 Apr. 2005, T-88/01, *Sniace v. Commission*, ECR, II, 1165.

213. A last question should be faced: determining which persons are the most frequent interveners in the EU proceedings. As it has been shown, the intervener may scarcely affect the result of the proceedings. Frequently, the intervener is a person politically bound to one of the main parties: a Member State who wants to support an important national firm, or another Member State, whose firms have opposite interests and therefore supports the defendant EU institution. Almost the same may be noted about the organization of consumers, the trade unions, the territorial public bodies. Generally, the future intervener is fully informed about the controversy and therefore may prepare its application quickly.

§10. Joinder

214. The President of the court may, at any time, after hearing the parties, the Judge-Rapporteur and the Advocate-General, order that two or more cases concerning the same subject matter, on account of the connection between them, be joined for the purposes of the written or oral procedure or of the final judgment. The joined cases may always be subsequently disjoined. The President may decide alone or refer these questions to the court.[345]

In the EU proceedings, the notion of connection seems to exclude the event of a merely personal connection (as the Rules speak of cases 'concerning the same subject matter') and to be limited to the event of the objective connection, where more claims are based on the same grounds and the same facts. One may think of the event where separately many firms request the review of the same measure of an EU institution (e.g., the same measure orders different penalties to many firms because of the same antitrust conduct), or of the event of different actions for annulment, brought on the basis of different grounds, against the same act.

In practice, the Luxembourg judges join cases also beyond these limits, for example, in cases where the same points of law are in debate.

The joining of cases may be ordered either in the written or in the oral stage. The decision has the form of an order, against which no appeal may be brought.

Before the CJ, the Rules only provide joinder between cases of 'the same type': it implies the impossibility to join a direct action with a preliminary proceeding.

345. Articles 54 RP CJ, 68 RP GC.

Chapter 3. Evidence

§1. General Features

I. The Burden of Proof

215. Also in the EU procedural law the burden of proving facts is on the shoulder of he/she who wants to allege them, like in the legal orders of the Member States. The case law of the Luxembourg courts has always held this rule, even if it is not openly written in the EU sources, not only for the claimant, but also for the defendant, with reference to its objections.[346]

As it is well known, burden of proof refers, on the one hand, to the conduct of the judge, who may reject a claim if the facts, on which it is based, are not proved and, on the other hand, to the activity which the party bearing the burden is called to do, just to reach the goal of the necessary demonstration.

216. Under the latter perspective, the intervention of the judge in the matter of the burden of proof is quite important in the EU proceedings.

Of course, no court may change the substantive rules of law affecting the burden of proof. Usually, then, it is a task of the applicant and the defendant to offer evidence in support of the respective claim or defence.[347] Yet, the judge has remarkable powers of its own motion and may order one of the parties to produce all documents and to supply any information which he/she considers desirable, taking formal note of any refusal; and that happens, even if the requested party is not substantially burdened of the proof.

In fact, it should be recalled that in the EU system a remarkable difference exists, between the legal and natural persons (so-called private parties), on the one hand, and the Member States and the EU institutions, on the other hand. Frequently, only the strong parties may physically accede to certain documents whose existence may only be alleged, but not directly proved, by the weaker party (which usually is the private one). Here, the activity of the court in the management of evidence may put the parties in better conditions of equality.

II. Powers of the Courts and Powers of the Parties in Taking Evidence

217. In the EU proceedings, the parties are entitled to introduce any kind of evidence, within the limits of the Rules of Procedure, to present documents and to request the courts to hear witnesses or experts or prescribe any other measure of

---

346. *See*, *inter alia*, CJ, 5 Dec. 1979, joined cases 116 and 124/77, *Amylum and Tunnel Refineries v. Council and Commission*, ECR, 3497; CJ, 13 Dec.. 1989, C-169/88, *Prelle v. Commission*, ECR, 4335; CJ, 2 Mar. 1994, C-53/92 P, *Hilti v. Commission*, ECR, I, 667; CJ, 16 Sep. 1997, C-362/95 P, *Blackspur v. Commission and Council*, ECR, I, 4775; CJ, 12 May 2005, C-287/03, *Commission v. Belgium*, ECR, I, 3671; CJ, 22 Nov. 2012, C-89/11, *E.ON Energie v. Commission*; GC, 17 Nov. 2016, T-157/16 P, *Fedtke v. CESE*. With regard to the defendant, *see* CJ, 11 Jul. 1984, 51/83, *Commission v. Italy*, ECR, 2793.

347. Articles 120, 124, 128, and 132 RP CJ; Arts 76, 81, and 85 RP GC.

inquiry. The courts may prescribe the measures of inquiry which they consider appropriate, not only on application by the parties but also of their own motion. The courts may order measures of organization of procedure too, although these institutes are to be placed, strictly speaking, out and before evidence, and not considered a part of it.

The two described powers (of the party and of the courts) coexist, and the question is how to fix the respective limitation, taking into account the rule of the burden of the proof.

218. Looking at the question carefully, it may be said that the powers of the courts do not arrive at the point of annulling the burden of the proof borne by the parties. The courts may (and shall) intervene in taking evidence actively, only when the party, who is charged by the burden of the proof, shows to have complied with its duty, by means of the greatest effort possible for it, to set out documents and requests for evidence, but, at the same time, not to be able to give a full and direct demonstration of the issue, because of the material lack of the information, which the proof relies on. When the activity of the party reaches this breakpoint, the activity of the court is possible; both searching evidence actively or, more frequently, by the inversion of the burden of the proof, which is achieved through an order to the opposite party to supply the relevant documents or information.

Should the courts simply ascertain that the facts, on which a claim or an objection are based, are not sufficiently proved, they would not be compelled to take evidence of their own motion. In these cases, the rule of the burden of the proof should be applied, with the consequence that the claim (or the objection) should be rejected.

On this point, the CJ has stressed that if the applicant requests the exhibition of a document, which seems to be relevant to decide the case, but which is not in his/her possession, even if he/she is in degree to point out some elements of it (such as the date or the content), the judge may not dismiss such request, on the ground that the very existence of such document may not be deduced by the statements of the case. In fact, the possibility that the documents exist is a reason enough to enable the court to order the party (or the third party), which is assumed to be in possession of it, to produce it in the case. So, the claim might not be rejected because of the lack of proof.[348] In the meantime, it is not possible to prevent a European judge from ordering an investigation procedure, by virtue of a presumed infringement of the rules governing the burden of proof.[349]

---

348. CJ, 4 Mar. 1999, C-119/97 P, *Ufex and others v. Commission*, ECR, I, 1341. In literature, R. Bonatti, 'Nuove prospettive sui poteri istruttori del giudice comunitario', *Riv. trim. dir. proc. civ.* (2001): 579 et seq.; C. Volpin, '"The Ball is in Your Court". Evidential Burden of Proof and the Proof-Proximity Principle in EU Competition Law', *Comm. M. L. Rev.* (2014), 1159 et seq.
349. CJ, 27 Oct. 2011, C-47/10 P, *Republic of Austria v. Scheucher-Fleisch*, ECR, I, 10707.

The EU proceedings are therefore nearer to an adversary system than to an inquisitorial system, as the concrete conduct of the courts confirms and as the structure of the EU judicial protection brings about. The first task of the Luxembourg judges is the fair application of the EU law, more than the search of truth in the single case.[350]

As it has been stressed, both parties and courts concur in bringing evidence. The parties may freely produce documents and request for the prescription of any measure of inquiry; the courts shall prescribe such measures, after an evaluation about the relevance in the case and the formal admissibility of the measures requested.

Even when prescribing some measures of inquiry of their own motion, the EU courts are compelled to hear the parties, if the measure, which is to be prescribed, is oral testimony, the commissioning of an expert's report or the inspection of the place or of the thing in question. The issue of this confrontation is not only as to whether the measure should be prescribed or not, but also the contents of it (so, which facts are to be proved, which questions are to be put to witnesses, and so on). It is an interesting application of the right to be heard in a matter of evidence, which enriches the role of the parties before the EU courts.[351]

Although this rule is not present in the new procedural regulation of the Court but only in that of the General Court, it can suppose that this lack can be explained by the greater simplicity of the evidence in front of the CJ where such measures of inquiry are more rarely applied.

III. The Principle of Free Evaluation

219. The principle of free evaluation of the evidence rules the preparatory inquiry in the EU proceedings. The courts shall appreciate the evidence brought into the case by the parties or of their own motion, on a rational basis; their convincement may not be bound by legal provisions.

The freedom in the evaluation of evidence is coherent with the existence of wide powers for the courts in fact-finding. It does not mean that the courts are free in the administration of evidence, because, on the contrary, they are restrained to those measures of inquiry, which are established by the Rules of Procedure. However, the courts are free to take into consideration any kind of documentary evidence, even if referred to facts which should be usually proved by one of the measures of inquiry. For instance, the courts may appreciate, in order to decide the case, written statements by third parties, even if these persons have not been called as witnesses in the case.

220. The EU judges may also use presumptions (both presumptions of law and rebuttable presumptions) to assess the truth of facts.

---

350. P. Biavati, *Accertamento dei fatti e tecniche probatorie nel processo comunitario* (Milan: Giuffrè, 1992).
351. Article 92 RP GC.

As in the legal orders of the Member States, the Luxembourg courts know and apply the law, while they ignore the facts. As far as it concerns facts, any information about the case is brought by the activity of the parties or by the courts, of their own motion (even if the latter situation is practically unusual). Of course, the courts may hold the existence of notorious facts, without taking any evidence. Determining what is notorious is to be made at the light of the EU legal order (for instance, some facts which could be notorious for a national judge should be alleged and proved before the EU courts).

221. On the other hand, as far as it concerns the law, the EU courts know and apply the EU law, and not the single national laws; the existence of national rules, if relevant, is to be alleged and proved. Yet, the national legal orders are included in the knowledge of the law of the EU courts, as far as they concur in the formation of the EU law; this is the case, for instance, of the principles of law common to the Member States or the fundamental human rights.

Besides, on the one hand, the EU courts are not obliged to be informed on the administrative Acts referring to individuals, which are to be included in the documentary evidence by the parties. On the other hand, strictly speaking, they are not even obliged to know their case law (or the case law of another EU judiciary body), by which they are not bound (despite all that may be said on the importance of precedents in the EU case law). This means that it is helpful for the parties pointing out the favourable precedents, if any.

§2. The Preparatory Inquiry

222. In the written stage of the proceedings, the parties shall state the nature of any evidence in support to their claims or objections, in the application and in the defence, or in the reply and the rejoinder, provided they give reasons for the delay in offering it. Third parties shall do it in the statement in intervention.[352] The possibility to introduce evidence is not closed at this stage; the EU proceedings have practically no time limits as far as concerning the production of evidence in support of the claims of the parties.

Both parties and courts may be active in requesting or prescribing measures of inquiry. The admission of no measure of inquiry is conditioned to the prior activity of the parties.[353]

223. The decision on the admissibility and relevance of the measures of inquiry requested by the parties, and as whether measures of inquiry should be prescribed of the court's own motion is usually taken at the end of the written stage, on recommendation of the Judge-Rapporteur and after the measures of organization of the procedure, if any. Yet, the EU courts may prescribe measures of inquiry all the proceedings along.[354]

352. Articles 120, 124, 128, 132 RP CJ; Arts 76, 81, 85, 145 RP GC.
353. Article 64 RP CJ; Art. 88 RP GC.
354. Article 63 RP CJ and Art. 88 RP GC.

The EU courts prescribe the appropriate measures of inquiry after hearing the Advocate-General, by means of an order setting out the facts to be proved. Before the General Court decides on oral testimony, the commissioning of an expert's report and an inspection, the parties shall be heard. The order shall be served on the parties. The measures of inquiry are undertaken by the courts in the composition to decide the case, or the task to undertake them is entrusted to the Judge-Rapporteur. The Advocate-General shall take part in the measures of inquiry and the parties shall be entitled to attend them.

224. It is important to stress the adversarial feature of the EU proceedings as far as it concerns evidence. The opposite party is fully informed about every request for measures of inquiry and every document alleged in the case; the oral measures are practised at the presence of the parties. The Judge shall only take into consideration those procedural documents and items which have been made available to the representatives of the parties and on which they have been given an opportunity of expressing their views.[355]

Evidence may always be submitted in rebuttal and previous evidence may be amplified.

225. When the preparatory inquiry is closed, the CJ may prescribe a period within which the parties may lodge written observations, just to discuss what came out in taking evidence. After that period has expired, the President fixes the date for the opening of the oral procedure.[356]

Besides, exceptionally, the parties may produce or offer further evidence after the closing of the written part of the procedure. They must give reasons for the delay in submitting such evidence. As a consequence, the President may prescribe a time limit within which the other party may comment on such evidence.[357]

§3. Admissibility and Relevance of the Measures of Inquiry: Treatment of Confidential Information, Items, and Documents

226. Evidence may be taken, only where the issues, which the measures of inquiry aim to demonstrate, are relevant for the decision of the case. This is true both for the measures requested by parties and as an internal limit to the powers of the courts.

Even if the EU proceedings are ruled by the principle of free evaluation by the judge, nevertheless, it cannot be held that any kind of measure of inquiry may be admitted. On the contrary, some limits exist and especially the following ones: (a) the courts may not admit measures of inquiry, not included in the bill of the Statutes and of the Rules of Procedure; (b) the courts may not admit the measures included in the mentioned bill, out of the limits of application of each of them (for instance,

355. Articles 65(3) RP CJ; Arts 64 and 92(6) RP GC.
356. Article 75 RP CJ.
357. Article 128 RP CJ; Art. 86 RP GC.

no oral testimony by a party might be administrated); (c) the courts may not admit documentary evidence, if it deals with documents obtained out of legality or protected by confidentiality.

227. From the point of view of confidentiality, some kinds of situations may be pointed out which deserve protection: national security, trade, medical or professional secret, administrative confidentiality.

If a document is secret or confidential, some consequences may come over the proceedings. The document may be physically taken off the dossier of the case, or the party may be allowed to refuse to produce it, notwithstanding the request of the judge. The leave not to produce the document is given by an order of the courts.

It may also happen that a party has interest to bring a document on the table of the court, but at the same time to avoid that any other party be informed of it, exactly on grounds of confidentiality. Now, usually the courts shall take into consideration only those documents which every other party may examine: the right to be heard of the parties and the adversary principle compel to do so. But in some cases a different choice is made by the Rules of Procedure.[358]

The question of the confidentiality of documents is quite important and frequent, above all in antitrust cases. The protection of trade secret is on the opposite side of the right of defence. On the one hand, too much care for the defence might lead to real abuses, for instance, where a party would bring a case, not aiming to win it, but with the purpose to obtain access to relevant economic and commercial documents, the knowledge of which might be very important in the market strategies. On the other hand, no possibility to see the documents might be an obstacle to the protection of the rights.

The case law of the General Court, often called to decide on this subject, has been fixing some general criteria to verify the confidentiality of documents. According to the Kirchberg judges, data may be communicated, depending on how recent and aggregate they are. Of course, it should be repeated that usually each party may see any documents produced by the other party, and that the decision to omit secret or confidential documents is an exception.[359]

Some more rules about the subject are included in the Rules of Procedure of the General Court (even if they seem to be general and not specific rules, therefore, applicable by every EU court). Where a document is protected by confidentiality, the courts shall take into consideration only those documents which have been made available, if not to the parties, to the lawyers on which they have been given the opportunity of expressing their views.

First of all, during the stage of examination of confidentiality of certain information and material, this information or material shall not be communicated to that other party. Then, the General Court, if it concludes in the examination that certain information or material produced before it is relevant in order for it to rule on the

358. Article 131 RP CJ; Art. 144 RP GC; Art. 6 Instructions to the Registrar of the GC.

359. GC, 19 Jun. 1996, ord., joined cases T-134/94 and others, *Nmh Stahlwerke and others v. Commission*, ECR, II, 537; GC, 3 Jun. 1997, ord., T-102/96, *Gencor v. Commission*, ECR, II, 879; GC, 22 Feb. 2005, ord., T-383/03, *Hynix v. Council*, ECR, II, 621; GC, 15 Jun. 2006, ord., T-271/03, *Deutsche Telekom v. Commission*, ECR, II, 1747. *See* in literature N. De Boer, 'Secret evidence and due process rights under EU law: ZZ', *Comm. M. L. Rev.* (2014): 1235 et seq.

case and is confidential vis-à-vis the other main parties, shall weigh that confidentiality against the requirements linked to the right to effective judicial protection, particularly observance of the adversarial principle. After weighing up the matters, the General Court may decide not to communicate such information or material, specifying, by reasoned order, the procedures enabling the other main party, to the greatest extent possible, to make his/her views known, including ordering the production of a non-confidential version or a non-confidential summary of the information or material, containing the essential content thereof. Otherwise, the Court may decide to bring the confidential information or material to the attention of the other main party, making its disclosure subject, if necessary, to the giving of specific undertakings.[360]

Lastly, where a document to which access has been denied by an EU institution has been produced by that institution in proceedings related to the legality of that denial, that document shall not be communicated to the other parties.[361]

These rules may be applied also in joined cases.[362] In fact, above all in the antitrust cases, situations are frequent, where many firms challenge the same act: where cases are joined, a third party to one of the proceedings (but principal party in another of them) would be entitled to be informed about relevant economic data of a competitor, even if it is formally allied in the review of a decision of the EU institution. This is why the EU procedural rules face the question, with the purpose to avoid abuses of the proceedings.[363]

Specific rules state the treatment of information or material pertaining to the security of the Union or that of one or more of its Member States or to the conduct of their international relations.[364]

§4. MEASURES OF INQUIRY

I. Measures of Inquiry in the EU Legal System

228. The measures of inquiry which may be adopted in the EU proceedings are the following ones: the personal appearance of the parties; a request for information and production of documents; oral testimony; the commissioning of an expert's report; an inspection of the place or thing in question.[365] These measures are not exhaustive of the sources for the conviction of the judge, because also written evidence (documents or material objects) has to be considered.

360. Article 103 RP GC.
361. Article 104 RP GC. R.W. Davis, 'The Court of Justice and the Right of Public Access to Community-Held Documents', *Eur. L. R.* (2000): 303 et seq.; C. Rasia, 'Il nuovo regolamento di procedura del Tribunale dell'Unione europea', *Riv. trim. dir. proc. civ.* (2016): 613 et seq.
362. Article 68(4) RP GC.
363. GC 30 Apr. 2014, T-468/08, *Tisza Erőmű v. Commission.*
364. Article 105 RP GC.
365. Articles 24, 25, 26, 32 of the Statute; Art. 64(2) RP CJ; Art. 91 RP GC.

The EU judges may not prescribe, either on application of the parties, or of their own motion, forms of measures of inquiry which are not filed in the Rules of Procedure. Yet, according to the rule of free and reasonable evaluation of evidence, they may take into consideration any relevant evidence submitted to them, even if coming by atypical means.

229. The Kirchberg courts rarely prescribe measures of inquiry. The absolutely dominating evidence in the EU proceedings is the written one (statistics, letters, reports, administrative documents), while oral testimony or commissioning of expert's reports are not frequent. The most common measure of inquiry is the request for information and production of documents; in fact, by this measure the delivery to the courts of documents and paper is achieved and facts may be proved without any relevant organizational effort.[366]

230. No specific rule is prescribed as far as it concerns the personal appearance of the parties and the inspection (except that the parties should be heard before the prescription of the latter). Any practical disposition about them is contained in the order which prescribes them, save the application of the general rules about the carrying out of evidence.

231. The request for information and production of documents is adopted by a simple letter by the Registrar. The answers, the observations, and the documents which are so achieved are put at disposition of the parties, just to make possible any submission in rebuttal, fully respected the right to be heard, except only the case of confidentiality.

The courts are free as far as it concerns both the choice of the contents of the request and the choice of the persons whom the request is addressed to (which may be the parties to the proceedings or third persons), and the mixing of the two points above (different questions may be put to different persons). The judge is so enabled to intervene on the burden of the proof because then he/she may take formal note of any answer or of any refusal.[367] So, for instance, the request to the defendant EU institution of information and documents which the applicant party may not produce compels the defendant to be active in the proceedings, even if it could expect that the claim should be rejected because of a lack of proof.

II. Oral Testimony

232. Article 26 of the Statute rules oral testimony: witnesses may be heard under conditions laid down in the Rules of Procedure. Such measure of inquiry is shaped

366. P. Biavati, 'La richiesta di informazioni nel processo comunitario', *Riv. trim. dir. proc. civ.* (1989): 181 et seq.
367. Article 24 of the Statute.

according the lines of the continental European legal orders and not following the experience of the common law systems.[368] Usually, the courts may prescribe it after hearing the parties.

Witnesses may be heard before the court or the sole designed Judge-Rapporteur; the Advocate-General shall take part in the administration of the measure and the parties may be present, if they so wish. The witness shall be summoned by an order of the court, even where the measure has been ordered by application by a party.

Such order shall contain the date fixed for the hearing, the name, description, and address of the witness, an indication of the facts about which the witness is to be examined. The order shall be served on the parties and the witnesses.

At the hearing, after the identity of the witness has been established, the President (or the designated judge) shall inform him/her that he/she will be required to vouch the truth of his/her evidence in the manner laid down in the Rules of Procedure. After the witness has given his/her main evidence, the President may put questions to him/her, at the request of a party or of his/her own motion. The other judges and the Advocate-General may do likewise. Subject to the control of the President, questions may be put to witnesses by representatives of the parties. As it is clear, this pattern of oral testimony is very far from the Anglo-Saxon cross-examination.

After giving his/her evidence (and not before) the witness shall take the oath. The court may, after hearing the parties, exempt a witness from taking the oath.

233. The Registrar shall draw up minutes in which the evidence of each witness is reproduced. The minutes shall be signed by the President (or by the Judge-Rapporteur responsible for conducting the examination of the witness) and by the Registrar. Before the minutes are thus signed, witnesses must be given the opportunity to check the content of the minutes and to sign them. The minutes shall constitute an official record. If, without good reason, a witness who has been duly summoned fails to appear before the court or, without good reason, refuses to give evidence, a pecuniary penalty may be imposed upon him/her.

234. An objection to a witness may be raised by one of the parties within two weeks after service of the order summoning the witness. The statement of objection must set out the grounds of objection and indicate the nature of any evidence offered. The matter shall be resolved by the court.

235. The Rules of Procedure state that witnesses are entitled to the reimbursement of their travel and subsistence expenses and also to compensation for loss of earnings. They are paid by the cashier of the EU court concerned, after they have carried out their duties.[369] The EU court may also issue letters rogatory for the examination of witnesses.[370]

Oral testimony is not frequently prescribed in the EU proceedings. The structure of judicial litigation at Luxembourg and the concrete conduct of the courts usually

368. Article 26 of the Statute; Art. 47 RP CJ; Art. 68 RP GC.
369. Article 73 RP CJ; Art. 100 RP GC.
370. Article 29 of the Statute; Arts 1–3 of the Supplementary rules CJ; Art. 101 RP GC.

bring about the use of written evidence. Sometimes, written testimonies, above all from persons informed on the facts, are admitted.

III. Expert's Report

236. The commissioning of an expert's report, like the oral testimony, is not frequently prescribed, even if the issues discussed before the EU courts might often suggest its use (such as in antitrust cases or in cases relating the features of the European market of determined goods).[371]

Experts are individuals or even bodies, authorities, committees, or other organizations, chosen by the courts with the task to give them a technical and impartial opinion, which nevertheless is not binding for the judge.[372]

The commissioning of an expert's report may be ordered by the courts on application by the parties or of their own motion. The courts, after hearing the parties, appoint the expert by an order which defines his/her task and sets a time limit within which he/she is to make his/her report. It is possible that the expert is chosen on agreement of the parties. No private expert is allowed; the parties may not influence the work of the expert.

The expert shall receive all the documents necessary for carrying out his/her task, together with a copy of the order. He/she shall be under the supervision of the Judge-Rapporteur, who may be present during his/her investigation and who shall be informed of his/her progress in carrying out his/her task. Moreover, the courts may request the parties or one of them to lodge security for the costs of the report. The parties may be present at the measure of inquiry.

The expert may give his/her opinion only on points which have been expressly referred to him/her. At his/her request, the court may order the examination of witnesses. After the expert has made his/her report, the court may order that he/she is examined, the parties having been given notice to attend. Questions may be put to the expert by the representatives of the parties. In this way, the right to be heard of the parties is somehow protected, although no adversarial confrontation is given while the expert is working. Yet, these questions are to be considered a stage in taking evidence; afterwards, it will be possible to put questions to the expert at the oral hearing.

The same rules of the oral testimony are applied to the expert's report, as far as it concerns the oath of the expert, the objections by the parties, letters rogatory.

IV. Documentary Evidence

237. Written documents are the most frequent kind of evidence in the EU proceedings. The parties may produce documents all the proceedings along and even at the oral hearing; the courts may order that documents be produced.

371. E. Barbier De La Serre & A.L. Sibony, 'Expert Evidence Before the EC Courts', *Comm. M. L. Rev.* (2008): 941 et seq.
372. Article 25 of the Statute; Arts 70–73 RP CJ; Arts 96–101 RP GC.

Very different kinds of documents may be found in the EU praxis: schedules, reports, statistics, technical or scientific papers, administrative Acts, letters, and so on. Some documents are a direct demonstration of facts, because they refer what historically happened and were formed before the proceedings and independently from them. Other documents are written just to be produced in the proceedings and they often take the place of the corresponding measures of inquiry (although the evaluation of them by the courts may rather be different); so, a private report may aim to take the place of an expert's report commissioned by the courts or written statements by third persons may try to avoid the prescription of oral testimony. It is important to observe that the latter group of documents is not forbidden and may enter to form the dossier of a party before the courts.

The prevailing of written evidence may be explained by more than one reason. It derives from the difficulty to organize measures of inquiry in multinational proceedings, such as those before the EU courts, because of the problems arising from transfers and language limitations; it derives also from the peculiar features of the EU judicial protection where facts to be proved are rarely the matter of an individual testimony.

Chapter 4. The Oral Stage and the Decision

§1. The Oral Stage

238. Pursuant to the Statute, an oral procedure is a mandatory part of the EU proceedings. The oral procedure shall consist of the hearing by the Court of agents, advisers and lawyers, and of the submissions of the Advocate-General, as well as the hearing, if any, of witnesses and experts.[373] The hearing in court shall be public, unless the court, of its own motion or on application by the parties, decides otherwise for serious reasons.[374]

Yet, the recent evolution of the EU proceedings, under the pressure of the increasing workload, leads to omit the oral stage in many cases.

239. The Rules of Procedure before the CJ and the General Court (with a slight difference between each other), despite the main orality rule, provide that, upon proposal from the Judge-Rapporteur and after hearing the Advocate-General, the Court may decide not to hold a hearing if it considers, on reading the written pleadings or observations lodged during the written part of the procedure, that it has sufficient information to give a ruling.[375]

The omission may take place whenever an evolution of the court and the silence of the parties coincide. The rules refer to the criteria that the court may avoid a hearing if it deems to be suitably informed about the case, after the written phase.

The Rules of the General Court, which originally always envisaged an oral hearing, with some specific exceptions, have progressively adapted to the CJ ones. However, a difference remains: the Rules of the General Court seem to condition the General Court decision to leave out the oral phase to the lack of a request from one of the parties, a requirement which is absent in Rules of the CJ.[376]

It has to be observed that there is neither an absolute power of the Court, as far as it concerns the omission of the oral stage, nor an absolute right of the parties to obtain it. Should a party submit an application explaining the reasons which justify the oral hearing, the Court ought to decide to fix it. Yet, if the grounds set out by the party are manifestly unfounded (because there is no reason to discuss the case in the oral hearing and the written stage has already put the parties in degree to comply with their defence fully), the Court may dismiss the request and decide the case without the hearing.

As one can see, there is great flexibility about this point, and obviously also the danger of any discretionary and unfair decision of the Court, against which no remedy is given to the parties.

Before the CJ, the oral part of the procedure may be omitted also in the preliminary interpretation proceedings, after the statement of case or written observations have been submitted, on a report of the Judge-Rapporteur, provided that none of the entitled persons has submitted an application setting out the reasons for which

373. Article 20 of the Statute.
374. Article 31 of the Statute.
375. Article 76 RP CJ and Art. 106 RP GC.
376. *See* Art. 106(3) RP GC.

he/she wishes to be heard, or where the answer to the question referred to the Court admits of no reasonable doubt or may be clearly deduced from existing case law or where the question is identical to another one on which the Court has already ruled.[377] It should be underlined that the oral hearing always takes place after the request for a hearing, in the preliminary proceedings, where it has been submitted, stating reasons, by an interested person who did not participate in the written part of the procedure.[378]

Pursuant to Article 20(5) of the Statute, where it considers that the case raises no new point of law, the Court may decide, after hearing the Advocate-General, that the case shall be determined without a submission from the Advocate-General. This rule makes the oral stage more simple. Yet, it should be remarked that no perfect correspondence exists between the two phenomena, that is, omitting the oral hearing and excluding the submission from the Advocate-General (even if the former is coherent with the latter); in fact, it is possible that the oral hearing is omitted and a submission is presented or that the parties discuss the case effectively at the oral hearing, but no submission from the Advocate-General is required.

It must be added that the oral stage is also omitted in other cases where simplified proceedings have place or where the right for the parties to be heard is not fully realized; this is the case of fast proceedings, proceedings by default, proceedings to rectificate, or for failure to adjudicate.

240. On the contrary, the General Court decides to declare the action manifestly well founded by reasoned order in which reference is made to the relevant case law. This is possible when the CJ or the General Court has already ruled on one or more questions of law identical to those raised by the pleas in law of the action and the facts have been established. This decision is an omission of the oral stage.[379]

§2. The Oral Hearing

241. As soon as the preparatory inquiry has been completed, or on the basis of the sole preliminary report, the President of the court fixes the date for the opening of the oral procedure. The decision is served to the parties.

The case list shall be established by the President. The order in which the cases are to be dealt with follows priority criteria. Usually, it shall deal with the cases before it in the order in which they become ready for examination. The President may, in special circumstances, decide that a case be given priority over others, or he/she may defer a case to be dealt with at a later date. Yet, sometimes this order may be changed. The President may order that a case be given priority over others as the proceedings for interim measures or the expedited procedures or the urgent preliminary ruling procedure.[380]

377. Articles 76 and 99 RP CJ.
378. Article 76(3) RP CJ.
379. Article 132 RP GC.
380. Article 34 of the Statute; Arts 53 and 56 RP CJ; Arts 67 and 107 RP GC.

The hearing takes place before the formation of the court established for each single case.

The oral procedure must not necessarily be concluded in one hearing only, but it may include more hearings, like in the cases where measures of inquiry or measures of organization of procedure are to be instituted. In such cases, the EU courts take usually care to fix the hearings in the following and near dates, to avoid to the lawyers more transfers to Luxembourg.

242. After the amendment, the reading of the report presented by the Judge-Rapporteur is no longer provided. In practice, for a long time the written text of the report has been given to the parties some time before the hearing.

Oral proceedings are opened and directed by the President, who shall be responsible for the proper conduct of the hearing. The central moment is the presentation of the oral statements of the parties, which may address the courts only through their agents, advisers or lawyers.[381]

The oral debate gives the lawyers the possibility to stress the strong points of their pleas and arguments, already dealt with in the written statements; to comment the results of the preparatory inquiry or to request to enlarge and complete it; to put into light those points, which appear to be interesting to the President; to the Advocate-General and to each judge, who may put questions to the agents or lawyers of the parties in the course of the hearing.[382]

243. The EU courts take a lot of care in ensuring that the oral hearing may be at the same time well-ordered and fruitful. In the practice directions, the lawyers are suggested not to repeat arguments already treated in the written statements and to limit their speeches in a reasonable time. Usually, the duration of the pleadings is no longer than half an hour. On the contrary, the EU courts request that new arguments are explained, if any (for instance, those relating to new developments in the case law), and that the questions, put by the judges, receive an answer. The lawyers dress the gown and may also use the gowns they dress before the national courts.

It should be remarked that the effectiveness of the oral debate encounters the limit coming from the language barriers. The service of simultaneous translation, through the work of many and qualified interprets, lets any judge understand what the lawyers and agents say in their national language; it is clear, however, that the brightness of the pleading is surely limited by the translation, even if a technically perfect one. Consequently, in practice, the lawyers use to deliver to the interprets a translated copy or at least a written summary of their speech.

244. During the oral stage, new documents may be produced and new measures of inquiry may be instituted or completed.[383]

The last step of the oral procedure consists of the presentation of the submission (obviously, if not excluded) from the Advocate-General, which is limited, in practice, to the lecture of the operative part of it. The parties have no right to reply to

381. Articles 80–81 RP CJ; Art 110 RP GC.
382. Article 32 of the Statute.
383. Article 88 RP GC.

the submission, which is somehow more the first step of the delivering of the judgment, than the last one of the oral stage. The submission from the Advocate-General, according to the case law of the CJ, is outside the oral debate and with it a member of the institution carries out its task. So, parties are not allowed to submit written observation to reply to the submission presented by the Advocate-General.[384]

245. The main difference between the CJ and the General Court, as far as it concerns the oral hearing, consists in the role played by the Advocate-General. In fact, before the General Court, three ways are possible: (a) no judge is appointed as Advocate-General (and this is what it usually happens); (b) an Advocate-General is appointed and presents a written submission; (c) an Advocate-General is appointed and presents its submission in oral way.[385] The choice, as whether a written or an oral submission is to be presented, depends upon a discretionary evaluation by the Advocate-General.

246. After the delivery of the opinion of the Advocate-General, the President shall declare the oral procedure closed. Yet, the court may order the reopening of it, after hearing the Advocate-General.[386]

The reopening of the oral procedure may let the court grant the parties the right to be heard on the arguments of the submission of the Advocate-General, just to ensure the right of the defence, because of the lack of the possibility to reply to such submission. It may be ordered whenever clarifications are necessary or where the case is going to be decided on the bases of an argument, on which the parties have not discussed.[387] According to the Rules of the Procedure of the General Court, the Court may order the reopening of the oral part of the procedure if it considers that it lacks sufficient information, or where the case must be decided on the basis of an argument which has not been debated between the parties, or where requested by a main party who is relying on facts which are of such a nature as to be a decisive factor for the decision of the General Court but which it was unable to put forward before the oral part of the procedure was closed.[388]

The Registrar shall draw up minutes of every oral hearing. The minutes shall be signed by the President and by the Registrar and shall constitute an official record. The parties may inspect the minutes at the registry and obtain copies of them, at their own expense.[389]

---

384. CJ, 4 Feb. 2000, ord., C-17/98, *Emesa Sugar*, ECR, I, 665; CJ, 14 Dec. 2004, ord., C-210/03, *Swedish Match*, ECR, I, 11893. *See* N. Marsch & A.C. Sanders, 'Gibt es ein Recht der Parteien auf Stellungnahme zu den Schlussanträgen des Generalanwalts? Zu Vereinbarkeit des Verfahrens vor dem EuGH mit Art. 6.I EMRK', *Eu. R.* (2008): 345 et seq. Now, *see* Art. 82 RP CJ.
385. Article 53 of the Statute; Arts 111–112 RP GC.
386. Article 83 RP CJ; Art. 113 RP GC.
387. CJ, 29 Apr. 2004, C-181/02 P, *Commission v. Kwaerner Warnow*, ECR, I, 5703; CJ, 11 Jul. 2006, C-432/04, *Commission v. Cresson*, ECR, I, 6387; CJ, 16 Dec. 2008, C-210/06, *Cartesio*, ECR, I, 9641; CJ, 29 Jun. 2010, C-28/08 P *Commission v. Bavarian Lager,* ECR, I, 378.
388. Article 113 RP GC.
389. Article 84 RP CJ.

§3. The Closing of the Proceedings

247. As soon as the oral procedure has been closed and any measure of inquiry has been administrated, the EU courts rule the case.

248. The courts deliberate in closed session. Only those judges who were present at the oral proceedings may take part in the deliberations. Neither the Advocate-General, nor the Registrar (save in case of administrative decisions) enter the closed session. Since the Registrar is not present, the minutes are drawn up by the less senior judge in the office and are signed by this judge and by the President.[390]

The deliberations of the courts shall be and shall remain secret.[391] This means that not the result of the deliberation, but the way in which the decision has been taken remains secret. So, nobody can know which opinion each judge expressed in the closed session, or how the majority to decide was reached; on the contrary, the judgments are public and everybody may read them, requesting a copy from the Registry or watching the European courts report or, now, the website of the EU judiciary.

249. No great difference exists between the EU Rules of Procedure and the national procedure rules about the closed session. Every judge taking part in the deliberations shall state his/her opinion and the reasons for it; the conclusions reached by the majority of the judges after final discussion shall determine the decision of the court. Votes shall be cast in reverse order to the common order of precedence; in other words, the less senior judge in the office votes first, and then the more senior judges vote. Differences of view on the substance, wording or order of questions, or on the interpretation of a vote shall be settled by decision of the court.

In the practice, the closed sessions begin with a first meeting where every judge states his/her point of view. Then, the Judge-Rapporteur prepares a project of the judgment, which is afterwards discussed and approved.

250. The multilingual feature of the EU proceedings comes out also as far as it concerns the closed sessions. Whatever may be the official language of the case, the judges ought to understand each other, without the help of interpreters. They usually speak French or English.

251. No space is given to dissenting opinions in the EU system. Many reasons lead to this choice: the protection of the independence of the judges (whose national government might demand to take a certain position); the respect to the authority of the EU judicial bodies; the purpose to make compromise solutions easier. It should be added that the submission of the Advocate-General, when different from the final judgment, is the expression of a minority and dissenting (but at the same time, very authoritative) point of view.

---

390. Article 32 RP CJ; Art. 21 RP GC.
391. Article 35 of the Statute.

252. The proceedings may be closed with a judgment or an order.

The Luxembourg courts deliver a judgment to decide on the merits of the case and often on the questions of competence and admissibility of the claim. The cases where they decide by an order are more and more frequent. Orders are given whenever the case must go on, with a further inquiry or the reopening of the oral stage. In some cases, a judgment may decide a preliminary question, without deciding the whole subject matter of the case.

§4. The Delivery of the Decision

253. The judgment is delivered in open court; the parties are given notice to attend to hear it. Therefore, after the oral hearing and save the reopening of the oral procedure or the prescription that a previous inquiry be repeated or expanded, a new hearing is always fixed, just to let the parties hear the judgment. In the practice, only the operative part of the judgment is read.[392]

254. The original of the judgment, signed by the President, by the judges who took part in the deliberation and by the Registrar, is sealed and deposited at the Registry. Then, the parties are served with certified copies of the judgment. The Registrar records on the original of the judgment the date on which it was delivered; which is absolutely important, because the judgment shall be binding exactly from the date of its delivery.

After being delivered, the judgment is translated into the other official languages and published by the Registrar in the European courts report.

255. Usually, the judgments define the case; it means that the decision deals with the whole subject matter submitted to the judges. Yet, it is also possible that the judgment does not define the case.[393] In fact, there exists a logical sequence between the different questions (e.g., the admissibility and the merits of a claim, or the right to recover damages and the amount of them). So, the courts may decide only a part of the merits of the subject matter, or state on a preliminary point, without any prejudice for the merits. In these cases, the judgment does not close the proceedings, but supposes their following prosecution; at the end, the final judgment will be delivered.

If the judgment does not close the case, no decision is taken about the costs; such point will be faced in the final judgment. It must be highlighted that over the past few years, the CJ of the EU has focused on the protection of personal data in the context of publications relating to court proceedings before the European judges. In fact, due to the increasing use of new technologies and the publication obligations of the decisions, anonymity becomes much more difficult to ensure if the notice that a relevant case has been brought has already been published in the OJEU. This is

392. Articles 86–88 RP CJ; Arts 116–118 RP GC.
393. *See* Art. 56 of the Statute.

certainly the result of the entry into force of the new general regulation on the protection of personal data, the so-called GDPR (EU Regulation No. 2016/679).[394]

In particular, in case of preliminary ruling proceedings, as ruled in Article 95 of the Rules of procedure,[395] where anonymity has been granted by the referring court or tribunal, the CJ will respect that anonymity in the preliminary ruling proceedings pending before it. Since 1 July 2018,[396] the names of individuals mentioned in preliminary ruling cases have been replaced by random initials in all material published in connection with those cases. Where a person considers it necessary that certain personal data should not be disclosed in published material relating to a case brought before the CJ, the Registrar shall ensure that parts of the judgment are rendered anonymous. Clearly, in order to be effective, that request must be made at the earliest possible stage of the proceedings. The Registrar then replaces the parties' names with random initials, thus ensuring anonymity.

The circumstances in which an application may be submitted to the Registrar are set out in the Decision of the CJ, 1 October 2019, establishing an internal supervision mechanism regarding the processing of personal data by the CJ when acting in its judicial capacity.[397]

§5. No Need to Adjudicate

256. In some cases, the subject matter has been so modified during the proceedings, that there is no longer need to adjudicate on the claim.[398]

The decision about no need to adjudicate may be taken at the closing of the ordinary proceedings (after the written and oral stage) or in a fast procedure (where there exists any absolute bar to proceeding with an action or declare that the action has become devoid of purpose). Anyway, the parties should be previously heard. The decision is taken in the form of an order.

The most frequent cases of no need to adjudicate are the following ones: the claim has lost its object, since the challenged measure has been revoked or modified, or the challenged measure had no (or may not have any more) effect in prejudice to the applicant.

394. Regulation (EU) No. 2016/679 of the European Parliament and of the Council of 27 Apr. 2016 on the protection of natural persons with regard to the processing of personal data and on the free movement of such data and repealing Directive No. 95/46/EC (General Data Protection Regulation), in O.J.E.U., L 119, 1, 4 May 2016.

395. Article 95 RP CJ.

396. ECJ, Press Release No. 96/18.

397. *See* Decision of the Court of Justice, 1 Oct. 2019. in O.J.E.U., C 383/02, 2, 11 Nov. 2019. As stated in Art. 1 of this Decision, if a natural person submits an application to the Registrar of the Court of Justice requesting the Registrar to adopt a decision in his capacity as person responsible for the processing of personal data by the Court of Justice when acting in its judicial capacity, the Registrar shall notify the person concerned of his decision within two months from the date on which the application was submitted. Within two months, a complaint may then be made in respect of the Registrar's decision to a committee established within the Court of Justice that is responsible for ensuring the compliance with the rules on data protection.

398. Article 149 RP CJ; Arts. 130–131 RP GC; relating to the matter of costs, Arts 142 RP CJ, 137, and 103(6) RP GC.

§6. THE ENFORCEABILITY OF THE JUDGMENTS

257. Establishing the effects of the Luxembourg courts' judgments is a quite important issue, not only as it concerns the EU proceedings but, more in general, to understand the institutional architecture of the Union correctly. In fact, the level of efficiency of the judicial decisions to affect the substantial positions of natural or legal persons and their aptitude to be enforced even against the will of the party concerned is a basic and perhaps decisive element to qualify the phenomenon of the European integration exactly.

Aware of the importance of this issue, the TFEU takes it into consideration, stating that the judgments of the CJ of the EU shall be enforceable under the conditions established by the Treaty itself. Obviously, this includes the decisions from each judicial body of the EU.[399]

258. Judgments are binding from the date of their delivery.[400] The orders deciding on the merits are more and more frequent and they are also binding from the date of their service.[401]

Therefore, the decisions of the EU courts are immediately binding for the persons concerned. If one deals with declaratory or constitutive judgments, such effects are produced without any need for further enforcement steps. On the contrary, where one deals with decisions condemning anybody, the binding effect is immediately produced and the judgment (or the order) has the substantial nature of enforcing title, but, if the defeated party omits to comply with the decision and the successful party wishes to enforce the decision, enforcement proceedings should be initiated, pursuant to the provisions of the treaties, which refer to the rules of civil procedure in force in the Member State in the territory of which the enforcement is carried out.[402]

259. The Statute establishes two important exceptions to the rule of the binding (and so enforcing) force of the judgments of the General Court from the date of the delivery.[403]

First, an appeal shall not have suspensory effect, but it remains save the possibility of the CJ to order that application of the contested Act be suspended and, however, to prescribe any necessary interim measure.

Then, the EU legal order takes care to grant the legal certainty with reference to the annulment of the EU regulations. In fact, the decisions of the General Court declaring a regulation to be void shall take effect only as from the date of expiry of the period to bring an appeal or, if an appeal has been brought, as from the date of dismissal of the appeal (and, therefore, where they get the force of res judicata). No prejudice is given, however, to the right of a party to apply to the CJ to obtain the

399. Article 280 TFEU (and prior Art. 244 EC). *See also* Art. 159 EAEC.
400. Article 91 RP CJ; Art. 123 RP GC.
401. Article 91(2) RP CJ; Art. 121(2) RP GC.
402. Articles 299 TFEU and 164 EAEC.
403. Article 60 of the Statute.

interim suspension of the effects of the regulation which has been declared void or for the prescription of any other interim measure.

§7. Res Judicata

260. The binding or enforcing effect should be distinguished from the effect of res judicata of the EU judgments or orders.

In this exposition of the EU procedural law, the issue of the effects of the judgment shall be based on the continental notion of res judicata. Therefore, one must distinguish between a procedural and a substantial meaning of res judicata. In the first meaning, res judicata means that no more ordinary appeal against the judgment may be brought and no more decision on the same subject matter of the judgment may be applied for. In the second meaning, res judicata means that the controversy is finally ended and the substantial relations between the parties are finally defined.

261. The effect of res judicata in the substantial meaning for the EU decisions may be drawn by the general system of the treaties (even if no specific rule deals with it): as the jurisdiction on certain matters has been given to the EU courts, the judgments of the courts must necessarily be endowed not only with binding force but also with final stability.

Some difficult questions arise about the jurisdiction of annulment. The statement that an Act is annulled has effects not only for the claimant and the EU institution, but, where it is a regulation or any other Act with general effects, also for any person in the EU legal order, because for them such annulment is not only a historical event, but it is a fact determining changes (positive or negative) in their sphere of rights.

Where a controversy has been decided with the effects of res judicata, the parties may apply no longer for a new successive decision on the same subject matter and the exception of res judicata may be raised by the defendant. Of course, one should ascertain which is the subject matter really involved in the first judgment and, therefore, which is the real effect of res judicata on the claim, which is afterwards brought.

The EU case law takes care not to extend the principle of res judicata too much.[404] The Luxembourg courts have been stating that the force of res judicata extends only to matters of fact and law actually or necessarily settled by the judicial decision in question and to pleas which have been effectively discussed in the proceedings.[405]

Also the orders deciding on the merits after fast proceedings, where they are not appealed or after the dismissal of the appeal, have the effect of res judicata in the substantial meaning, and the same claim may not be brought again.

404. L. Querzola, 'Spunti sui limiti oggettivi del giudicato comunitario', *Riv. trim. dir. proc. civ.* (1998): 332 et seq.

405. CJ, 28 Nov. 1996, ord., C-277/95 P, *Lenz v. Commission*, ECR, I, 6109; GC, 20 Apr. 1999, ord., joined cases T-305/94 and others, *Limburgse Vinyl Maatschappij v. Commission*, ECR, II, 931 (the appeal on which is CJ, 15 Oct. 2002, joined cases C-238/99 P and others, ECR, I, 8375); GC, 13 Feb. 2003, T-333/01, *Meyer v. Commission*, ECR, II, 117.

A peculiar feature of the question of res judicata deals with the preliminary rulings: no substantial res judicata exists in such cases, because the subject matter of such decisions (both of interpretation and of validity) is only an issue of law, and not a controversy of fact. Moreover, the CJ might always change its positions about the preliminary reference, and no stability at all may be held.

262. As far as it concerns the procedural meaning of res judicata, the existence of many jurisdictional bodies has brought about an ordinary course of the proceedings: an instance of decision only where the competence to deal with the case belongs to the CJ, and two or more instances, taking into account the referring cases back to the first court, where the competence is given to the General Court with the possibility to bring an appeal before the upper court. Such ordinary way is distinguished by the exceptional review procedures.

In fact, while the decisions of the CJ may not be appealed and may be controlled only by means of (and within the limits of) the exceptional review procedures, the decisions of the General Court are subject both to an ordinary appeal before the CJ (even if only on the basis of the grounds established by the Statute) and to the exceptional review procedures, which have the aim to modify or sometimes only to correct or to interpret the will already expressed by the judges.

The third-party proceedings and the revision are surely exceptional and not ordinary means of review of the judgments. In the past, such feature had been discussed, with the aim to grant somehow a way of control against the judgments of the CJ; but now the difference between them and the ordinary appeals is clear, as appeals look for a change of the decision on the same pleas of fact and law discussed in the proceedings in first instance, while third-party proceedings and revision introduce a claim which is absolutely different from the original subject matter of the case (exactly, the prejudice to the rights of a third party, or the discovery of a new fact justifying the revision).

The introduction of a review procedure, pursuant to the rules laid down in the Statute, against the decisions of the General Court acting as a judge of appeal against the decisions of the specialized courts or in matter of preliminary rulings, fixes the moment of the final stability of such decisions when the review procedure has been ended (or where it may be no longer proposed). In fact, despite the wording of the treaty ('decisions … may exceptionally be subject to review'), such review should be considered a step in the ordinary way of the proceedings. This may be held because the first Advocate-General shall examine every judgment delivered by the General Court acting as a judge of appeal; because he/she may propose the review only within a short and pre-determined time limit; because sometimes the judgments of the CJ in the review may affect the substantial rights of the parties and, lastly, because the review aims to modify the judgment on a point of law, which affects a plea already included in the case. Therefore, whenever the review is still possible, no res judicata may exist.[406]

So, it may be stated that res judicata exists, as far as it concerns the General Court, when no ordinary appeal may be brought and, as far as it concerns the specialized courts, when not even the (so-called exceptional) review may be proposed.

406. Article 62b of the Statute.

Where the CJ decides in one instance only, the delivering of the judgment brings about res judicata in the formal meaning, notwithstanding the possibility of any exceptional review procedure.

§8. The EU Enforcing Titles

I. The Enforcing Title

263. The EU jurisdiction is able to give a decision, which is binding and has the force of res judicata. Now, the problem of the concrete enforcement of such decisions has to be studied.

Since the power to enforce its own provisions is the fundamental test of the efficiency of any legal system, the consideration of the point of the enforcement shows the weakness of the EU, whose courts may give autonomous provisions, but cannot enforce them, unless by means of the enforcement organization of each Member State.

It can be surely affirmed that the EU legal order produces binding (judicial or administrative) provisions, some of which are enforceable and have the nature of enforcing titles. The enforcement is made pursuant to the national procedural rules and under the control of the national authorities, save the question of the stay of the enforcement, which remains in the exclusive power of the Luxembourg courts.

264. Usually, the role of enforcer is played by the EU institutions, who are endowed with relevant political and economic powers, which may compel the opposite party to fulfil its obligations, as far as they have been set in the enforcing title. So, even if the enforcement proceedings are not fully effective or however are in the hands of the national judicial or administrative bodies, one must not think that the EU be lacking of compulsory force.

265. The enforcing titles, deriving from judicial proceedings in the EU system, are the following ones:

(a) the condemnation decisions of the CJ, which shall be enforceable under the conditions laid down in the treaties;[407]
(b) the condemnation decisions of the General Court;[408]
(c) the condemnation decisions of the specialized courts (until yesterday, the decisions of the Civil Servants Tribunal);
(d) other judicial enforceable provisions, such as interim orders, orders relating to costs, orders which impose pecuniary penalties to witnesses which fail to appear before the courts or refuse to give evidence without good reason, orders to refund to the Registrar sums advanced by way of legal aid.

407. Articles 280, 299, 254 TFEU; Art. 164 EAEC.
408. Article 225 RP GC.

It should be noted that there exist also enforcing titles not deriving from judicial proceedings, such as (to give an example) the decisions of the Commission and the Council which impose a pecuniary obligation on persons other than Member States.[409]

It deserves to be stressed that pursuant to the EU procedural rules not only the judgments, but also the orders may be enforcing titles. At the same time, not every judicial decision may be enforced, but only those containing a provision of condemnation, which may be enforced by generic or specific way.

In the context of the EU jurisdiction, decisions bringing about a condemnation on the merits are possible, only where the courts have full substantive jurisdiction (and so, actions for damages for non-contractual liability of the EU, disputes between the EU institutions and their agents, actions in matter of pecuniary penalties, actions brought pursuant to arbitration clauses). The judgments deciding on the costs of the cases are enforcing titles, independently from the kind of action, in the context of which they are delivered.

266. All the enforcing titles deriving from the EU system are considered titles in the national legal orders. In fact, pursuant to the treaties, enforcement shall be governed by the rules of civil procedure in force in the State, in the territory of which it is carried out and the order for its enforcement shall be appended to the decision, without other formality than verification of the authenticity of the decision, by the national authority designated by the government of each Member State for this purpose.[410]

II. The Enforcement Proceedings

267. As it has been remarked, the enforcement proceedings are governed by the rules of civil procedure in force in the Member State, where they are carried out.

The first step consists in obtaining the order for the enforcement of the EU enforcing title. The EU jurisdiction has no power to order the national enforcing authorities, whose cooperation is necessary. Yet, appending such order to the decision requires no free assessment by the national bodies, who may only ascertain the authenticity of the decision.

As far as it concerns the place of the enforcement, the creditor may choose any Member State, where such enforcement may be foreseeably fruitful; enforcement proceedings may be begun also in more Member States, in the event of unsuccessful result.

268. In the enforcement proceedings brought in force of an EU enforcing title, the applicant is the person whose rights are ascertained in the decision. Every person belonging to the EU system may be subject to the enforcement proceedings; so, individuals (natural or legal persons), as well as the Member States and the EU institutions themselves. Yet, it must be said that enforcement against the EU institutions

409. Article 299 TFEU.
410. Articles 299 TFEU and 164 EAEC.

and the Member States may be brought only on the basis of an enforcing title deriving from a judicial provision (and not from an administrative decision).

269. With regard to EU, the Protocol on the Privileges and the Immunities of the Union, signed in Brussels, 8 April 1965, and now alleged to the treaties,[411] has to be considered. Pursuant to the Protocol, which aims to protect the rights of the Union against any possible interference by third bodies and, above all, by the Member States, some limits are established as far as it concerns the admissibility of enforcement proceedings against the Union and its institutions (included the ECB).

Article 1 of the Protocol states that the premises and buildings of the Union shall be inviolable; they shall be exempt from search, requisition, confiscation, or expropriation. The property and assets of the Union shall not be the subject of any administrative or legal measure of constraint, without the prior authorization of the CJ. Therefore, who wishes to enforce a judgment (even if it were an EU court judgment) against the Union (e.g., to distrain certain goods or assets) shall lodge an application to the Court, in order to be authorized. It has to be said that such event is absolutely unusual and that the EU institutions use to give up the protection which the Protocol grants them. However, the lack of proper authorization would make the enforcement inadmissible.

It should be underlined that, when speaking of the Union as the subject of an enforcement, one must refer not only to the institutions, but also to bodies, offices, or agencies of the Union.

270. Also with regard to the Member States more specification is necessary. In fact, a Member State may never be compelled to enact a judgment which condemns it; such State has to comply with the prescriptions of any EU jurisdictional decision referring to it, but it takes the appropriate measures by a quite autonomous way. Of course, this is true, save the hypothesis in which a Member State takes part to proceedings at the same level of a legal private person.

Besides, it is helpful to remind that the CJ, where a Member State fails to fulfil an obligation under the treaties and then it does not take the necessary measures to comply with the judgment assessing such infringement, may impose, on application by the Commission, a lump sum or penalty payment.[412]

As far as it concerns the rules governing the enforcement of an enforcing title formed in the EU system, the treaties refer to the national rules of civil procedure of the State in which the enforcement is to be carried out.

Regarding the delicate task of sharing the functions relating to the enforcement proceedings between the EU jurisdiction and the national jurisdictions, the treaties state that enforcement may be suspended only by a decision of the EU courts, while the courts of the country concerned shall have jurisdiction over complaints that

---

411. Protocol No. 7, alleged to the EU and TFEU treaties. *See* C. Schmidt, 'Le Protocole sur les privilèges et immunités des Communautés européennes', *Cah. dr. eur.* (1991): 67 et seq.

412. Article 260 TFEU. The Court's first interpretation and application of Art. 260(3) TFEU was rendered on 8 Jul. 2019 (CJ, 8 Jul. 2019, C-543/17, *Commission v. Belgium*, ECR, 573). In the mentioned case, the Court imposed on Belgium a financial penalty for failure to fulfil with the obligation under EU law. Recently, CJ, 16 Jul. 2020, C-549/18, *Commission v. Romania*, ECR, 563 and CJ, 16 Jul., C-550/18, *Commission v. Ireland (Fight against money laundering)*, ECR, 564.

enforcement is being carried out in an irregular manner. In other words, it is for the national courts to review the legality of the enforcement proceedings, in accordance with the procedural rules of their respective States. The national judges have jurisdiction to decide on any claim or opposition concerning the legality of the way in which the enforcement is carried out, but they have no power to stay the enforcement, because, in doing so, they would violate the sphere of the EU jurisdiction.

It should be noted that some hypotheses exist, in which the EU courts have jurisdiction about the legality of the enforcing title. It deals with the following cases:

(a) when administrative measures by the EU institutions are challenged, which impose penalties and are at the same time enforcing titles, pursuant to Article 299 TFEU;
(b) when an appeal or an exceptional review is brought against a jurisdictional decision.

In these cases, the EU courts have jurisdiction both to decide on the merits and to stay the enforcement.

§9. Discontinuance

271. The EU proceedings are not always closed by a decision, but they may also arrive at the end without any assessment on the case, because of an activity of one or both parties, which give up to the request to get the controversy decided. In such event, the EU courts take the situation into account and order the case to be removed from the register.

The Rules of Procedure govern two different cases of discontinuance of the proceedings. The first one concerns the event of the settlement of the dispute, reached by the parties outside the proceedings, which brings about the final giving up to the claim. The second one follows the mere wish of the applicant to discontinue the proceedings and lets the party the possibility – where the proper requirements exist – to begin the case once again.

272. The first kind of discontinuance is the following one. If, before the court has given its decision, the parties reach a settlement of their dispute and intimate to the court the abandonment of their claims, the court shall order the case to be removed from the register.[413]

Because of its structure, this kind of discontinuance, based on the agreement of the parties, may not be applied to the claims for annulment and inactivity; in fact, in these cases the unilateral will of the applicant to give up the claim is sufficient to get the same result.

413. Articles 141 RP CJ and 136, 138 RP GC.

273. The second kind of discontinuance has place where the applicant informs the court in writing or at the hearing that he/she wishes to discontinue the proceedings. In this event, the President of the court shall order the case to be removed from the register, giving the proper decision as to costs.[414]

A party who discontinues the proceedings shall be compelled to bear the costs, if they have been applied for in the observations of the other party on the discontinuance. However, upon application of the party who discontinues the case, the costs shall be borne by the other party, if this appears justified by the conduct of that party. Where the parties have come to an agreement on costs, the decision as to costs shall be in accordance with that agreement, and if costs are not applied for, the parties shall bear their own costs.

274. It should be remarked that no discontinuance is possible in the preliminary rulings. Nevertheless, the parties may discontinue the national proceedings and therefore take away the CJ's task to decide.

§10. The Amicable Settlement of Disputes

275. The proceedings may be closed also by an amicable settlement of the disputes before the judge. The Rules of Procedure of the General Court (and, before, those of the CST) take this event widely into consideration in matter of staff cases.[415]

The goal to settle the litigation, more than to state principles of law is at the basis of the rule, pursuant to which the General Court may, at all stages of the procedure, examine the possibilities of an amicable settlement of the dispute between the parties (usually, a servant and a EU institution), propose one or more solutions capable to put an end to the dispute, and adopt appropriate measures with a view to facilitating such settlement. The way to reach the goal is fully discretionary.

Where the parties come to an agreement before the court, they may request that the terms of the agreement be recorded in a document signed by the Judge-Rapporteur and the Registrar, which shall constitute an official record. The case shall be removed from the register by reasoned order.

Two other important rules should be underlined. First, the President shall give a decision as to costs in accordance with the agreement or, failing that, at his discretion. Second, confidentiality is protected: no opinion expressed, suggestion made, proposal put forward, concession made, or document drawn up for the purposes of the amicable settlement may be relied on as evidence by the General Court or the parties in the contentious proceedings. It might be doubtful whether the judges will be really able to forget all that they have heard and set off any impression received at that stage.

Moreover, both sets of Rules state that before the Court has given its decision, when the main parties reach an out-of-court settlement of their dispute and inform

---

414. Articles 148 RP CJ, 125 RP GC.
415. Articles 125a and et seq. RP GC.

the Court of the abandonment of their claims, the President shall order the case to be removed from the register and shall give a decision as to costs.[416]

§11. Proceedings by Default

276. The proceedings before the EU courts have been described, up to now, thinking that all the concerned parties take part to them effectively. Yet, it may happen that the party, on which the application is served, does not want to defend itself, by lodging a defence within the established period or lodges statements not complying with the Rules of Procedure. In these cases, proceedings by default have place.

In the EU proceedings, default depends upon the omitting of a regular and valid presence before the courts; there is no default, therefore, if the party, who has lodged its defence, should not appear (by means of its lawyers or agents) at the oral hearing. Being present before the courts consists in the formal validity of the first statement in the case.

277. The Rules of Procedure are slightly different, but fix two requirements for the beginning of the proceedings by default: an application initiating the case has been duly served on a defendant and the defendant has failed to lodge a defence to such application in the proper form within the time prescribed.[417] Should these two requirements exist, it is a choice of the applicant to apply to the court for judgment by default. For the Rules of the CJ (but not for the Rules of the General Court) this second application is served on the defendant; the claimant requests the granting of the form of order sought, without the written stage. While the CJ may decide to open the oral procedure on application, or not, and so deciding on the basis of the application and the annexed documents, the General Court, without the oral procedure, shall give judgment in favour of the applicant, unless it is clear that the Court has no jurisdiction to hear and determine the action or that the action is manifestly inadmissible or manifestly lacking any foundation in law.

278. Anyway, before giving judgment by default, the courts shall consider whether the application initiating proceedings is admissible, whether the appropriate formalities have been complied with, and whether the application appears well founded; it may order a preparatory inquiry. It should be noted that the mere fact of default does not bring about the success of the claimant at any event. The claim might be rejected because inadmissible, or because of the lack of competence of the court, or because the facts alleged by the claimant are not proved.

If the requirements for the proceedings by default exist, the courts shall deliver the judgment, which may admit or reject the claim (for grounds of admissibility or on the merits). Unless the requirements exist, the courts shall not dismiss the claim, but shall order that the application initiating the proceedings be served again.

416. Articles 147 RP CJ, 124 RP GC.
417. Article 41 of the Statute; Art. 152 RP CJ; Art. 123 RP GC.

The proceedings by default are therefore much more simple than the ordinary proceedings, since there is no written stage and the oral one too may be omitted. The oral phase will certainly be omitted before the General Court.

§12. The Expedited Procedure

279. The EU judiciary has been trying to get the delivering of judgments faster, with the aim to face the increasing workload without increasing the number of the judges, which is held to be politically incorrect. Besides the forms of faster procedure of managing the controversies, an expedited procedure has been introduced.[418]

This kind of procedure is a structural variety of the ordinary proceedings, which, in the very beginning of the case, may enter the expedite way. It is not a special form of procedure, because it is not referring to a determined matter. It is better to speak of a reserved lane, where the court may direct the development of the case, because of grounds connected to some single controversies and not to some kinds of litigation (which is a further expression of flexibility). The expedite procedure derogates from the common procedural provisions, but where nothing is especially established, such provisions shall be, however, applied.

280. Two requirements should exist to justify the adoption of the expedited procedure, the first of which being an application by a party and the second the particular urgency of the case, which requires the court to give its ruling with the minimum of delay.

As far as it concerns the first requirement, the decision to apply the expedite procedure is taken by the President of the CJ or by the General Court, on application by one of the main parties (claimant or defendant, but not intervener), on the basis of a recommendation by the Judge-Rapporteur, and after hearing the other party and the Advocate-General. The application for a case to be decided under an expedited procedure shall be made by a separate document lodged at the same time as the application initiating the proceedings or the defence.

Exceptionally, the court may also take a decision to apply the expedite procedure on their own motion, after hearing the parties, the Judge-Rapporteur and the Advocate-General.

The second requirement consists in dealing within a short time and in the particular urgency to decide the case on the merits. Any urgency which might bring about interim measures is ruled under the apposite special form of procedure. Until 2012, the Rules of Procedure of the CJ (but not those of the General Court) stressed that the decision to apply the expedite procedure should be taken exceptionally.

418. Articles 133–136 RP CJ; Art. 151–155 RP GC. *See* E. Barbier de la Sierre, 'Accelerated and Expedited Procedure Before the EC Courts: A Review of the Practice', *Comm. M. L. Rev.* (2006): 783 et seq.

281. The expedited procedure has the following features: the written stage is strongly limited and more space is given to the oral hearing. The originating application and the defence may be supplemented by a reply and a rejoinder and an intervener may lodge a statement in intervention only if the President considers this to be necessary (or, before the General Court, if the court so allows, by way of measures of organization of procedure). It is to be noted that, before the General Court, where the applicant has requested that the case should be decided under an expedited procedure, the period prescribed for the lodging of the defence shall be one month only. If the General Court decides not to adopt the expedite procedure, the defendant shall be granted an additional period of one month in order to lodge or, as the case may be, supplement the defence.

Once the decision to adjudicate under an expedited procedure has been taken, a date for the hearing is fixed, with priority; such date shall be communicated forthwith to the parties.

The choice for the expedited procedure does not forbid that measures of inquiry may be undertaken. The possibility for the parties to supplement their arguments and offer further evidence moves into the oral stage, even if the parties must give reasons for the delay in offering such further evidence. But it must be observed that the short time itself for the defence might be a good reason. The date of the hearing may be postponed, where measures of inquiry or where measures of organization of procedure so require.

The court shall decide the case by delivering a judgment (like in the ordinary proceedings) after hearing (before the CJ) the Advocate-General.

Part IV. Special Forms of Procedure

Chapter 1. General Features

282. In these pages, it has been often noted that the EU proceedings are ruled pursuant to the same pattern, notwithstanding the specificity of each kind of action. A claim for annulment or a suit for damages are subject to the same procedural rules, and concretely the Statute and the Rules of Procedure. This brings about a strong character of unity in the EU judicial system.

The Statute and the Rules of Procedure draw an ordinary form of proceedings, which should be applied whenever no express derogation is established. But some special forms of procedure exist which are different from the ordinary proceedings, where the peculiar features are connected to a specific matter of litigation. Both these requirements (peculiar characters and specific matter) must coexist; if not, one cannot speak of special forms of procedure, but only of varieties of the ordinary proceedings.

283. The main special forms of procedure are to be described in the following lines. Some other ones are to be briefly recalled now:

(a) Claims against decisions of the Arbitration Committee EAEC.
The EAEC Treaty states in matter of the granting of patents, provisionally protected patent rights or utility models relating to inventions directly connected with nuclear research. The controversies in this matter are submitted to an Arbitration Committee, whose decisions may be appealed before the CJ, with the purpose to annul them on the basis of grounds concerning the formal validity of the decision and the interpretation of the rules of the Treaty given by the Committee. The procedure has some particular features and is characterized by the simplification of the proceedings and the lack of any preparatory inquiry.[419]
(b) The procedure on the requests for an opinion.[420]
(c) The procedures concerning the applications under Articles 103, 104, and 105 of the EAEC Treaty, about the decisions of the CJ about the compatibility with the provisions of the Treaty of any draft agreement or contract with a third State, an

419. Article 18 EAEC; Art. 22 of the Statute; Art. 201 RP CJ.
420. Article 196 RP CJ.

international organization or a national of a third State, concluded either by Member States or by persons or undertakings of the Member States, in matter of atomic energy.[421]

(d) The procedures provided for by the EEA Agreement.
It should be reminded that the Agreement on the EEA provides about the jurisdictional protection of the contracting parties. Especially, the right of the States, which are not member of the Union but parties to the Agreement, is established, to submit a request to the CJ to state on the interpretation of any rule of the Agreement, which is identical to any EU rule, if a dispute on the matter arises; moreover, the right is provided for any court or tribunal of an EFTA State (being not member of the Union) and for the EFTA Surveillance Authority to raise a question of preliminary interpretation of any rule of the Agreement, which is identical to any EU rule, before the CJ. The requests for interpretation which may be directly submitted to the CJ and the preliminary rulings are ruled by general provisions on preliminary ruling.[422]

421. Articles 202 and 203 RP CJ.
422. Article 204 RP CJ; Art. 111(3) of the EEA Agreement.

Chapter 2. Interim Relief

§1. The Urgency Powers of the EU Courts

284. The treaties give the EU courts a number of decision powers, with the purpose to grant the protection of the rights of the parties, while waiting for the final decision on the merits of the case, or the settlement of the controversy about the enforcement of a title.[423]

Three hypotheses of urgency powers are considered by the treaties:

(1) the power of suspending the execution of a measure of an EU institution, while proceedings are pending;[424]
(2) the power to prescribe interim atypical measures;[425]
(3) the power to suspend the enforcement of an enforcing title (an administrative Act or a final judicial decision).[426]

There must also be added a fourth hypothesis (which may not be included in any of the three above), concerning the power of the courts acting as judges of appeal to suspend the enforcement of the decisions of the judges acting in first instance. In fact, the decisions of the General Court are judicial acts, and not administrative measures by the EU institutions.[427]

285. The urgency powers of the EU courts are not a kind of autonomous competence, but an accessory power to already existing competence to state on the merits. The EU courts may suspend the execution of an Act or prescribe interim measures only where they have competence and/or jurisdiction to decide the substance of the controversy.

Besides, not any kind of competence brings about the possibility to exercise the urgency powers. This is true, for example, for the actions for annulment, but not for the merely declaratory actions or the preliminary rulings.

---

423. P. Oliver, 'Interim Measures: Some Recent Developments', *Comm. M. L. Rev.* (1992): 7 et seq.; J.L. Da Cruz Vilaça, 'La procédure en référé comme instrument de protection juridictionelle des particuliers en droit communautaire', *Scritti in onore di G.F. Mancini*, vol. II (Milan: Giuffrè, 1998): 257 et seq.; C. Morviducci, 'Fumus boni iuris e misure cautelari nel processo comunitario', *Riv. it. dir. pubbl. com.* (1999): 705 et seq.; D.M. Tomasevic, 'Usage du référé devant la Cour de justice à l'encontre des Etats membres de la Communauté européenne', *Revue du Marché unique européen* (1999): n. 4, 25 et seq.; L. Querzola, 'Appunti sulle condizioni per la concessione della tutela cautelare nell'ordinamento comunitario', *Riv. trim. dir. proc. civ.* (2001): 501 et seq.; L. Querzola, 'La tutela cautelare nel processo comunitario: il bilanciamento degli interessi è di nuovo il fulcro della decisione', *Riv. trim. dir. proc. civ.* (2004): 317 et seq.; F. Castillo De La Torre, 'Interim Measures in Community Courts: Recent Trends', *Comm. M. L. Rev.* (2007): 273 et seq.
424. Articles 278 TFEU and 157 EAEC.
425. Articles 279 TFEU and 158 EAEC.
426. Articles 280 and 299 TFEU; Art. 164 EAEC.
427. Article 60 of the Statute.

286. Two fundamental features define the interim measures in the EU system: they are strictly related to the substance of the case and provisional in view of the decision on the merits.

As far as it concerns the first feature, the Rules of Procedure state that an application to suspend the operation of any measure adopted by an institution shall be admissible only if the applicant is challenging that measure in proceedings before that judicial body, while an application for the adoption of any other interim measure shall be admissible only if it is made by a party to a case before that judicial body and relates to that case.[428] So, one can speak of ancillary nature of interim relief.

As far as it concerns the second feature, the Statute states that any interim ruling shall be provisional and shall in no way prejudice the decision on the substance of the case.[429] According to the settled case law of the EU courts, the application for an interim measure has to be dismissed, where the challenged Act is no longer producing effects.[430]

§2. The Suspension of the Execution of the EU Measures

287. It is a general rule, stated by the treaties, that actions brought before the EU courts shall not have suspensory effect. The challenged Acts are binding and enforceable; their legality is presumed, up to a different decision delivered by the judges. Yet the courts may, if they consider that circumstances so require, order that application of the contested Act be suspended.[431]

A necessarily link exists between the request for the suspension and the claim on the merits. An application for the suspension, lodged without a previous claim to get the annulment, would not be admissible.

In order to determine which Acts may be suspended, two requirements are to be considered: it must deal with Acts which may be challenged and which are producing effects, which may be suspended.

As far as it concerns the first condition, the admissibility of the application for the suspension is strictly linked to the admissibility of the application on the merits. As to the second requirement, suspension is possible in the claims for annulment, where one may find an Act, which the applicant requests the elimination of and the provisional stay of the effects of which is applied for. For the same reason, no suspension may be requested in merely declaratory actions (and above all in the preliminary references or in the actions for condemnation).

428. Article 160 RP CJ; Art. 156 RP GC.

429. Article 39 of the Statute. *See*, in the case law, *inter alia*, GC, 1 Aug. 2001, ord., 1 Aug. 2001, T-132/01 R, *Euroalliages and others v. Commission*, ECR, II, 2307; GC, 12 Jul. 2002, ord., T-163/02 R, *Montan v. Commission;* GC 23 Jan. 2012, T-607/11, *Henkel v. Commission.*

430. CJ, 22 May 1978, ord., 92/78 R, *Simmenthal v. Commission*, ECR, 1129; CJ, 5 Feb. 1982, ord., 10/82 R, *Mogensen and others v. Commission*, ECR, 325; CJ, 13 Dec. 1984, ord., 292/84 R, *Scharf v. Commission*, ECR, 4349.

431. Article 278 TFEU; with some differences, Art. 157 EAEC.

§3. The Atypical Interim Measures

288. The treaties grant the EU courts the power to prescribe any necessary interim measures in any case before them.[432]

The interim measures are the most important expression of the urgency power of the Luxembourg judges. It concerns atypical measures, with many different possible contents, for which the features of the link to the substance of the case (so-called ancillary nature) and the provisional character are even more strictly required.

In fact, the procedural rules forbid to apply for interim measures not related with the controversy on the merits and state that interim orders may have only a provisional effect and shall lapse when final judgment is delivered.

The wider range of the interim atypical measures makes their field of application larger than the one possible for the suspension. They may be requested not only in the claims for annulment, but also in the suits for payment or damages. The EU case law has held as admissible the request for a provisional order of payment, in a claim for damages.[433] Only the merely declaratory actions are therefore excluded (besides, as usual, the preliminary references). In the light of Article 279 TFEU, the CJ has recently ordered a Member State to make a daily penalty payment of EUR 1,000,000, as an interim measure for not complying with an earlier interim order in the context of an action under Article 258 TFEU for failure to fulfil obligations brought by the Commission.[434] In particular, the order follows the Commission's request that the Member State be ordered to pay a daily penalty payment in order to deter it from delaying bringing its conduct into line with that order.[435]

§4. The Stay of the Enforcement

289. While the control on the legality of the enforcement proceedings relating to the EU enforcing titles is a competence of the national jurisdictions, the power of suspending the enforcement is given by the treaties to the EU courts alone. The

432. Article 279 TFEU.
433. GC, 21 Mar. 1997, ord., T-179/96 R, *Antonissen v. Council and Commission*, ECR, II, 425.
434. *See* CJ, 27 Oct. 2021, ord., C-204/2 R, *Commission v. Poland*, ECR, 878. In this case, Poland had not complied with its obligations under the order of 14 Jul. 2021 of the Vice-President of the Court: consequently, the Commission lodged an application requesting that Poland be ordered to pay a daily penalty payment in order to deter that Member State from delaying bringing its conduct into line with that order. The CJ states necessary to strengthen the effectiveness of the interim measures set out in that order by providing for the imposition of a periodic penalty payment on the Republic of Poland in order to deter that Member State from delaying bringing its conduct into line with that order.
435. This is not the first time: in the 1980s the Commission requested that France be ordered to cease the illegal conduct at issue without delay, but the request was granted (CJ, 29 Mar. 1980, ord., C-24/80 R, C-97/80 R, *Commission v. France*, ECR, 1319). *See also* CJ, 20 Nov. 2017, C-441/17 R, *Commission v. Poland,* ECR, 877, concerning the breach of environmental provisions, where the Court raised the possibility of such measure (subsequently not actually ordered) in the case of non-compliance with obligations.

national judge may assess the lack of legality of such enforcement, but may not stay it; this is why no national judge may interfere with the effects of the decisions of the Union.

The stay of the enforcement is the third hypothesis of the urgency power of the EU courts.

290. Yet, a relevant difference exists, between the stay of the enforcement and the two other kinds of urgency powers of the EU courts; basically, it deals with the lack of a link between the interim proceedings and the proceedings on the substance of the case. In fact, while the application for the suspension of the operation of an Act may be admitted only if the applicant is challenging such Act and the application for the adoption of any interim measure is admissible only if it is made by a party to a case before the EU court and relates to that case, when a party applies for the stay of the enforcement before the EU courts, the substance of the case (which is the plea of illegality of the enforcement proceedings) is managed by the national judge concerned.

The EU courts, when they are called to assess the legality of an Act (an administrative Act, as well as a judicial decision), are entitled to suspend the enforceability of the enforcing title only in few cases. So, the simultaneous existence of the national and the European competence (the former, as far as it concerns the review of the legality of the enforcement proceedings, and the latter, as far as it concerns the stay of the enforcement) is an unavoidable aspect.

This brings about that in matter of the stay of the enforcement, the EU rules, according to which proceedings on the substance of the case should be pending before the same EU court to which the granting of interim relief is requested, do not apply. The link between the interim proceedings and the substance of the case may be preserved only by means of an interpretation, which takes into account, at the same time, the jurisdiction of the national courts on the procedures relating to a review upon the illegality of the enforcement.

So, it may be held that an application to the stay of the enforcement before the EU courts is admissible, only when the proceedings contesting the legality of the enforcement have begun, even if before the national judge having jurisdiction. Correspondingly, it should be held that the application to the stay of such enforcement has to be however brought before the Luxembourg courts, even if no EU proceedings on that question exist. When, in the course of the enforcement proceedings before the national judge, the party concerned wishes to request the stay of the enforcement (because of the risk of an irreparable harm to it), it has to make an appropriate application before the EU courts, demonstrating, with regard to the link between the interim measure and the merits of the case, to have correctly initiated a suit contesting the legality of the way in which the enforcement is being carried out before the national judge.

291. Particular problems arise about the stay of the enforcement of enforcing titles consisting in judgments, when they still are subject to any form of appeal or review.

The EU decisions (of the CJ or the General Court) are immediately enforceable and neither appeals nor exceptional reviews have suspensory effect. So, if they are condemnation judgments, they let the party concerned begin the enforcement proceedings at once. But, since such enforcing titles may be appealed or reviewed, it is possible that the stay of the proceedings has place while a jurisdictional control is pending.

It should be noted that the stay of the enforcement of enforcing titles consisting in EU judgments may not be identified with any of the three classical other hypotheses of exercise of the interim power of the EU courts. In fact, it is different both from the suspension of the execution of the EU measures (because in that case the interim relief is sought when a decision on the legality of the Act reviewed has still to be made) and the mere stay of the enforcement (which not always allows the possibility to review the decision, which gives life to the enforcing title). The rules about such stay will be examined later, when dealing with the appeal and the review of the EU decisions. It is useful to stress immediately that the court concerned decides by way of summary procedure.

§5. The Conditions for Granting Interim Relief

292. The conditions for granting interim relief are fixed in the Rules of Procedure, as interpreted in the case law. It must be noted that the EU courts work in the view of assessing concrete cases and that this perspective is quite important while reading the orders in this matter.

Such conditions are the prima facie case, the urgency of adopting interim measures, the assessment of the opposite interests.

293. As far as it concerns the prima facie case, the judge should find that at least some of the pleas relied on by the applicant appear, at first sight, to be relevant and, in any event, not entirely unfounded.[436] According to the settled case law of the Court the fumus boni juris requirement is met where at least one of the pleas in law relied on by the applicant for interim measures in support of the main action appears, prima facie, not unfounded. That is the case, *inter alia*, where one of the pleas relied on reveals the existence of difficult legal issues, the solution to which is not immediately obvious and, therefore, calls for a detailed examination that cannot be carried out by the court hearing the application for interim relief, but must be the subject of the main proceedings, or where the discussion of issues by the parties reveals that there is a major legal disagreement whose resolution is not immediately obvious.[437] The question of the admissibility of the application should not be considered in the urgency proceedings. Yet, it is clear from established case law that, while the question of the admissibility of the main action should not, in principle, be examined in the context of proceedings for interim relief, so as not to prejudge the merits of the case, it may nevertheless be necessary, in order for an application

436. CJ, 20 Dec. 2019, ord. of the Vice President of the Court, C- 646/19 P(R), *Puigdemont i Casamajó and Oliveres v. European Parliament*, ECR, 1149; GC, 12 Aug. 2020, ord., T-162/20 R, *Indofil Industries (Netherlands) v. EFSA*, not published, ECR, 366, where the President of the GC dismissed the application on the ground that there was no prima facie case, without it being necessary to examine the condition relating to urgency or the weighing up of interests.

437. CJ, 17 Dec. 2018, ord., C-619/18 R, *Commission v. Poland*, ECR, 1021.

to suspend the operation of a measure to be declared admissible, for the applicant to prove the existence of certain matters permitting the conclusion that, prima facie, the main action to which his/her application for interim relief relates is admissible, so as to prevent him/her from obtaining, by way of proceedings for interim relief, the suspension of the operation of a measure which the court may subsequently refuse to annul, his/her main action having been ruled inadmissible. So, should the main claim be manifestly inadmissible or not founded, the interim application may be dismissed.[438]

294. According to settled case law, the urgency of an application for interim relief must be assessed in the light of the need for an interlocutory measure in order to avoid serious and irreparable damage to the party seeking the relief, while waiting for the decision on the substance of the case.[439] Where damage depends on the occurrence of a number of factors, it is enough for that damage to be foreseeable with a sufficient degree of probability. It is for the applicant to prove that it cannot wait for the outcome of the main proceedings without suffering damage that would entail serious and irreparable consequences.[440] It should be added that a damage affecting fundamental and political rights is always irreparable.[441]

Sometimes, the party in favour of which the interim relief is granted has the duty to give a security, to ensure an adequate protection for the opposite party, in case of subsequent dismissal of the claim in the substance; yet, it has to be stressed that the availability to give a security is no sufficient condition to obtain the adoption of the requested measure, unless a serious risk of irreparable damage exists.

Lastly, it should be pointed out that although it is firmly established that damage of a pecuniary nature cannot, save in exceptional circumstances, be regarded as irreparable, or even as being reparable only with difficulty, if it can ultimately be the subject of financial compensation, it is also settled case law that an interim measure is justified if it appears that, without that measure, the applicant would find itself in a position which could jeopardize its existence before final judgment in the main action or irremediably alter its position in the market.[442]

It is interesting to note that it should also be determined whether the pecuniary damage pleaded may be classified as serious in the light, in particular, of the size and turnover of the undertaking and of the characteristics of the group to which it

438. GC, 15 Mar. 1995, ord., T-6/95 R, *Cantine dei Colli Berici v. Commission,* ECR, II, 647; GC, 26 Sep. 1997, ord., T-183/97 R, *Micheli and others v. Commission*, ECR, II, 1473; GC, 5 Jul. 2001, ord., T-55/01, *Asahi Vet v. Commission*; GC, 2 Jun. 2015, ord., T-241/15 R, *Buge v. Parliament.*
439. CJ, 20 Nov. 2017, ord., C-441/17 R, *Commission v. Poland,* ECR, 877.
440. 1GC, 1 Dec. 1994, ord., T-353/94 R, *Postbank v. Commission*, ECR, II, 1141; GC, 3 Jun. 1996, ord., T-41/96 R, *Bayer v. Commission*, ECR, II, 381; GC, 15 Jul. 1998, ord., T-73/98 R, *Prayon-Rupel v. Commission*, ECR; II, 2769; GC, 20 Jul. 2006, ord., T-114/06, *Globe v. Commission,* ECR, II, 2627; GC, 22 Mar. 2018, ord., T-732/16 R, *Valencia Club de Fútbol v. Commission.*
441. GC, 2 May 2000, ord., T-17/00, *Rothley and others v. Parliament*, ECR, II, 2085.
442. GC, 28 May 2001, ord., T-53/01 R, *Poste Italiane v. Commission*, ECR, II, 1479; GC, 27 Jul. 2004, ord., T-148/04, *TQ3 v. Commission*, ECR, II, 3027; GC, 10 Nov. 2004, ord., T-316/04, *Wam v. Commission*, ECR, II, 3917; GC, 13 Jul. 2006, ord., T-11/06 R, *Romana Tabacchi v. Commission*, ECR, II, 2941; GC, 19 Jul. 2007, ord., T-31/07 R, *Du Pont de Nemours v. Commission*, ECR, II, 2767; GC, 14 Nov. 2012, ord., T-403/12, *Intrasoft International v. Commission.*

belongs.[443] The EU judges have included in the sphere of the interim protection also the situation of dismissed employees, with regard to the claim for the payment of a provisional salary up to the amount of the unemployment allowance.[444]

295. The case law of the Luxembourg courts has always been taking into account the balance of the opposite interests: granting an interim measure, while protecting it against a damage, must not cause an irreparable prejudice to the opposite party or to third parties. The global consideration of the different interests, included the good working of the EU system, should anyway be considered. Here, one may watch a kind of an administrative management of the interests, made by judiciary bodies. Many concrete cases might be quoted with this purpose. For example, in the so-called mad cow disease case, the CJ could not but recognize the paramount importance to be accorded to the protection of human health, in comparison with the reasons of free trade.[445]

296. The Rules of Procedure provide that applications for the adoption of interim measures must state the circumstances giving rise to urgency and the pleas of fact and law establishing a prima facie case for the measures sought. Those conditions are cumulative, so that an application for interim measures must be dismissed if any one of them is absent.[446]

The EU courts have always tried to remain free in the examination of such conditions, acting in a very discretionary way as far as it concerns the order in which the examination is made. According to the settled case law, in the context of that overall examination, the judge hearing the application enjoys a broad discretion and is free to determine, having regard to the specific circumstances of the case, the manner and order in which those various conditions are to be examined, there being no rule of EU law imposing a pre-established scheme of analysis within which the need to order interim measures must be analysed and assessed.

---

443. CJ, 15 Apr. 1998, ord., C-43/98 P-R, *Camar v. Commission and Council*, ECR, I, 1815; GC, 30 Jun. 1999, ord., T-13/99 R, *Pfizer Animal Health v. Council*, ECR, II, 1961; GC, 27 Feb. 2002, ord., T-132/01, *Euroalliages and others v. Commission*, ECR, II, 777; GC, 4 Dec. 2007, ord., T-326/07, *Cheminova and others v. Commission*, ECR, II, 4877; GC, 7 Dec. 2010, ord., T-385/10, *Arcelo-Mittar Wire France and Others v. Commission*, ECR II, 262; GC, 24 Jan. 2011, ord., T-370/10 R, *Rubinetterie Teorema v. Commission*, ECR, II, 9.

444. GC, 23 Nov. 1990, ord., T-45/90 R, *Speybrouck v. Parliament*, ECR, II, 705.

445. CJ, 12 Jul. 1996, ord., C-180/96, *United Kingdom v. Commission*, ECR, I, 3903; *see also* GC, 2 Mar. 2011, ord., T-392/09 R, *1. garantovaná a.s. v. Commission*, ECR, II, 33 (where the balance of the opposite interests was decisive for the interim application); GC, 16 Nov. 2012, ord., T-341/12 R, *Evonik Degussa v. Commission*; GC, 20 Jul. 2016, ord., T-729/15 R, *MSD Animal Health Innovation v. EMA*.

446. CJ, 14 Oct. 1996, ord., C-268/96 P-R, *SCK and FNK v. Commission*, ECR, I, 4971; GC, 1 Feb. 2001, ord., T-350/00 R, *Free Trade Foods v. Commission*, ECR, II, 493; CJ, 20 Nov. 2017, ord., C-441/17 R, *Commission v. Poland*, ECR, 877.

Sometimes the point of urgency and sometimes the one of prima facie have led the courts to decide and to grant the measure requested, even where the other condition might appear weak.[447] Obviously, this makes the concrete decision more appropriate, but at the same time less foreseeable, making the right of defence more uncertain.

§6. The Urgency Proceedings

297. The EU courts, when they are called to state about an interim measure (both a provisional one and on the stay of the enforcement), decide by way of a special procedure, which the Statute defines summary.[448]

The EU urgency proceedings may be considered as summary because of two elements: the power to decide is given to the President of the court alone and the more simple features of the management of the case.[449]

The power to decide, under the conditions laid down in the Rules of Procedure, may be also exercised by the Vice-President of the court.[450] Should the President and the Vice-President be prevented from attending, another judge shall take their place.

298. As it has been already noted, the interim application is not admissible independently from the main proceedings. Yet, it shall never be included in the application initiating the proceedings, not even where the urgency arises at the same time of the beginning of the action (like in the event of an application for the suspension of an Act). On the contrary, the interim application shall be made by a separate document, in accordance with the general provisions for the applications beginning the case. Such application shall state the subject matter of the proceedings, the circumstances giving rise to urgency and the pleas of fact and law establishing a prima facie case for the interim measure applied for. It shall contain all the evidence and offers of evidence available to justify the grant of interim measures.[451]

Should the request for an interim measure be submitted in the same application initiating the case, it would be inadmissible. Besides, the application for interim

---

447. CJ, 19 Jul. 1995, ord., C-149/95 P-R, *Commission v. Atlantic Container and others*, ECR, I, 2165; CJ, 21 Mar. 1997, ord., C-110/97 R, *Netherlands v. Council*, ECR, I, 1795; GC, 7 Jul. 2004, ord., T-37/04, *Região autónoma dos Açores v. Council,* ECR, II, 2153. The General Court underlined that in the context of that overall examination, the judge hearing the application enjoys a broad discretion and is free to determine, having regard to the specific circumstances of the case, the manner and order in which the various conditions (the prima facie case, the urgency of adopting interim measures, the assessment of the opposite interests) are to be examined, there being no rule of European law imposing a pre-established scheme of analysis within which the need to order interim measures must be analysed and assessed (GC, 9 Mar. 2011, ord., T-591/10 R, *Castiglioni v. Commission*, ECR, II, 47).

448. Article 39 of the Statute. *See* B. Pastor & E. Van Ginderachter, 'La procédure en référé', *Rev. trim. dr. eur.* (1989): 561 et seq.

449. Articles 160 and 161 RP CJ; Art. 157 RP GC.

450. *See* CJ, 20 Dec. 2019, ord., C- 646/19 P(R), *Puigdemont i Casamajó and Oliveres v. European Parliament*, ECR, 1149; CJ, 27 Oct. 2021, ord., C-204/21 R, *Commission v. Poland*, ECR, 878.

451. Article 160 RP CJ; Art. 156 RP GC.

relief must be sufficient in itself to enable the defendant to prepare his/her observations and the judge hearing the application to rule on it, where necessary, without other supporting information. In order to ensure legal certainty and the proper administration of justice, it is necessary, if such an application is to be admissible, that the essential elements of fact and law on which it is founded be set out in a coherent and comprehensible fashion in the application for interim relief itself. While the application may be supported and supplemented on specific points by references to particular passages in documents which are annexed to it, a general reference to other written documentation, even if it is annexed to the application for interim relief, cannot make up for the absence of essential elements in that application. A similar interpretation must be adopted regarding the presentation of observations on an application for interim relief which are lodged by a defendant.[452]

The application for interim relief may be brought at any moment of the proceedings concerning the merits of the case. Yet, while the application for atypical measures may really have place in different moments of the proceedings, the application for the suspension of an Act is logically placed at the very beginning of the proceedings.

The provisions about the lodging of the pleadings by telefax or other technical means of communication may find a very effective use in the summary procedures.

299. The application for interim relief is usually served on the opposite party and the President prescribes a short period within which that party may submit written or oral observations. Therefore, the defence may consist in lodging a written pleading or simply in the oral debate at the hearing.[453] Moreover, the President may grant the application even before the observations of the opposite party have been submitted; this decision may be varied or cancelled even without any application being made by any party.

The President may also order measures of organization of procedure and measures of inquiry. Yet, the structure of the summary proceedings, linked to the need for the applicant to bring prima facie case elements, makes the undertaking of complex measures of inquiry almost impossible. The effort of the applicant is that of alleging facts, whose existence itself may bring about an interim relief, and of producing written documents in support of them.

There are no subsequent stages (written stage, preparatory inquiry, oral stage) in the summary proceedings; yet, none of such stages is eliminated. An oral hearing is often (but not always) fixed, at the end of which the decision is taken. The right to be heard is sometimes limited, pursuant to a widely spread technique in matters of interim measures in the national procedural legislations. However, the defendant is usually put in the conditions to defend himself/herself adequately. The EU case law holds that the intervention of a third party is admissible.[454]

300. The need for a quick and summary assessment has to be counterbalanced by means of a certain variability of the interim measures. Therefore, on application

452. GC, 7 May 2002, ord., T-306/01, *Aden and others v. Council and Commission*, ECR, II, 2387.
453. Article 160 RP CJ; Art. 157 RP GC.
454. GC, 26 Jul. 2004, ord., T-201/04, *Microsoft v. Commission*, ECR, II, 2977.

by a party, the interim order may at any time be varied or cancelled on account of a change in circumstances.[455] As stated in Article 163 of the Rules of Procedure of the CJ, the order may at any time be varied or cancelled on account of a change in circumstances. This provision emphasizes the provisional nature of interim protection. Moreover, it shows that the protective measure does not cease to have effect only in the cases referred to in Article 162.[456]

In this respect, the CJ has recently ruled on the notion of 'change of circumstances', declaring that it refers in particular to the occurrence of any factual or legal element capable of calling into question the assessments of the judge hearing the application for interim measures as to the conditions to which the grant of a suspension or of interim relief is subject.[457]

The interim measures, even if decided in the adversary proceedings, have a precarious nature and they are always subject to the management by the judge of the interests coming into play.

Where the order is made without having previously heard the opposite party, the decision may be varied or cancelled also of the court's motion. But no appeal is left before the judge who granted the measure; the interim orders of the General Court may be appealed before the upper judge, while the interim measures of the CJ may never be appealed.

301. Other two rules complete the system of check and balance, which tries to take into account both the protection of the applicant and the positions of the defendant, since the interim relief is granted without having ascertained the issue on the merits. First, the enforcement of the order may be made conditional on the lodging by the applicant of security, of an amount and nature to be fixed in the light of the circumstances.[458]

Then, the order granting the application shall fix, where appropriate, a date on which the interim measure is to lapse, different from the date when the final judgment is delivered.

302. As it has already been noted, the summary proceedings are managed by the President of the judicial body concerned, who hears and decides on the application personally. Before the CJ, the President may decide on the application himself/herself or refer it to the Court, which shall give a decision immediately, after hearing the Advocate-General. Before the General Court, the President always decides

---

455. Article 163 RP CJ, Art. 158(2) RP GC.
456. Article 162 RP CJ.
457. CJ, 6 Oct. 2021, ord., C-204/2021 R, *Poland v. Commission*, ECR, 834. *See also* CJ, 20 Sep. 2021, C-121/21 R, *Czech Republic v. Poland*, ECR, 752. In *Poland v. Commission,* the Member State argued that a change of circumstances had occurred as a result of the ruling of the Constitutional Court of Poland. The latter had found an incompatibility between EU law and the Polish Constitution. The CJ held that the application was unfounded because, by the principle of the primacy of European Union law, the fact that a Member State invokes provisions of national law, even if they are of constitutional rank, cannot affect the unity and effectiveness of European Union law.
458. Article 162(2) RP CJ; Art. 158(2) RP GC.

alone; in the event that the President is absent or prevented from dealing with the case, the Vice-President of the court or another judge is designated, in accordance with the Rules of Procedure.[459]

303. The decision on the application shall take the form of a reasoned order; it is frequent to find interim orders consisting in many pages. The order is served on the parties forthwith. As it has been remarked, the order has only an interim and provisional effect and is without prejudice to the subsequent decision on the substance of the case. Nevertheless, should the interim relief be granted, the parties might draw remarkable elements in view of the final orientation of the court. The interim order is binding and is an enforcing title.

The contents of the order are different, above all as far as it concerns the interim atypical measures. It may be said that the form of order sought may never be the same of the claim in the main proceedings; for instance, an Act of an EU institution may be suspended, but not annulled.

It has already been noted that unless the order fixes the date on which the interim measure is to lapse, the measure shall lapse when final judgment is delivered. Obviously, this rule is applied when the application is granted. If the application for an interim relief is rejected, the party may make a further application on the basis of new facts.[460] Such rule is important above all before the CJ, where no appeal against the interim order is possible.

The costs relating to the summary procedure are to be decided in the final judgment on the substance of the case. Before the General Court, if it appears justified in the light of the circumstances of the case, a decision as to the costs relating to the proceedings for interim relief shall be given in the order.[461]

The parties to the proceedings may appeal to the upper court against any decision of the General Court, within two months of its notification.[462]

---

459. Article 161 RP CJ; Art. 157 RP GC.
460. Article 164 RP CJ; Art. 160 RP GC.
461. Article 158(5) RP GC.
462. Article 57(2) of the Statute.

Chapter 3. The Special Proceedings Relating to Intellectual Property Rights

§1. General Features

304. EU Regulations No. 1001/17 in matter of trademark, No. 2100/94 in matter of plant variety rights, and No. 6/02 in matter of designs have introduced new important remedies. Especially, the Kirchberg judges have been given jurisdiction to decide the controversies about the existence and the validity of the intellectual property rights (while it has been provided that the national courts have jurisdiction in matters of infringement of EU trademarks).[463]

The decisions of the EU offices (i.e., to say, the EU Intellectual Property Office or the Community Plant Variety Office) are subject to a control before the Board of Appeal, which has no jurisdictional nature (despite the presence of relevant procedural elements in its operating). The decisions of the Board of Appeal are subject to an action for annulment (and for modification) before the General Court, whose judgments may be obviously appealed before the CJ.

305. This matter has a remarkable importance under the point of view of quantity, since it represents about one-third of the workload of the General Court. But above all, it deserves to be studied because of the high degree of specialization requested to the judges and because these controversies, in the substance, are discussed between two individuals. This last aspect is now quite exceptional in the EU judicial system (which takes into consideration only cases between States and institutions, or individual and EU institutions), but it might open new perspectives in the European jurisdiction.

306. Also from the procedural point of view, it has immediately been clear that litigation in this matter implied some corrections. In fact, the true controversy is the one between two firms and the right to use or not a certain trademark. The position of the Office is somehow secondary, since the interest of the institution is that only one person may be entitled to use the trademark, no importance having for it which of the litigators be successful. Yet, since the proceedings begin because of an act or a conduct of the Office is challenged, it was necessary to avoid the substantial opposite party to occupy the uncomfortable place of a mere intervener and to allow it to be able to defend its positions fully. The EU case law is aware of the fact that these proceedings govern controversies between individuals. For example, it is settled that the Office may seek the same form of order of the applicant.[464]

463. L. Querzola, 'Proprietà intellettuale e tutela giurisdizionale comunitaria: quadro attuale e prospettive di evoluzione', *Riv. trim. dir. proc. civ.* (2002): 777 et seq.

464. *See*, *inter alia*, GC, 30 Jun. 2004, T-107/02, *GE Betz v. OHIM*, ECR, II, 1845; GC, 1 Feb. 2006, joined cases T-466/04 and T-467/04, *Dami v. OHIM*, ECR, II, 183; GC, 16 May 2007, T-137/05, *La Perla v. OHIM*, ECR, II, 47.

This is why the Statute has included the provision, pursuant to which the Rules of Procedure of the General Court may derogate from the common rules on intervention and procedure by default in order to take account of the specific features of litigation in the field of intellectual property.[465]

The special rules are applied to few, well-specified kinds of application: to proceedings brought against the Intellectual Property Office and against the Plant Variety Office, concerning the application of the rules relating to an intellectual property regime, and where prior proceedings before a Board of Appeal have been introduced. It may be held that such rules are applied also to proceedings in matter of designs.

Special proceedings have therefore been realized, the most important feature of which is to put the private parties, which are in contrast in the substantive controversy relating to the rights of intellectual property, on the same level.

The judicial proceedings are also strongly linked to the administrative ones before the Board of Appeal; in fact, only those who took part in the latter may exercise such powers as the main parties and the subject matter of the case is the same which had been discussed at the stage before the Board of Appeal. The Rules of the General Court provide that the pleadings lodged by the parties in proceedings may not change the subject matter of the proceedings before the Board of Appeal.[466]

§2. The Language of the Proceedings

307. The first special aspect is the language of the proceedings.[467] The general criterion, according to which the choice of the language of the procedure is given to the claimant, is quite corresponding to the need for judicial protection when the defendant is an institution, in degree to practise all the languages, by means of its agents. But, where the confrontation is substantially among two private parties, the rules on the language should be shaped in order to ensure the equality of weapons.

The Rules of Procedure state that the application shall be drafted in one of the official languages, according to the applicant's choice: this language shall become the language of the case if the applicant was the only party to the proceedings before the Board of Appeal, or if another party to those proceedings does not object to this within a period laid down for that purpose by the Registrar after the application has been lodged. If, within that period, the parties to the proceedings before the Board of Appeal agree on the choice of another official language, such second language becomes the language of the case.

In the event of an objection to the language of the application by a party to the proceedings before the Board of Appeal of the Office other than the applicant, the language of the decision that is contested before the General Court shall become the language of the case; in such cases, the Registrar shall ensure the translation of the application into the language of the case.

465. Articles 53, 40(4), and 41 of the Statute.

466. Article 188 RP GC. *See* GC, 27 Feb. 2018, T-166/15, *Gramberg v. EUIPO* (in matter of evidence submitted for the first time before the GC).

467. Article 45 RP GC.

These modifications of the common procedural rules about language have a clear meaning: in this matter, there are no two-party proceedings, where one of them is an EU institution, which may plead in every official language, but there are usually multi-party proceedings, almost two of which are individuals, using to practise a certain national language and which the necessary protection as far as it concerns the expression in the case is to be granted. It should be noted, *inter alia*, that the language applied by the Office are five only: French, English, German, Spanish, and Italian.[468]

§3. The Powers of the Interveners

308. Not all controversies in matters of intellectual property rights are multi-party controversies. For instance, while a decision of the Office on an application for the invalidity of a trademark supposes a conflict between the applicant and the proprietor of the trademark, the denial of registration of a new trademark brings about a litigation only between the applicant and the Office. Yet, the presence of more than two parties before the Board of Appeal is very frequent.

309. In fact, the most relevant difference with the common proceedings is the existence of a special kind of interveners (which might be called qualified, in order to distinguish them from all the other interveners), which are those persons who were parties to the proceedings before the Board of Appeal other than the applicant. The Rules of Procedure give these parties the possibility to defend and seek new and autonomous forms of order, and not only, therefore, to support the claims of one of the main parties. So, such interveners take part to the proceedings at the same level of the main parties.[469]

310. The due protection of the rights of these persons brings about that the application, even if containing a claim for annulment and/or modification of an Act of the institution and, therefore, directly brought against the Office, shall be served on the substantive opposite parties, which were parties to the proceedings before the Board of appeal. In fact, such parties are to be informed of the beginning of the case, without being obliged to look after the notices given in the Official Journal.

This is why the application shall contain the names of all the parties to the proceedings before the Board of Appeal and the addresses which they had given in the course of those proceedings; if not, the application shall be declared inadmissible.

The parties to the proceedings before the Board of appeal other than the applicant may participate, as interveners, in the proceedings before the General Court. They have not to prove their interest to the case, because such interest is always existing. They have the same procedural rights as the main parties and they may apply for a form of order and put forward pleas independently of those applied for and put forward by the main parties.

468. Article 146 EU Regulation No. 1011/17.
469. Articles 177,178, 179 RP GC.

Such interveners, in their responses lodged in the case, may also seek an order annulling or altering the decision of the Board of Appeal on a new point, not raised in the application and put forward pleas in law not raised in the application; in other words, they are entitled to challenge the Act for different and may be opposite grounds than those of the applicant, submitting a cross-claim.

The Rules of Procedure of the General Court provide that where an intellectual property right affected by the proceedings has been transferred to a third party by a party to the proceedings before the Board of Appeal of the Office (i.e., after a sale of business that also includes the sale of the trademark), the successor to that right may apply to replace the original party in the proceedings (just started) before the General Court. The application for replacement shall be served on the parties. The decision on the application for replacement shall take the form of a reasoned order of the President or shall be included in the decision closing the proceedings.[470]

311. The Office submits its response to the application within a time limit of two months from the service of the application. That time limit may, in exceptional circumstances, be extended by the President.[471]

Before the expiry of the time limit prescribed for the lodging of a response, a party to the proceedings before the Board of Appeal other than the applicant shall become a party to the proceedings before the General Court, as intervener, on lodging a procedural document. This document is autonomous from the response. The intervener loses the status of intervener before the General Court if he/she fails to respond to the application in the manner and within the time limit prescribed.

The Rules explain the position of the qualified interveners who do not want to defend but also contest the decision of the Office.

These parties may submit a cross-claim within the same time limit as that prescribed for the submission of a response, but it is submitted by a document separate from the response. The cross-claim shall seek an order annulling or altering the decision of the Board of Appeal on a point not raised in the application.[472]

312. In this landscape, where more protection is given to the individuals, some shadows still remain. The most relevant one is the rule, pursuant to which the cross-claim of the qualified intervener shall be deemed to be devoid of purpose if the applicant discontinues the main action or if the main action is declared manifestly inadmissible. The rule may be criticized; yet, it may be also explained, thinking that if two parties have grounds to challenge the same Act, some advantage is to be established in favour of him/her, who began the case first. Of course, such rule reduces the real autonomy of the qualified intervener.

Where a cross-claim is lodged, the other parties may submit a pleading confined to responding to the form of order sought, the pleas in law and arguments relied on in the cross-claim, within two months of its being served on them.

470. Articles 174, 175, 176 RP GC.
471. Article 180 RP GC.
472. Articles 182–184 RP GC.

The proceeding follows the common rules, with the possibility to decide without oral hearing and the respect of the maximum length of written pleadings.

The judgment of the General Court may be appealed before the CJ; both the main parties and the qualified interveners have peer standing to appeal.

Part V. Peculiar Aspects of the Proceedings in the Relationships Between the Judicial Bodies

Chapter 1. Questions of Jurisdiction and Competence

313. Up to the introduction of the CFI, the notion of competence in the Luxembourg proceedings had the meaning of jurisdiction. Where the CJ stated not to be competent to decide a certain case, it assessed to have no jurisdiction over that matter. In other words, it acknowledged not to be entitled to state upon that claim, which was out of the limits of the jurisdictional powers it had received by the treaties.

This hypothesis of lack of jurisdiction goes on being considered also in the nowadays system. The EU courts may dismiss a claim because they are lacking of the power to decide on that matter.[473]

314. The introduction of the CFI and the consequent distribution of tasks have given birth to a hypothesis of incompetence in the proper meaning, which has extended after the subsequent introduction of the judicial panels: it deals with the wrong lodging of the application initiating a case to one or to the other EU judicial body, where the subject matter of the litigation surely falls within the EU jurisdiction. It is interesting to note that the wording of the Statute still uses the expression 'jurisdiction', also where it deals with a question of competence.

The provisions of the Statute and the Rules of Procedure take care to give a solution to any possible conflict of jurisdiction and competence.

315. As far as it concerns the question of jurisdiction, the decisions on this point deal with a substantive issue. The EU courts decide by means of a judgment or a reasoned order, where it is clear that they have no jurisdiction to take cognizance of an action. The decisions of the General Court may be appealed before the upper court. Therefore, the last word on the jurisdiction belongs to the CJ.[474]

316. For what concerns the competence in the proper meaning (i.e., the division of the jurisdiction among the different bodies), three cases should be distinguished:

473. Article 53(1) RP CJ; Art. 126 RP GC.
474. Articles 56 and 58 of the Statute; Art. 53 RP CJ; Art. 126 RP GC.

a mere mistake in lodging an application, the finding that the court has no competence, the connection between more cases.[475]

Where an application or other procedural document addressed to one of the EU judicial bodies is lodged by mistake with the Registrar of another EU court, that Registrar transmits it immediately to the other Registrar.

The second and more relevant case is the following one. Where the General Court finds that it does not have competence to hear and determine an action in respect of which the CJ has competence, it shall refer that action to the CJ. Likewise, where the CJ finds that an action falls within the competence of the General Court, it shall refer that action to the General Court, whereupon the General Court may not decline jurisdiction. It must be noted that, in these events, there is no doubt that the EU courts have jurisdiction on the controversy, but it is discussed which of them has competence.

The decision which states the lack of competence and refers the case to the other judicial body is taken, by the CJ, by a judgment, save where the court manifestly lacks the competence; in such case the decision has the form of a reasoned order. The General Court decides by a reasoned order. The Rules of Procedure of the General Court also take into consideration the hypothesis of a decision, referring the case to another court because the case falls within the competence of that court, taken after a preliminary plea about the question, without going to the substance of the case.[476] Obviously, while the decision of the CJ may not be challenged, the one of the General Court may be appealed in the ordinary way.

317. The third hypothesis has place where more cases are connected. Where the CJ and the General Court are seized of cases in which the same relief is sought, the same issue of interpretation is raised, or the validity of the same Act is called in question, the General Court may, after hearing the parties, stay the proceedings before it, until such time as the CJ has delivered judgment; that is the natural consequence of the relationship between the two main EU judiciary bodies. But (and this second possibility affects the question of competence), where the action is one brought pursuant to Article 263 TFEU, the General Court may also decline its competence, so as to allow the CJ to rule on such actions. In the same circumstances, the CJ may also decide to stay the proceedings before it; in that event, the proceedings before the General Court shall continue, notwithstanding the contrary opinion of the General Court, if any.[477]

A peculiar solution is established, where a Member State and an institution of the Union are challenging the same Act, which is possible where the competence to decide on the actions brought by Member States is given to the General Court. In this event, no choice is given to the General Court, which shall anyway decline its competence, so that the CJ may rule on both applications.

It should be noted that declining of competence by the General Court, with the consequent transferring to the CJ of the case once brought before the General Court, gives a better protection to the applicant, who may defend its position before the

475. Article 54 of the Statute.
476. Article 130(1) RP GC.
477. *See* GC, 8 Mar. 2018, ord., T-46/18, *Comune di Milano v. Commission*.

Court, instead of being compelled to merely wait for the exit of the decision of the case (what happens in case of stay of the proceedings), without any possibility to influence such decision. Therefore, one may conclude that the choice between stay of the proceedings and decision on the lack of competence is not neutral as far as it concerns the right of defence of the parties.

Chapter 2. The Stay of Proceedings

§1. The Stay of Proceedings Before the CJ

318. Two hypotheses of stay of proceedings are possible before the CJ.[478]

The first case is where the CJ and the General Court are seized of cases in which the same relief is sought, the same issue of interpretation is raised or the validity of the same Act is called in question. Both courts may stay the proceedings before each of them, until such time as the other court has delivered judgment.

The second hypothesis, on the contrary, has a general character. In fact, the Rules refer to all other cases, without any other specification.

The stay in case of connected or identical claims is made by order, after hearing the Advocate-General alone (and not the parties, with a relevant breach to their right to be heard); in the other cases, the decision is adopted by the President, after hearing both the Judge-Rapporteur and the Advocate-General and, save the case of references for a preliminary ruling, the parties.

Of course, no appeal may be brought against the decision or order to stay proceedings; but the Court may revoke it.

§2. The Stay of Proceedings Before the General Court

319. The stay of proceedings has remarkably different features before those courts, whose decisions may be appealed before an upper court.

320. The General Court may stay proceedings pending before it in the following cases:[479]

(a) when an appeal before the CJ and an application initiating an exceptional review procedure (third-party proceedings, revision, interpretation) before the General Court contest the same judgment of the General Court, the General Court may, after hearing the parties, stay the proceedings until the CJ has delivered its judgment;
(b) in the cases of connected claims, pursuant to Article 54 of the Statute (considered above as far as it concerns the CJ);
(c) where an appeal is brought before the CJ against a decision of the General Court which does not close the proceedings (and so, disposing of the substantive issues in part only, disposing of a procedural issue concerning a plea of lack of competence or inadmissibility or dismissing an application to intervene), the General Court may stay proceedings, until the CJ has adjudicated the appeal.

478. Article 55 RP CJ.
479. Article 69 RP GC.

In these three hypotheses, the stay of proceedings is linked to the existence of proceedings before the CJ. But stay of proceedings may happen also at the joint request of the main parties and in other particular cases where the proper administration of justice so requires.

As it has been stressed, in some cases both the CJ and the General Court may stay proceedings, having the same subject matter or being however connected. Therefore, cases of conflict are possible.

Should the conflict be a positive one (if both courts decide to stay proceedings), the decision of the CJ prevails: if the Court decides to stay proceedings before it, the proceedings before the General Court shall necessarily continue, even if the General Court had also decided to stay them. On the contrary, should the conflict be a negative one (so, if both courts refuse to stay proceedings), the Rules of Procedure state no solution, except where the General Court decides to decline competence. Theoretically, one might arrive at two different and contrasting judgments. Yet, the party concerned has the right to appeal the judgment of the General Court before the CJ, with the obvious consequence that the opinion of the CJ prevails and no conflict between two final judgments is possible. The prevalence of the decisions of the CJ, in few words, is the basic solution to any hypothesis of conflict in this matter.

321. The decision to stay the proceedings is taken by the President after hearing the parties (and the Advocate-General, if designed).[480] The decision is served on the parties and may not be appealed. The stay of proceedings shall take effect on the date indicated in the decision of stay or, in the absence of such an indication, on the date of that decision. While proceedings are stayed, time shall cease to run for the purposes of prescribed time limits for all parties, except the time limit for an application to intervene by a third party; but interim measures may be requested. From the date of the resumption of proceedings, any suspended procedural time limits shall be replaced by new time limits and time shall begin to run from the date of that resumption.

The decision to stay may fix the length of the stay, or not. In the first case, at the end of the period, the proceedings go on automatically. In the second and more usual case, a decision ordering that the proceedings be resumed has to be adopted, in accordance with the same procedure as for the decision to stay; there is no doubt that any party may lodge an application for this purpose. The decision of resumption is served on the parties and may not be appealed. The stay shall end on the date indicated in the decision of resumption or, in the absence of such indication, on the date of the decision of resumption.

480. Articles 70–71 RP GC.

Chapter 3. Judgments Delivered When the Case Has Been Referred Back

322. Since the EU jurisdiction has been distributed, at least for some matters, on many judicial bodies, there has been introduced the case of a judgment delivered by a court after its decision has been set aside and the case referred back to it.

Pursuant to the Statute, if an appeal against a decision of the General Court is well founded, the CJ, after quashing such decision, may itself give final judgment in the matter or refer the case back to the General Court for judgment. So, a new stage in the proceedings begins: the General Court is free to decide on the merits, but it shall be bound by the decision of the CJ on points of law.[481]

323. The features of the proceedings where the case has been referred back are different, in accordance to the stage of the proceedings in which the appealed decision has been delivered. The issues of fact are not always already verified and in some cases new measures of inquiry or new measures of organization of procedure may be prescribed. Sometimes, the judgment consists in a re-consideration of the facts verified, at the light of the principle of law established by the upper court; in other cases, it deals with still uncompleted and open proceedings. That has influence, for example, on the formation of the courts.[482]

Generally, the procedure shall be conducted in accordance with the common provisions governing the proceedings at the first instance before the court to whom the case is referred back, with some specific points. So, all the rules about the written stage, the oral procedure, the preparatory inquiry, and the measures of organization of procedure apply, as well as all the rules referring to the language of the case, with the particular rules of the proceedings relating to intellectual property right.

324. Some specific points are to be underlined. Where the written procedure before the General Court has been completed when the judgment referring the case back to it is delivered, the course of the procedure shall be as follows. The decision of the CJ is served upon the parties, as usual. Within two months (not extendible time limit) of the service of the decision of the CJ, the parties may lodge their written observations on the conclusions to be drawn from the decision of the CJ for the outcome of the proceedings. Therefore, it is not possible to enlarge the subject matter of the proceeding, but only to highlight useful points of law or fact.

On the contrary, where the written procedure before the General Court had not been completed when the judgment referring the case back to the General Court was delivered, the case shall be resumed, at the stage which it has reached.

While in the first hypothesis the written statements have the goal of explaining the position of the parties after the setting aside of the first judgment, in the second case the parties may exercise their defence by means of the ordinary statements. In both cases, the General Court may, if the circumstances so justify, allow supplementary statements of written observations to be lodged.

481. Article 61 of the Statute.
482. Articles 215–219 RP GC.

These provisions may be clarified, if one takes into account that in the EU system the proceedings after the case has been referred to the General Court are governed by the principle of initiative of the court, so that the appeal before the upper court plays the role of linking the two stages of the proceedings at the first instance: the one prior and the one following the judgment of setting aside. In fact, the court concerned is seised of the case, not by the parties' motion, but by the judgment itself, referring the issue to it. The parties are allowed, but not compelled, to lodge the statements described above. Should the parties omit such lodgement, there is no discontinuance of the proceedings, but the court decides the controversy at any case, on the basis only of the Acts lodged before the judgment, then appealed.

The strong link between the two stages before the General Court and the proceedings on the appeal is confirmed by the rule, pursuant to which the General Court decides on the costs relating to the proceedings instituted before it and to the proceedings on the appeal before the CJ.

After the Treaty of Nice, it is also possible that the CJ reviews a judgment of the General Court, acting as a judge of appeal against a decision of a specialized court or (in the future) for a preliminary ruling. In this case, the provisions described above are adapted to such situation.[483]

It should be noted that not every case of annulment of the decision delivered at the first instance brings about the referring back of the case to the General Court.

For example, the case is referred back in the hypothesis of a final decision on the merits, set aside on the ground of a breach of the EU law. In this case, the General Court may state again, at the light of the principle of law, stated by the upper court.

In other cases, the case is referred back only under a procedural point of view, because the judge of appeal refers back to the General Court a case the decision of which has been set aside for procedural grounds, while no finding on the merits has ever been made. In the practice, here the case is referred back, with the task for the court seized of it to decide it on the substance for the first time.

On the contrary, the annulment of an interim decision gives no place to a new judgment, but only to the substitution of the measure stated by the General Court with the new measure ordered by the upper court (which, for instance, may order the suspension of an Act, which had not been ordered by the General Court).

Anyway, the referring back of the case after the setting aside of the judgment is never mandatory, because the CJ may itself give final judgment in the matter: here, the question is about the requirements which should exist to enable the Court to do it.

483. Articles 220–222 RP GC.

Part VI. The Proceedings of Appeal and Review of the Decisions

Chapter 1. General Outline

325. It has been possible to speak of EU appeal proceedings, only since 1986, when the European Single Act altered the institutional structure of the Communities, by introducing a jurisdiction with the task of hearing and determining some kinds of actions at first instance, with the provision that decisions given by the new judicial body were subjected to a right of appeal to the CJ on points of law only. The provision of the treaties was later enacted by the decision of the Council of 24 October 1988, which instituted the CFI and altered the Statutes, granting the CJ the task of judge of the appeals.

The appeal against the decisions of the General Court brought before the CJ may certainly be considered the ordinary pattern of any appeal in the EU system; yet, it is not the only way of challenging a decision of an EU judicial body before an upper court. In fact, after the Treaty of Nice, other forms of control are possible:

(a) appeals before the General Court against the decisions of the specialized courts, on points of law only or, when provided for in the regulation establishing the specialized court, also on matters of fact;[484]
(b) exceptional review before the CJ of the decisions given by the General Court on the appeals brought before it against decisions of the specialized courts, under the conditions and within the limits laid down by the Statute, where there is a serious risk of the unity or consistency of EU law being affected;[485]
(c) exceptional review before the CJ of the decisions given by the General Court on questions referred for a preliminary ruling, under the conditions and within the limits laid down by the Statute, where there is a serious risk of the unity or consistency of the EU law being affected.[486]

The judicial protection for the litigators is therefore remarkably grown up and the parties to the EU proceedings have been granted more than that 'essential minimum', which accompanied the institution of the CFI. At the same time, until 2016, the choice made for the appeals before the General Court against the judgments of

484. Article 257 TFEU; Arts 192–214 RP GC.
485. Articles 256(2) TFEU.
486. Articles 256(3) TFEU.

the CST joined the pattern, widely ruled and concretely experimented, of the appeals before the CJ against the decisions of the General Court. Such pattern did not consist in a double full level of jurisdiction on the merits, since the appeal before the upper court might here be brought only on points of law, without any review of the issues of fact. Yet, pursuant to the text of the treaties, it may not be excluded that for the future specialized tribunals a right of appeal also on matters of fact might be introduced.

In the consideration of the ways of control in the EU system, one must also take into account the exceptional review procedures, which are brought before the same court which made the challenged judgment and which were present also in the ordinary text of the Statutes and the Rules of Procedure of the CJ alone: the third-party proceedings, the revision, the application to set aside a judgment by default, the interpretation, the rectification, and the failure to adjudicate.

Chapter 2. The Ordinary Proceedings of Appeal Against the Decisions of the General Court

§1. General Features

326. As stressed above, the ordinary appeal proceedings do not consist in a double full level of jurisdiction on the merits, but in a review of legality, which may be compared with the application before the Supreme Courts in the European national continental systems (like the *Cour de Cassation* in France).[487]

In fact, any appeal to the CJ is limited to points of law and it shall lie on the grounds of lack of competence of the General Court, a breach of procedure which adversely affects the interests of the appellant as well as the infringement of the EU law by the General Court. So, it deals with a review on the legality, which does not affect the findings on the facts, made by the General Court in its decisions.

Therefore, the CJ, if the appeal is well founded and the decision of the General Court is quashed, may not only refer the case back to the General Court for the judgment on the merits (as in the usual scheme of any appeal on the mere legality), but also itself gives the final judgment in the matter, where the state of the proceedings so permits. In this event, once affirmed the principle of law to be applied in the case, the CJ may go to find facts and consequently decide on the substance of the case.

So, the CJ as a judge of appeal works like a national Supreme Court, with the power to decide on the merits, where it is proper.

It should be added that the EU ordinary appeal is governed by the principle of the transmission to the upper court of the power to decide as much subject matter, as the parties wish; in fact, the CJ may state on the decision of the General Court, as far as the parties (the applicant, but also the defendant or the interveners) want to challenge it. With regard to that, the Rules of Procedure take into account the possibility that the appeal seeks to set aside the decision of the General Court only in part.[488] The possibility of any enlargement of the subject matter of the case in the stage of appeal is to be absolutely excluded.

Lastly, it is useful to underline that the EU system has made the choice not to put limitations to the right to appeal against the decisions of the General Court. No prior form of control or need for a leave to appeal has been introduced (save the common requirements as far as it concerns the admissibility of the application). The political will to grant the parties a greater protection is at the base of this option.

---

487. L. Scambiato, 'La natura del giudizio dinanzi alla Corte di giustizia delle Comunità europee avverso le decisioni del Tribunale di primo grado nel processo comunitario', *Riv. it. dir. pubbl. com.* (1995): 1049 et seq.; P.J. Rideau & F. Picod, 'Le pourvoi sur les questions de droit', *Revue du Marché commun* (1995): 585 et seq.; M. Gros, 'Le pourvoi devant la Cour de justice des Communautés européennes', *L'actualitè juridique: droit administratif* (1995): 589 et seq.; S. Sonelli, 'Appeal on Points of Law in the Community system: A Review', *Comm. M. L. Rev.* (1998): 871 et seq.; C. Fardet, 'Le "réexamen" des décisions du Tribunal de première instance', *Revue du Marché commun* (2004): 184 et seq.
488. Articles 169, 170, 178 RP CJ.

§2. The Decisions Which May Be Appealed

327. The decisions of the General Court against which an ordinary appeal may be brought before the CJ are the following ones:[489]

(a) final decisions closing the proceedings (disposing on the merits or only on procedural questions);
(b) decisions disposing of the substantive issues in part only;
(c) decisions disposing of a procedural preliminary issue concerning a plea of lack of competence or inadmissibility;
(d) decisions dismissing an application to intervene;
(e) decisions made in matter of interim protection and stay of the enforcement.

These decisions may be made in form of judgment or of order.

328. With regard to the decisions closing the proceedings, it should be noted that such category includes all the final judgments of the General Court, either wholly disposing on the merits, or stopping at a decision on a procedural question, which closes the proceedings; for example, dismissing the claim on grounds of lack of jurisdiction or inadmissibility. In general, it may be held that any decision closing the proceedings may be appealed: included the orders in matter of discontinuance and no need to adjudicate.

Of course, against the orders of the General Court dismissing the claim, because the action is manifestly inadmissible or manifestly lacking any foundation in law, an appeal may be brought, both where such orders have been made after the whole development of the proceedings, and where they have been delivered after fast proceedings or after a party has applied for a decision on a preliminary issue not going to the substance of the case.

329. Where the General Court has decided on an application about a preliminary issue without going to the substance of the case, it is obviously possible an order stating the existence of the jurisdiction, the competence or the admissibility. In this event, the right of appeal is granted the party opposing the continuation of the proceedings on the merits. In such cases, the General Court disposes the continuation of the proceedings before it, notwithstanding the appeal before the CJ, which might quash the challenged decision and, consequently, the proceedings on the merits. One may think, for example, of an order stating the admissibility of the claim, which is then quashed by the CJ. In this situation, the General Court may stay the proceedings, but it is not compelled to do so. Should the proceedings not be stayed, the effects of the judgment of the CJ would have effects beyond the preliminary question, with all the delicate consequences deriving from it.

330. The EU legal order admits, without exceptions, the possibility to bring an appeal against decisions which do not close the proceedings.

489. Articles 56 and 57 of the Statute.

331. The decisions dismissing applications to intervene may be appealed, while, on the contrary, no appeal may be brought against those ones admitting such applications. The reason is clear: the third party excluded shall be put into conditions to contest the unfavourable decision immediately, since, if not, it loses any possibility of protection in those proceedings. With regard to the intervener who has been admitted, the opposing parties, who hold that such intervention was inadmissible, are entitled to appeal the judgment of the General Court on the ground of a breach of procedure, if that really affects their interests.

332. Lastly, the decisions of the General Court in matter of interim measures and of suspension of the enforcement of the challenged Acts may be appealed: both those decisions granting the measure requested and those dismissing the interim application. The EU proceedings, therefore, grant the immediate appeal against any interim measure. Yet, it has to be noted that, as it regards only points of law, the EU appeal may scarcely upset the decision of the CFI, which is necessarily based (above all with regard to the urgency) on grounds of fact. In fact, the praxis has shown the weak efficacy, as far as it concerns the results, of the appeals against the interim orders: such appeals are usually unsuccessful.

333. Any other decision of the General Court is out of the sphere of the appeal: so, the decisions extending time limits, the orders admitting or dismissing requests about the undertaking of measures of inquiry, the orders in matter of legal aid. Yet, even if these decisions may not be appealed directly, an appeal may be brought against the final judgment, under the point of view of a breach of procedure, where such decisions have caused a prejudice to a party, which then has lost the case exactly because of them.

Pursuant to the Statute, no appeal shall lie regarding only the amount of the costs or the party ordered to pay them. Obviously, the point of the decision about costs may be appealed, if any other part of the decision is challenged.[490]

§3. Time Limits to Bring Appeal

334. The decisions of the General Court (both those disposing in whole or in part of the merits and those disposing of procedural issues) are notified by the Registrar to all parties as well as all Member States and the EU institutions, even if they did not intervene in the case before the General Court.[491]

Usually, an appeal may be brought within two months of such notification. Such time limit is extended on account of distance by a single period of ten days.[492] A time limit of two months from the notification of the decisions concerned is also provided with regard to the appeal against the decisions in interim matter or suspending the enforcement of Acts. On the contrary, only two weeks are given to he/she who wishes to appeal a decision dismissing an application to intervene; here,

490. Article 58(2) of the Statute.
491. Article 55 of the Statute.
492. Articles 56(1), 57, and 45 of the Statute; Art. 51 RP CJ.

the time limit is shorter because the due composition of the parties to the proceedings has to be assessed as soon as possible.

§4. Standing for Appeal

335. As a general rule, the ordinary appeal may be brought by any party which has been unsuccessful, in whole or in part, in its submissions. However, interveners (where they are private parties) may bring such an appeal only where the decision of the General Court directly affects them.[493]

The EU proceedings are so following the prevailing line in the national civil proceedings. A remarkable difference exists, when the EU proceedings take into account the position of the Member States and the EU institutions. So, with the exception of cases relating to disputes between the Union and its servants (whose political weight is smaller), an appeal may also be brought against the judgments of the General Court by Member States and EU institutions which were not party to the proceedings.

It deals with a peculiar right, linked to the stronger position of States and institutions in the EU system. The goal is that of giving these persons the possibility not only to orient the case law of the CJ in important issues, but also to get a decision altered or quashed, where affecting their interests. Yet, this right is limited where the question has a lower political importance. So, only the third party whose application to intervene has been dismissed, may appeal the decision concerned; at the same time, only the parties to the proceedings may appeal the decisions about interim measures.

It has to be underlined, nevertheless, that the Member States and the EU institutions, when appealing, are in the same position as Member States or institutions which intervened at first instance (and not as the main parties to the proceedings).

§5. The Grounds for Appeal

336. The ordinary appeal before the CJ against the decisions of the General Court has two main features: it may be brought only on points of law and on specific grounds.

Pursuant to the Statute, an appeal to the CJ shall be limited to points of law. It shall lie on the following grounds:[494]

(a) lack of competence of the General Court;
(b) breach of procedure before the General Court, which adversely affects the interests of the appellant;
(c) infringement of the EU law.

493. Article 56(2) of the Statute.
494. Article 58 of the Statute.

337. With regard to the lack of competence of the General Court, the decisions of the judicial body of first instance may be appealed because of vices relating not only the competence strictly speaking (and so, the sharing of the jurisdiction between the judicial bodies, with regard to which the supremacy of the CJ in the resolution of conflicts is so stated again), but also the lack of jurisdiction.

338. As far as it concerns the breaches of procedure, the wording of the Statute requires that it deals with breaches which really bring a prejudice to the party. So, not every formal infringement of procedural rules may lead to an appeal, but only those vices which have been relevant in the conviction of the General Court, or, however, may let the party think that should the procedure had been followed correctly, the decision of the judges might have been different.

One can think of breaches of the right to be heard or of vices in the preparatory inquiry. For example, grounds for appeal are: any violation of the right of defence;[495] the refusal to re-open the oral stage and admit the measures of organization of procedure and the measures of inquiry requested by a party;[496] the lack of compliance with the law with regard to the hearing of a witness.[497] A decision of the General Court may also be appealed because of the statement of reasons is lacking or insufficient.[498]

Having the possibility to appeal a judgment because of procedural breaches increases the judicial protection for the parties: such breaches become grounds of challenging the decision. The parties concerned may raise preliminary objections about those vices and the decisions of the judges (e.g., as whether repeating a previous inquiry or not) may be object of an appeal.

339. The third ground has a general and wide feature: the infringement of the EU substantive law (since the procedural law is considered within the ground mentioned above). The vice has to consist in a wrong or incorrect application or interpretation of the EU rules, and not in a wrong evaluation of the facts. There is no doubt that the EU legislator has wanted to forbid the parties to bring issues of fact before the CJ, whose task is clearly limited to the points of law only. Any jurist is well aware, how difficult is distinguishing between issues of fact and issues of law. Yet, the CJ has always chosen a very rigorous conduct; its case law has excluded any evaluation of the facts, even if taking into account the concrete situations of the controversies. It has held that one should distinguish between the evaluation, on the one hand, and the qualification in law of the facts, on the other hand: the former belongs to the General Court alone, while the latter may be the object of an

495. CJ, 10 Jan. 2002, C-480/99 P, *Plant and others v. Commission and South Wales Small Mines Association*, ECR, I, 265; CJ, 24 Sep. 2002, joined cases C-74/00 P and C-75/00 P, *Falck v. Commission*, ECR, I, 7869.

496. CJ, 8 Jul. 1999, C-227/92 P, *Hoechst v. Commission*, ECR, I, 4443.

497. CJ, 26 Apr. 1993, ord., C-244/92 P, *Kupka-Floridi v. ESC*, ECR, I, 2041.

498. *See, inter alia*, CJ, 17 Dec. 1992, C-68/91 P, *Moritz v. Commission*, ECR, I, 6849; CJ, 14 May 1998, C-259/96 P, *Council v. De Nil and Impens*, ECR, I, 2915; CJ, 11 Sep. 2003, C-197/99 P, *Belgium and others v. Commission and others*, ECR, I, 8461; CJ, 29 Sep. 2011, C-521/09 P, *Elf Aquitaine v. Commission*, ECR. I, 8947.

appeal.[499] The evaluation of evidence by the General Court is included in the evaluation of the facts and, therefore, remains outside any possible appeal. Yet, there are at least two exceptions to this rule. First, the General Court may have been mistaken with regard to the application of the procedural rules about evidence.[500] Second, the General Court might have distorted the clear sense of the evidence before it. In that regard, it must be pointed out that, in accordance with the case law of the CJ, complaints based on findings of fact and on the assessment of those facts in the judgment under appeal are admissible on appeal where the appellant submits that the General Court has made findings of fact which the documents in the file show to be substantially incorrect or that it has distorted the clear sense of the evidence before it. It should be recalled that there is distortion of the clear sense of the evidence where, without recourse to new evidence, the assessment of the existing evidence appears to be clearly incorrect.[501]

§6. The Filtering Mechanism for Appeals

340. Regulation (EU, Euratom) No. 2019/629 introduced a new procedure which let the CJ decide whether an appeal should be allowed to proceed.[502]

In order to improve the functioning of the CJ, which has seen a huge increase in the number of cases brought before it, the Council adopted a new filtering mechanism for appeals by changing the Statute of the EU.[503]

Moreover, the aim of the reform is to make the proceedings more efficient and to improve legal protection in the EU and it is based on the fact that European judges find that many appeals are dismissed by the Court because 'they are patently unfounded or on the ground that they are manifestly inadmissible'.[504]

---

499. CJ, 16 Mar. 2000, C-284/98 P, *Parliament v. Bieber*, ECR, I, 1527; CJ, 29 Apr. 2004, C-470/00 P, *Parliament v. Ripa di Meana and others*, ECR, I, 4167; CJ, 3 Mar. 2005, C-499/03 P, *Biegi v. Commission*, ECR, I, 1751; CJ, 1 Jun. 2006, joined cases C-442/03 P and C-471/03 P, *P&O European Ferries v. Commission*, ECR, I, 4845; CJ, 10 Jul. 2008, *Bertelsmann and Sony v. Commission*, C-413/06 P, ECR, I, 4951.

500. CJ, 4 Mar. 1999, C-119/97 P, *Ufex and others v. Commission*, ECR, I, 1341; CJ, 15 Jun. 2000, C-237/98 P, *Dorsch Consult v. Council and Commission*, ECR, I, 4549; CJ, 12 Feb. 2003, ord., C-399/02 P-R, *Marcuccio v. Commission*, ECR, I, 1417; CJ, 10 Jul. 2008, *Bertelsmann and Sony v. Commission*, C-413/06 P, ECR, I, 4951.

501. CJ, 15 Jun. 2000, C-13/99 P, *TEAM v. Commission*, ECR, I, 4671; CJ, 20 Sep. 2001, ord., C-1/01 P, *Asia Motor France v. Commission*, ECR, I, 6349; CJ, 2 Oct. 2003, C-182/99 P, *Salzgitter v. Commission*, ECR, I, 10761; CJ, 18 Jul. 2007, C-326/05, *Industrias Quimicas del Vallés v. Commissione*, ECR, I, 6557; CJ, 17 Jun. 2010, C- 413/08 P, *Lafarge v. Commission*, ECR, I, 5361; CJ, 24 Jan. 2013, C-73/11 P, *Frucona Košice v. Commission*; GC, 9 Jun. 2015, T-556/14 P, *Navarra v. Commission*.

502. CJ, 24 Oct. 2019, ord., C-614/19 P, *Dr. Ing. h.c. F. Porsche AG v. Ufficio dell'Unione europea per la proprietà intellettuale (EUIPO)*, ECR, 904; CJ, 16 Sep. 2019, C-444/19 P *Kiku/OCVV*, ECR, 746, not published.
See in literature C. Rasia, 'L'introduzione del "filtro" nel giudizio di impugnazione avanti alla Corte di Giustizia dopo la riforma del 2019', *Riv. trim. dir. proc. civ.* (2020).

503. In accordance with the letter from the President of the ECJ of 13 Jul. 2018.

504. *See* Recital No. 4 of the Regulation (EU, Euratom) No. 2019/629, 17 Apr. 2019, in O.J.E.U., L 111, 1, 25 Apr. 2019.

For these reasons, it was necessary to modify the Statute and approve a set of amendments to the Court's Rules of Procedure whereby the Court allows an appeal to proceed only where it raises an issue that is significant with regard to the unity, consistency or development of Union law.[505] By doing so, the CJ is able to concentrate on the cases that require its full attention, without focusing on others that are manifestly inadmissible.

Article 58a[506] states that an appeal brought against a decision of the General Court concerning a decision of an independent board of appeal of one of the offices and agencies of the Union listed in Article 58a (namely the European Union Intellectual Property Office, the Community Plant Variety Office; the European Chemicals Agency and the EU Aviation Safety Agency) shall not proceed unless the CJ first decides that it should be allowed to do so.

This mechanism shall also apply to appeals brought against decisions of the General Court concerning a decision of an independent board of appeal, set up after 1 May 2019 within any other office or agency of the Union, which has to be seized before an action can be brought before the General Court.

Lastly, Article 58a provides that an appeal shall be allowed to proceed, wholly or in part, in accordance with the detailed rules set out in the Rules of Procedure, where it raises an issue that is significant with respect to the unity, consistency or development of Union law. By introducing this procedure, the legislator clearly wants to ensure the uniform interpretation of the Union law, as stated by the CJ in its decision, even before the above-cited reform.[507] In fact, the Court wants to give relevance to cases which may constitute a precedent in future decisions.

The Statute lays down the cases in which an appeal is admissible which are left to the Rules of Procedure of the CJ, where the legislator introduced a new section with two articles.[508] According to Article 170a, the appellant needs to annex to the appeal a request that the appeal be allowed to proceed, setting out the issue raised by the appeal that is significant with respect to the unity, consistency or development of EU law and containing all the information necessary to enable the CJ to rule on that request.[509]

The CJ has to rule as soon as possible on the request that the appeal be allowed to proceed and the decision as to whether the appeal should be allowed to proceed or not has to be reasoned and published.[510]

On a proposal from the Judge-Rapporteur and after hearing the Advocate General, the decision on that request is taken by a dedicated Chamber established for that purpose, presided over by the Vice-President of the Court and including also

505. This principle is highlighted in CJ, 24 Oct. 2019, ord., C-614/19 P, *Dr. Ing. h.c. F. Porsche AG v. Ufficio dell'Unione europea per la proprietà intellettuale (EUIPO)*, ECR, 904.

506. Article 58a Statute CJ.

507. CJ, 17 Dec. 2009, C-197/09 RX-II, *M. v. Emea, paragraph 62;* CJ, 19 Sep. 2013, C-579/12, *Commission v. Strack,* para. 59, 61; CJ, 8 Feb. 2013, C-334/12 *RX-II, Arango Jaramillo v. BEI*, para. 52.

508. *See* Arts 170a and 170b RP CJ.

509. *See*, CJ, 24 Oct. 2019, ord., C-614/19 P, *Dr. Ing. h.c. F. Porsche AG v. Ufficio dell'Unione europea per la proprietà intellettuale (EUIPO)*, ECR, 904; CJ, 16 Sep. 2019, C-444/19 P *Kiku/OCVV*, ECR, 746, not published.; CJ, 7 Oct. 2019, C-586/19 P, *L'Oréal v. Office de l'Union européenne pour la propriété intellectuelle (EUIPO),* ECR, 845.

510. Article 170b RP CJ.

the Judge-Rapporteur and the President of the Chamber of three Judges to which the Judge-Rapporteur is attached on the date on which the request is made.

Where the CJ decides that the appeal should be allowed to proceed, wholly or in part, having regard to the criteria set out in the third paragraph of Article 58a of the Statute, the proceedings shall continue in accordance with Articles 171–190a of these Rules.

The request that the appeal be allowed to proceed cannot exceed the length of seven pages and has to be drawn up taking into account all the formal requirements contained in the Practice Directions to parties concerning cases brought before the Court, adopted on the basis of these Rules.

In the drafting of any request, the parties have to respect the summary of the subject matter of the dispute, in order to ensure the smooth running of proceedings and thus their effectiveness. This recommendation was adopted by the European legislator some time ago with practical guidance to national judges and parties. Today, for the first time, a provision of the Rules of Procedure sets a maximum number of pages of a document. This is a binding solution which makes the party drafting the document more responsible, forcing them to concentrate on the essential aspects of the case and, at the same time, easing the workload of the translation services.

The Rules of Procedure lay down rules that have to be observed by the parties. Article 170a(3) states that if the request that the appeal be allowed to proceed does not comply with the requirements previously set out, the Registrar will prescribe a reasonable time limit within which the appellant is to put the request in order. The rules provide for the possibility of regularizing an application for admission which has already been lodged. This possibility has to be exercised within a short period set by the Registrar; otherwise, the application will be declared inadmissible. In fact, if the appellant fails to put the request in order within the time limit prescribed, the Vice-President of the Court will decide, upon proposal from the Judge-Rapporteur and after hearing the Advocate General, whether the non-compliance with that formal requirement renders the appeal formally inadmissible.

Chapter 3. The Development of the Appeal Proceedings

§1. General Features

341. The ordinary appeal proceedings in the EU system are mainly governed by the same common Rules of Procedure in the proceedings at the first or single instance. Yet, there are some peculiarities, which have the goal to ensure a quicker and more simple management of the cases. Under this point of view, the procedure might be perhaps considered as even too simple, with a remarkable limitation of the powers of defence of the parties.

The appeal proceedings have no preparatory inquiry, because their goal is discussing points of law only and new findings of the fact are not admitted.

§2. The Application

342. The appeal against the decisions of the General Court is brought by means of an application lodged at the Registry of the CJ or at one of the General Courts, indifferently. The Registry of the General Court transmits to the Registry of the CJ the papers in the case at first instance and, where necessary, the appeal.[511]

Pursuant to the Rules of Procedure, an appeal shall contain:[512]

(a) the name and address of the appellant;
(b) a reference to the decision of the General Court appealed against;
(c) the names of the other parties to the relevant case before the General Court;
(d) the pleas in law and legal arguments relied on, and a summary of those pleas in law;
(e) the form of order sought by the appellant.

With regard to the application initiating the proceedings at first or single instance, the requirement of the evidence offered in support fails. In fact, the CJ as a judge of appeal may not find the facts in a different way than the General Court and, above all, may not undertake measures of inquiry or administrate new evidence.

The appeal shall state the date on which the decision appealed against was served on the appellant. The application shall state an address for service at Luxemburg (or in addition to, or instead of that, a statement that the lawyer or agent agrees that service is to be effected on him/her by telefax or any other technical means of communication). The lawyer acting for a party must also lodge at the Registry a certificate that he/she is authorized to practise.

It may be useful to remind that there are applied the rules, according to which the application may be received at the Registry within the proper time limits by telefax

511. Article 167 RP CJ.
512. Article 168 RP CJ.

or other technical means of communication, provided that the signed original of the application, accompanied by the necessary annexes, is lodged no later than ten days thereafter.

The control of the requirements of the application is made by the Registrar and by the Court. This point is very important, since, should the appeal be found inadmissible, the short time limit to bring it usually forbids the party concerned to lodge a new appeal.

Should the application be lacking of the statement of the address for service at Luxembourg or of the declaration by the lawyer or agent to agree that service is to be effected on him/her by telefax or other technical means of communication, there is no inadmissibility, but all service on the party concerned shall be effected by registered letter and shall be deemed to be duly effected by the lodging of the registered letter at the post office of Luxembourg.

If an appeal does not comply with the other requirements, the Registrar shall prescribe a reasonable time limit within which the appellant is to put the appeal in order. If the appellant fails to put the appeal in order within the prescribed time limit, the CJ, after hearing the Judge-Rapporteur and the Advocate-General, decides whether the non-compliance with that formal requirement renders the appeal formally inadmissible. These rules may not be applied out of these narrow cases; therefore, another hypothesis of formal non-compliance of the application will bring no prejudice to the appellant.

343. With regard to the substantive requirements of the appeal, it is a task of the CJ to take them into consideration and to decide consequently. So, an appeal lacking of the pleas in law or the form of order sought will be dismissed as inadmissible.

Like the application initiating the proceedings at first or single instance, also the appeal may be held admissible only if complies with the requirement of the necessary precision. Moreover, the appeal has to make clear which are the challenged points of the judgment and the legal arguments relied on. A quite generic criticism to the decision of the General Court would be inadmissible, because it aims to get a full review of the judgment, which is not coherent with the features of the EU appeal, which concerns only points of law. On the contrary, the appellant shall state exactly where, according to his/her opinion, the General Court has been mistaken in law.

Many a time the CJ has stressed, in its settled case law, that an application merely repeating or copying the pleas and the arguments brought at first instance, including those openly dismissed by the General Court, does not comply with the Rules of Procedure and is therefore inadmissible. In fact, such an application is not really an appeal, because it does not contain any specific challenge of the reasoning of the General Court.[513] Of course, it is not forbidden for the appellant to defend again his/her positions in law, where the General Court has not admitted them.

---

513. CJ, 1 Feb. 2001, ord., joined cases C-300/99 P and C-388/99 P, *Area Cova v. Council,* ECR, I, 983; CJ, 19 Jan. 2006, C-240/03 P, *Comunità montana della Valnerina v. Commission,* ECR, I, 731.

344. Notice of the appeal shall be served on all the parties to the proceedings before the General Court. If any case of formal non-compliance exists, service shall be effected as soon as the appeal has been put in order or the Court has however declared it inadmissible.

In the appeal proceedings, the language of the case is the language of the decision of the General Court, against which the appeal is brought.[514]

§3. The Response of the Opposite Party and the Cross-Appeal

345. Any party to the proceedings before the General Court (but above all the successful party) may lodge a response within two months after service on it of notice of the appeal; such time limit shall not be extended.

The content of the response is somehow a mirror of the appeal. In fact, a response shall contain: (a) the name and address of the part lodging it; (b) the date on which notice of the appeal was served on him/her; (c) the pleas in law and legal arguments relied on; (d) the form of order sought by the respondent. The common rules about the address for service, the certificate of the lawyer, and the possibility to send the pleading to the Registry by telefax or other technical means of communication apply (exactly like for the appellant).[515]

346. The Rules of Procedure state the cross-appeal clearly. Any party having an interest may submit a cross-appeal within the same time limit as that prescribed for the submission of a response, but by means of a document separate. If the cross-appeal is not introduced by a document separate and distinct from the response, it must be dismissed as manifestly inadmissible.[516]

The content of the cross-appeal is similar to the content of the response, but it is different in the form of order sought.

The cross-appeal may be brought by the main parties to the proceedings at first instance and to the interveners. The basic requirement is that such parties have been unsuccessful, in whole or (where the parties were only two) in part. The difference between the appeal and the cross-appeal is only temporal: the appeal is introduced at first.

A cross-appeal is deemed to be devoid of purpose if: (a) the appellant discontinues his/her appeal; (b) the appeal is declared manifestly inadmissible for non-compliance with the time limit for lodging an appeal; (c) the appeal is declared manifestly inadmissible on the sole ground that it is not directed against a final decision of the General Court.[517]

514. Article 37 RP CJ.
515. Article 173 RP CJ.
516. CJ, 30 Jan. 2014, ord., C-422/12 P, *Industrias Alen v. The Clorox Company.*
517. Article 183 RP CJ.

§4. The Subject Matter of the Appeal Proceedings

347. A logical consideration, deriving from the features of the EU appeal, would lead to deny that the CJ might discuss new issues, not examined before the General Court. Yet, some problems arise about this point, because the Rules are not completely clear.

The Rules of Procedure state the possible contents of the appeal and of the response. The conclusions of the appeal may seek: (a) to set aside, in whole or in part, the decision of the General Court; (b) the same form of order, in whole or in part, as that sought at first instance. No different form of order may be sought. The conclusions of the response seek to have the appeal allowed or dismissed, in whole or in part. Finally, the cross-appeal seeks to have set aside, in whole or in part, the decision of the General Court or an express or implied decision relating to the admissibility of the action before the General Court.[518]

It has to be underlined that the opposite party may have been unsuccessful in part at the first instance and therefore may seek the form of order dismissed by the General Court (e.g., where a penalty for an undertaking has been established, but the EU Commission was seeking for a greater amount of it); besides, more than one party may have been unsuccessful, therefore new conclusions against the same decision may be brought, joining those of the main appellant.

The decision is set aside with specific pleas. The pleas in law and legal arguments relied on shall identify precisely those points in the grounds of the decision of the General Court which are contested.

These Rules are expression both of the principle, according to which the whole of the matter of the first instance is brought to the jurisdiction of the appeal court, and of the right, for the party against whom the appeal has been brought, to appeal the decision on its own account, where it had also been unsuccessful. But, even if they forbid new claims, they do not face the question of new pleas, which remains open.

Now, pursuant to the Rules of Procedure, neither the application of the appellant nor the cross-appeal may change the subject matter of the proceedings before the General Court. But it deals with a quite generic wording, which does not forbid the introduction of new pleas. Moreover, in the appeal proceedings the rule applies, pursuant to which no new plea in law may be introduced in the course of the proceedings, unless it is based on new matters; therefore, one might admit that new pleas might be introduced in the statements initiating the proceedings of appeal.

Even if the Rules are a bit uncertain, it has to be noted that the settled case law of the CJ has been, up to now, very severe and rigorous, prohibiting any enlargement of the subject matter of the case.[519]

Lastly, the prohibition of new pleas does not bring about the exclusion of new arguments in law; very often, such arguments are the strongpoint of the appeals.

518. Articles 169–170, 174, and 178 RP CJ.

519. CJ, 18 Mar. 1993, C-35/92 P, *Parliament v. Frederiksen*, ECR, I, 991; CJ, 17 Sep. 1996, ord., C-19/95 P, *San Marco v. Commission*, ECR, I, 4435; CJ, 27 Jun. 2002, ord., C-274/00 P, *Simon v. Commission*; ECR, I, 5999; CJ, 11 Feb. 2004, ord., C-180/03 P, *Latino v. Commission*, ECR, I, 1587; CJ, 2 Apr. 2009, C-202/07 P, *France Télécom v. Commission*, ECR, I, 2369.

§5. THE WRITTEN STAGE AND THE ORAL STAGE

348. Since the case has been widely discussed at first instance and the questions arising in the proceedings of appeal may affect only points of law, usually in the EU system only two statements are allowed: the application of the appellant, on the one hand, and the response of the defendant (or of the other parties), on the other hand. Yet, sometimes further statements are allowed. In fact, the appeal and the response may be supplemented by a reply and a rejoinder where the President, on a duly reasoned application submitted by the appellant within seven days of service of the response, considers it necessary, after hearing the Judge-Rapporteur and the Advocate-General, in particular to enable the appellant to present his/her views on a plea of inadmissibility or on new matters relied on in the response. The current law is more restrictive than the past rule, which allowed the submission of a reply in order to enable the appellant to put forward his/her point of view or in order to provide a basis for the decision on the appeal.[520]

In such an event, the President fixes the date by which the reply is to be produced and, upon service of that pleading, the date by which the rejoinder is to be produced. Obviously, a rejoinder may be only granted where the appellant has been allowed to submit his/her reply. The President may limit the number of pages and the subject matter of those pleadings.

A reply is also possible in another case, which requires no authorization. Where a cross-appeal is brought, the applicant at the first instance or any other party to the relevant case before the General Court having an interest in the cross-appeal being allowed or dismissed may submit a response, which must be limited to the pleas in law relied on in that cross-appeal, within two months after its being served on him/her. These cross-appeal and the response thereto may be supplemented by a reply and a rejoinder only where the President considers it necessary.

349. Once closed the written (and usually very simple) stage, the proceedings of appeal go on without any preparatory inquiry (because the case deals only with points of law) and, sometimes, without the oral stage.

Even if the procedure ought to consist of a written and an oral part, the CJ, having heard the Advocate-General and the parties, may dispense with the oral procedure.[521]

After the submission of the pleadings (as above described), once all the arguments in law of the parties are on the table of the Court, the President fixes the date for the preliminary report by the Judge-Rapporteur. In the appeal proceedings, the report has to orient the Court (nothing having to be decided with regard to evidence) about two main questions: the formation of the Court and the decision, as whether to dispense with the oral procedure.

According the Rules of Procedure, on a proposal from the Judge-Rapporteur and after hearing the Advocate-General, the Court may decide not to hold a hearing if it considers, on reading the written pleadings, that it has sufficient information to give a ruling. Nevertheless, any party is entitled to submit an application setting out

520. Article 175 RP CJ.
521. Article 59 of the Statute.

the reasons for which it wishes to be heard, within a period of three weeks (which may be extended by the President) from notification to the party of the close of the written procedure.[522]

It should be remarked that the decision without the oral hearing is often preferred by the CJ, because of evident reasons of economy in its case management. The parties are rarely in degree to submit new arguments, after the proceedings at first instance and after the pleadings in the written stage.

It is not enough for the party concerned to state that it was not in degree to defend itself fully in the written stage, but a reasoned explanation is required: the party concerned ought to convict the judges that the oral discussion will bring some new aspects in order to provide a basis for the decision on the appeal (and so, it deals with the same condition required to be allowed to lodge a reply). However, the right of defence is a basic principle in the EU system; so, should a doubt remain about the true utility of an oral hearing, the CJ shall fix it.

The oral stage is then governed by the same rules as at first instance. The rules on expedited procedures, joining of cases, service, time limits, prohibition of new pleas in law, discontinuance, intervention, exceptional review, interim measures apply. On the contrary, the rules on preliminary issues and judgment in default do not apply to appeal proceedings.[523]

§6. Complex Litigation

350. The hypothesis of proceedings of appeal where more than two parties are present is not rare.

More than two parties are present in the appeal proceedings, whenever so was at first instance. The CJ has many a times repeated that all the persons who have been party to the proceedings at first instance are party to those of appeal, the interveners being included.[524]

A second hypothesis has place, where an appeal has been brought by a Member State or an EU institution, which were not party to the proceedings at first instance.

A third group of cases consists of the application, in the appeal proceedings, of the rules about the joining of cases for grounds of connection and the intervention of third parties. It should be noted that intervention is possible in such proceedings: an application to intervene made to the Court in appeal proceedings shall be lodged before the expiry of a period of one month running from the publication on the Official Journal of the notice relating to the application initiating the proceedings.[525]

522. Article 76 RP CJ.
523. Article 190 RP CJ.
524. CJ, 22 Dec. 1993, C-244/91 P, *Pincherle v. Commission*, ECR, I, 6965; CJ, 14 Feb. 1996, ord., C-245/95 P, *Commission v. Ntn and Koyo Seiko*, ECR, I, 553.
525. Article 190(2) RP CJ.

§7. The Suspension of the Appealed Decision

351. An appeal to the CJ has no suspensory effect of the decisions of the General Court.[526] This rule is coherent with the nature of legality review (and not a new decision on the merits) of the EU appeal. Yet, the Court is entitled to use its general power, deriving from the treaties, to suspend the enforcement of the Acts challenged and to order the proper interim measures, also with regard to the appealed judgments.

Therefore, the appellant may request to the Court a measure suspending the effects of the decision against which the appeal has been brought. The rules governing the interim proceedings apply to this matter.[527]

So, the appellant may submit an application, by a separate document, to suspend the operation of the decision or for the adoption of any other interim measure. The President or the Court decide on the application, after hearing the parties, by an order which may not be appealed, making the enforcement of the order conditional on the lodging of security, where appropriate. The general criteria to grant an interim measures apply. It is clear that the burden is particularly heavy to the applicant, who has to state a prima facie case in his/her favour, having an unfavourable finding of the General Court against himself/herself.

526. Article 60(1) of the Statute.
527. Articles 160–166 RP CJ.

Chapter 4. The Decision on the Appeal and the Decision to Refer the Case Back to the First Instance

352. At the end of the proceedings, the Court decides on the appeal. The possibilities are the following ones: the appeal may be dismissed (by an order, where it is manifestly inadmissible or clearly unfounded, or by a judgment), or it may be admitted (by a final decision on the merits by the Court itself or by a decision quashing the judgment and referring the case back to the General Court). The dismissal or the granting of the appeal may also be partial.

The need to face the workload of the CJ is the main reason for the introduction of the possibility to decide the appeal, in whole or in part, by a simple reasoned order, instead of by a judgment, where the appeal is clearly inadmissible or unfounded or manifestly well-founded.

The Court so decides acting on a report from the Judge-Rapporteur and after hearing the Advocate-General and, in case of manifestly well-founded appeal, after also hearing the parties.

First, the order which rejects the claim must be considered.

The clear lack of foundation has regard to the contents of the grounds of appeal. The clear inadmissibility is a large hypothesis, also including the cases of incompetence or lack of jurisdiction.

The order may be made at any moment of the proceedings. The most logical moment is at the end of the written stage, after the preliminary report. A dismissal of the appeal may be made also before, immediately after the simple reading of the application. It deals with another example of the tendency of the EU procedural law to prefer forms of fast proceedings.

Second, the order which admits the claim occurs where the Court has already ruled on one or more questions of law identical to those raised by the pleas in law of the appeal or cross-appeal. Here the Court decides by reasoned order in which reference is made to the relevant case law.

If the CJ rejects the appeal, the appealed decision has the force of procedural and substantive (when appropriate) res judicata. It should be especially reminded that decisions of the General Court annulling a regulation take effect from that date.[528]

353. When the appeal is upheld, the Court quashes the decision of the General Court. As it has already been noted, it may either give final judgment on the matter, where the state of the proceedings so permits, or refer the case back to the General Court for judgment.[529] As a matter of fact, the Court has a true choice, only where a decision of the General Court on the substance of the controversy is quashed; in any other case, the General Court is called to decide. Because of evident reasons of economy in the case management, the Rules of Procedure state where the appellant

528. Article 60(2) of the Statute.
529. Article 61 of the Statute.

requests that the case be referred back to the General Court if the decision appealed against is set aside, he/she shall set out the reasons why the state of the proceedings does not permit a decision by the CJ.[530]

354. With regard to the criterion, in base to which the Court may opt to give the judgment or to refer back the case to the General Court, it is difficult to point out a clear statement. Surely, the CJ may not administrate a preparatory inquiry, acting as an appeal judge. So, where the appeal decision supposes new finding about facts (for instance, because of a breach of procedure, which has made impossible to administrate evidence correctly), the Court shall refer the case back to the General Court. On the contrary, where facts are properly found and the decision has been quashed only because of an infringement of the law, so that the case may be easily decided in application of the right principle of law, the Court shall save time and energies and shall give itself the final judgment. The CJ holds that is appropriate for it to avail itself of that possibility, where it has all the information necessary to rule on the substance of the case.

It may also be reminded that, where a case is referred back to the General Court, the General Court shall be bound by the decision of the CJ on points of law.

The Statute takes care to limit the possible prejudice coming upon the parties, as a consequence of an appeal brought by a Member State or an EU institution, which were not parties to the proceedings at first instance. In fact, where such an appeal is well founded, the Court may, if it considers this necessary, state which of the effects of the decision of the General Court which has been quashed shall be considered as definitive in respect of the parties to litigation.[531]

As far as it concerns costs of the appeal proceedings, if the decision is quashed and the case is referred back to the General Court, the General Court shall decide on this matter; on the contrary, where the appeal is dismissed or where it is well founded and the Court itself gives final judgment on the case, the Court shall make a decision as to costs. The rules about costs are the same as at first instance, save some exceptions.[532]

The appeal judgments and orders are binding from the date of their delivery, but they may be challenged by means of the exceptional review procedures, such as revision, third-party proceedings, interpretation, rectification and failure to adjudicate.[533]

530. Article 170(2) RP CJ.
531. Article 61(3) of the Statute.
532. Article 184 RP CJ.
533. Article 91 RP CJ.

Chapter 5. Appeal Against the Decisions of the CST

355. Since 1 September 2016, the jurisdiction over litigation between the Union and its servants has belonged to the General Court, after the dissolution of the CST whose Rules of Procedure have to continue to apply to the appeals against decisions of the CST of which the General Court is seized as at 31 August 2016 or which are brought after that date.

Since this discipline is no longer in force, it will not be analysed.

Chapter 6. The Exceptional Review of the Decisions of the General Court Before the CJ

356. The general rule introduced by the Treaty of Nice about this matter has been more detailed by the amendments to the Statute made by the decision of the Council, 3 October 2005. Pursuant to the Declaration No. 13 alleged to the final Act of the Treaty of Nice, the amendments have established the role of the parties to the review proceedings before the Court, in order to protect their rights; the effects of the review on the judgment made by the decision of the General Court; the effects of the review decision of the CJ on the litigation among the parties.

357. It is necessary to distinguish between the two hypotheses of exceptional review pursuant to Article 256(2) and to Article 256(3) TFEU: review against the decisions of the General Court acting as appeal judge against the decisions of the specialized courts; review against the decisions given by the General Court on questions referred for a preliminary ruling.

After the dissolution of the CST in 2016, both cases are only theoretically possible.

The rules on the proceedings are common to both hypotheses; on the contrary, the rules referring to effects of the review decision are remarkably different.

358. With regard to the proceedings, the General Court shall inform the CJ, as soon as the date for the delivery of a decision which might be reviewed is fixed; then, the decision shall be communicated immediately upon its delivery, as shall the file in the case, which shall be made available forthwith to the first Advocate-General. This machinery is necessary, because the parties have no power to request a review.

In fact, it is to the first Advocate-General the task to propose that the CJ reviews the decision of the General Court, where he/she considers that there is a serious risk of the unity or consistency of EU law being affected.[534] The proposal must be made within a determined time limit, which is one month of delivery of the decision by the General Court. Within one month of receiving such proposal, the CJ shall decide whether or not the decision should be reviewed. Pursuant to the Statute, the Court gives a ruling on the questions which are subject to review by means of an urgent procedure on the basis of the file forwarded to it by the General Court. No party is admitted to the proceedings, in this first sub-stage.[535]

Concretely, the decision shall be taken by a special Chamber set up for this purpose, composed by five judges: the President of the Court and four of the Presidents of the Chambers of five judges. The decision of the special Chamber is notified to the parties and other interested parties and, where it has admitted the review in matter of preliminary rulings, is made object of a notice in the Official Journal and is communicated to the national court concerned.

---

534. *See* case CJ, 17 Dec. 2009, C-197/09 RX-II, *M. v. Emea*, already quoted; CJ, 19 Sep. 2013, C-579/12, *Commission v. Strack*.

535. Articles 62 and 62a of the Statute; Arts 191 ff. RP CJ.

Where the Court holds that the decision of the General Court is to be reviewed, a new stage begins; here, all the interested persons are called to take part. The language of the case is the language of the decision of the General Court subject to review. The parties to the proceedings before the General Court (included all those who are entitled to submit observations in the preliminary proceedings) may lodge statements or written observations relating to questions which are subject to review, within one month of the notification to them of the decision to review the decision of the General Court.

The first Advocate-General shall assign the review to an Advocate-General. The Judge-Rapporteur presents a general report, containing recommendations as to whether any preparatory steps should be taken, as to the formation of the Court to which the case should be assigned and as to whether a hearing should take place (which is a further protection for the parties). Lastly, the decision is given.

359. The question about the effects of the beginning itself of the review proceedings and of the judgment granting the exceptional review is to be faced. Here, the two hypotheses above described run through quite different ways.[536]

360. In the cases where a decision given by the General Court as appeal judge against a decision of the specialized courts is challenged, proposals for review and decisions to open the review procedure shall not have suspensory effect. It deals with a very logical provision, consistent with the general rule, which denies suspensory effects to the EU appeals.

If the CJ finds that the decision of the General Court affects the unity or consistency of the EU law, it refers the case back to the General Court, which shall be bound by the points of law decided by the CJ. At the same time, it may state which of the effects of the decision of the General Court are to be considered as definitive in respect of the parties to the litigation. If, however, having regard to the result of the review, the outcome of the proceedings flows from the findings of fact on which the decision of the General Court was based, the Court gives final judgment.

It is important to underline that the EU legislator has opted for a solution, intermediate between considering the review decision as a mere declaration of a principle of law or granting the parties the full right to use the decision.

This peculiar structure of the review pursuant to Article 256(2) TFEU (and, above all, the short time limit for the proposal by the first Advocate-General, the fact that all decisions concerned are examined by the first Advocate-General, and the identity between the subject matter of the review and a point of law which was already included in the controversy) leads to consider it as an ordinary way of challenging decisions, even if the parties are not entitled to bring it. Therefore, as it has already been noted, the decision by the General Court given after an appeal against a decision of the specialized courts, has effects of procedural res judicata only when the exceptional review may no longer be introduced or where the decision of the CJ has confirmed the reviewed decision.

536. Article 62b of the Statute.

Obviously, it is nevertheless clear that the EU judicial policy aims to make the exceptional review a really extraordinary remedy: the main goal is not that of granting the parties a further protection (even if this is not fully excluded), but only to close the system, by giving the CJ the power of a final and global control. The effects on the parties are unforeseeable, since they depend on discretionary choices by the Court (which, however, shall surely apply a rule of reason in such matter, admitting the parties to have benefit from the review of clearly wrong decisions of the General Court).

361. In the cases where the review concerns a decision given by the General Court in matter of preliminary reference, the answers given by the General Court to the questions submitted to it shall take effect upon expiry of the period of one month prescribed for the proposal by the first Advocate-General or of one month prescribed for the decision of the CJ whether or not open the review procedure. Should a review procedure be opened, the answers subject to review shall take effect following that procedure, unless the Court decides otherwise.

Since the preliminary rulings have no effect of res judicata, here the question of the effects of the review decision is more simple. In fact, if the CJ finds that the preliminary decision of the General Court affects the unity or consistency of the EU law, the answer given by the CJ to the questions submitted to review shall be substituted for that given by the General Court.

Chapter 7. The Third-Party Proceedings

362. The third-party proceedings are one of the exceptional remedies provided against the judgments of the EU courts. Like the revision, they are not an obstacle to the force of res judicata of the decisions; unlike the revision, they may not be brought by the parties to the proceedings, but only by third parties.

Also in the EU system, the force of res judicata in the direct actions is limited to the parties to the proceedings. Therefore, it might happen that an unlawful prejudice be caused to the rights of a third party, to which a judicial protection is given, within the limits fixed by the Statute.

Member States, institutions, bodies, offices and agencies of the Union and any other natural or legal person may, in cases and under conditions to be determined by the Rules of Procedure, institute third-party proceedings to contest a judgment rendered without their being heard, where the judgment is prejudicial to their rights, before the same EU court which delivered the judgment.[537]

The application initiating third-party proceedings must be lodged within two months of the publication of the judgment in the Official Journal. But, since such publication is not mandatory, where the judgment has not been published, no time limit is established.

363. It is not easy to point out which persons have standing to institute third-party proceedings.

Yet, some statements are clear. First of all, those persons who were parties to the proceedings where the judgment was rendered are obviously excluded; especially, if the defendant has not been correctly called to take part to the proceedings, the judgment may be appealed because of a breach of procedure, but no third-party proceedings are admitted.[538] Besides, only those persons which could not take part to the proceedings have standing; consequently, no third-party proceedings may be instituted by those persons which were in degree to intervene and did not do it. Lastly, pursuant to the Statute, standing is acknowledged to persons which have not been heard in the proceedings.

So, it is possible to hold that third-party proceedings may be instituted by those persons, which were third parties in respect to the main controversy, which might have correctly intervened (with regard to the requirements for intervention), but who were not in degree to do it, because of objective grounds.

It is quite evident that third-party proceedings may be rarely introduced.

364. The application initiating third-party proceedings shall specify the judgment or order contested, state how that decision is prejudicial to the rights of the third party and indicate the reasons for which the third party was unable to take part in the original case.[539]

---

537. Article 42 of the Statute.
538. Articles 157 RP CJ, 167 RP GC.
539. *Ibid.*

That supposes that the res judicata, in the case concerned, has effects beyond the sphere of rights of the main parties and also affects a true right (and not a mere interest) of the third party. Consequently, no third-party proceedings may be instituted against decisions rendered in preliminary rulings. Moreover, the prejudice has to be concrete.

The application must be made against all parties to the original case. The common rules governing ordinary proceedings apply (and so, written stage, preparatory inquiry, when appropriate, and oral hearing). But before the General Court the procedure is quite simple in the written stage: the application for interpretation shall be served on the other parties, who may submit written observations within the time limit prescribed by the President. After giving the parties an opportunity to submit their observations, the General Court shall decide on the application.

On application by the third party, the EU court may order a stay of execution of the judgment or order; such decision is taken by a reasoned order, which may not be appealed. The court concerned has to assess the admissibility of the third-party proceedings and then to decide on the merits. Should the requirements for the institution of the third-party proceedings be lacking, the application is dismissed, without going to the substance of the case.

365. Where the application is well founded, the contested judgment or order shall be varied on the points on which the submissions of the third party are upheld. The original of the decision in the third-party proceedings shall be annexed to the original of the contested judgment or order and a note of the decision in the third-party proceedings shall be made in the margin of the original of the contested judgment or order.

Chapter 8. Revision

366. After the judgment has got the effects of procedural res judicata, a new decision on the merits of the controversy may be obtained by the parties, by means of an application for revision, according to the conditions laid down by the Statute and the Rules of Procedure.[540]

The structure of revision consists of two different stages: first, the EU court concerned shall give a judgment, as whether the requirements to open revision exist or not. If the revision is opened, ordinary proceedings on the merits of the case begin.

Only the parties to the case where the decision was rendered (and so, main parties and interveners) may make an application for revision. Revision may be requested against judgments (but not preliminary rulings)[541] and against orders.[542]

Two different time limits are established for revision. On the one hand, the application is to be made within three months of the date on which the facts on which the application is based came to the applicant's knowledge. On the other hand, no application for revision may be made after the lapse of ten years from the date of the judgment. So, the application for revision may be made when the judgment or order has already got the effect of res judicata, but the right to introduce it is prejudiced in consequence of the expiry of the time limit of ten years.

367. The conditions for the application for revision are to be considered.

An application for revision may be made only on discovery of a fact which is of such a nature as to be a decisive factor, and which, when the judgment or order was given, was unknown to the EU court concerned and to the party claiming the revision.

Before the case law of the CJ has interpreted the provisions of the Statute and has pointed out three requirements for the admissibility of an application for revision. The new fact, which leads to re-open the litigation on the merits, has to be happened before the date of the judgment, the revision of which is claimed; it has to be absolutely unknown both to the court and to the applicant; it has to be a decisive factor, with regard to the solution of the case.[543] Nowadays, these circumstances are provided by the Rules of Procedure of the General Court.[544]

368. The application for revision is to be lodged before the same EU court and the case is assigned to the same formation, which delivered the contested decision.

The first stage of the revision proceedings begins with the lodging of an application where, in addition to the common elements, the claimant shall specify the judgment or order contested, indicate the points on which the decision is contested,

540. Article 44 of the Statute.

541. CJ, 28 Apr. 1998, ord., C-116/96 rev., *Reisebüro Binder*, ECR, I, 1889.

542. For example, against orders rejecting the claim (e.g., in fast proceedings), *see* CJ, 5 Mar. 1998, C-199/94 P and C-200/94 rev., *Inpesca v. Commission*, ECR, I, 831.

543. CJ, 10 Jan. 1980, 116/78 rev., *Bellintani and others v. Commission*, ECR, I, 23; CJ, 24 Nov. 1983, 107/79 rev., *Schuerer v. Commission*, ECR, I, 3805; CJ, 23 Oct.1985, 267/80 rev., *Riseria modenese v. Council, Commission and Birra Peroni*, ECR, 3499; CJ, 5 Mar. 1998, *Inpesca v. Commission* (quoted above); GC, 29 Nov. 2017, ord., T-217/11 rev., *Staelen v. Ombudsman*.

544. Article 169 RP GC.

set out the facts on which the application is based and, above all, indicate the nature of the evidence to show that there are facts justifying revision of the judgment or order and that the time limits above mentioned have been observed. The application must be made against all parties to the case in which the contested decision was given.

The goal of this first stage is to establish, as whether the claim for revision is admissible. The procedure is quite simple. The written stage consists only in the presentation of written observations by the opposite parties (no reply or rejoinder being possible). No oral hearing is fixed: the EU court gives in the form of a judgment its decision on the admissibility of the application in closed session, after hearing the Advocate-General. Theoretically, a preparatory inquiry, according to the common rules on such matter, is possible; in practice, the proof of the new fact is usually a document and many a times the fact itself is a document. The order on the admissibility is given without prejudice to the decision on the substance.

If the EU court finds the application admissible, it opens the revision and it shall proceed to consider the substance of the application, pursuant to the ordinary Rules of Procedure. It should be noted that opening the revision does not mean that the original decision be always revised. Like as for the third-party proceedings, the original of the revising decision is annexed to the original of the judgment or order revised and a note of the revising judgment shall be made in the margin of the original of the decision revised.

Chapter 9. Application to Set Aside Judgments by Default

369. The judgment given by default is enforceable, but not final; in fact, an application to set it aside may be made, within one month from the date in which it has been served, before the same EU court which delivered it. The EU court may grant a stay of execution of the contested judgment until it has decided on the application.[545]

Such application is not an appeal, even if it has the goal to annul a decision. In fact, after the application has been served, the President of the court concerned shall prescribe a period within which the other party may submit its written observations; then, the proceedings go on according to the common Rules of Procedure and the party against which the judgment was given in default, may be heard and defend its reasons.

545. Article 41 of the Statute; Art. 156 RP CJ; Art. 166 RP GC.

Chapter 10. Interpretation of Judgments and Orders

370. Interpretation of judgments is a proper remedy for those legal orders which, because of the lack of a complete system of appeal, must face the problem how to make clear the true will of the judges, where any difficulty in reading a judicial provision arises. This is the case of the EU system, where, since many matters are still decided at a single instance, by a court whose judgments may not be reviewed, a due remedy is needed.

Pursuant to the Statute, if the meaning or scope of a judgment is in doubt, the CJ shall construe it on application by any party or any EU institution establishing an interest therein.[546]

An application for interpretation does neither aim to review the judgment, nor to a revision taking into account new facts, nor to complete the decision, but it has the purpose to make clear the exact meaning of the decision whose contents are not in discussion and so without changing anything already assessed. This is why it is made to the same EU court which delivered the decision.

The judgments and orders are subject to interpretation, even if they may also be appealed. The coexistence of appeal and interpretation puts in light better that interpretation is a remedy, the purpose of which is not that of challenging the judgment.[547]

Only the parties to the original proceedings (interveners included) and the EU institutions have standing to request the interpretation of a judgment or order. The Member States or any other private person have no standing. Moreover, the EU institutions are requested to show a concrete interest in the case and may not freely claim the interpretation. So, it is not possible to use interpretation to get an abstract clarification (e.g., as far as it concerns to know whether a certain judgment might be considered an appropriate precedent for another case), but only to clarify a concrete decision.

Therefore, interpretation has regard more to the operative part of the judgment, than to the grounds for the decision; the doubt about the meaning or scope of the judgment might also derive from a discrepancy between the reasoning of the EU court concerned and the operative part of the judgment.

371. The proceedings relating to the applications for interpretation are more simple than the ordinary proceedings, since the subject matter of the case is less complicated: it does not deal to find new facts or discuss new questions of law, but only define better the meaning or the scope of a decision already rendered and not challenged.

No time limit for initiating interpretation proceedings is established. Yet, after a reasonable period from the delivering of the judgment (and however, after the judgment has been enacted or enforced), no concrete interest seems to exist any longer, with the consequence that an application would be held inadmissible. The Rules of

546. Article 43 of the Statute.
547. Article 158 RP CJ; Art. 168 RP GC.

Procedure state that an application for interpretation must be submitted within two years after the date of delivery of the judgment or service of the order.[548]

The proceedings begin with the lodging of an application, which has to comply with all the common requirements prescribed by the Rules of Procedure and, in addition, has to specify the decision in question and the passages of which interpretation is sought. The judge shall only specify the points which are not clear, but no claim to get a global explanation of the decision would be admissible. As usual in the field of the exceptional controls, the application must be made against all the parties to the case in which the decision was given. The EU courts decide after having given the parties an opportunity to submit their observations, and after hearing the Advocate-General.

The original of the interpreting decision is annexed to the original of the decision interpreted. A note of the interpreting decision is made in the margin of the original of the decision interpreted. The effects of the interpreting decision are produced in respect of any party affected by the passage of the decision, the interpretation of which has been given.

548. Article 158 RP CJ; Art. 168 RP GC.

Chapter 11. Rectification of Judgments and Orders

372. Should an EU judicial body have incurred in clerical mistakes, errors in calculation and obvious slips in writing a judgment or order, rectification is allowed. Such rectification has not the purpose to change what the judges have already stated, but only to set aside some unwilling mistakes, turning the wording of the decision to the exact will of the court. Rectification may be made also where the decision has already got the effect of procedural res judicata.

The court concerned may rectify mistakes and slips not only on application by a party made within two weeks after delivery of the judgment or service of the order, but also of its own motion. The parties have the right to be heard; they are duly notified by the Registrar and they may lodge written observations within a period prescribed by the President, where the request for rectification concerns the operative part or one of the grounds constituting the necessary support for the operative part. In other cases (i.e., a wrong name in the grounds), the court decides without hearing the parties. No oral hearing is fixed and the EU courts give their decision by way of an order.[549]

As usual, the original of the rectification order is annexed to the original of the rectified judgment and a note of this order is made in the margin of the original of the rectified decision.

549. Article 154 RP CJ; Art. 164 RP GC.

Chapter 12. Failure to Adjudicate

373. If the EU Court has failed to adjudicate on a specific head of claim or on costs, any party wishing to rely on that may apply to the Court to supplement its decision. In this case, it is necessary to complete the decision, by adding a point which the judge has wrongly omitted.

An application to the Court to supplement its decision may be made by any party within a month after service (and not delivery) of the judgment. No supplement proceedings of the courts' motion are possible. The application shall be served on the opposite party and the President shall prescribe a period within which that party may lodge written observations. There is no oral hearing; after the observations have been lodged, the Court shall decide both on the admissibility and on the substance of the application.[550] The EU court gives its decision in the form of an order.

550. Article 155 RP CJ; Art. 165 RP GC.

Selected Bibliography

In English

Albors, A. & L. Lorens. *Private Parties in European Community Law*. Oxford: Clarendon Press, 1996.

Arnull, A. *The European Union and Its Court of Justice*. 2nd edn. Oxford: Oxford University Press, 2006.

Barents R., *Remedies and Procedures Before the EU Courts*. Alphen aan den Rijn: Wolters Kluwer, 2016.

Bebr, G. *Development of Judicial Control of the European Communities*. The Hague: Martinus Nijhoff, 1981.

Brown, L.N. & T. Kennedy. *The Court of Justice of the European Communities*, 5th edn. London: Sweet & Maxwell, 2000.

De Burca, G. & J.H.H. Weiler (eds). *The European Court of Justice*. Oxford: Oxford University Press, 2001.

Guinchard, E. & M.P. Granger (eds). *The New EU Judiciary*. Alphen aan den Rijn: Wolters Kluwer, 2018.

Kapteyn, P. J. G., et al. *Introduction to Law of the European Union and European Communities*. London: Kluwer Law International, 2009.

Kilpatrick, C., T. Novitz & P. Skidmore (eds). *The Future of Remedies in Europe*. Oxford: Hart Publishing, 2000.

Lasok, K.P.E. *The European Court of Justice: Practice and Procedure*. 2nd edn. London: Butterworths, 1994.

Lenaerts, K., I. Maselis & K. Gutman. *EU Procedural Law*. Oxford: Oxford University Press, 2014.

Prete, L. *Infringement Proceedings in EU Law*. Alphen aan den Rijn: Wolters Kluwer, 2017.

Usher, J.A. *European Court Practice*. London: Sweet & Maxwell, 1983.

Weatherill, S. *Cases and Materials on EU Law*. 12th edn. Oxford: Oxford University Press, 2016.

Other Languages

Amalfitano, C. & M. Condinanzi. *La Corte di giustizia dell'Unione europea oltre i trattati: la riforma organizzativa e processuale del triennio 2012–2015*. Milan: Giuffrè, 2018.

Selected Bibliography

Amalfitano, C., M. Condinanzi & P. Iannuccelli. *Le regole del processo dinanzi al giudice dell'Unione europea.* Naples: Editoriale scientifica, 2017.

Bergerés, M.C. *Contentieux communautaire.* 3rd edn. Paris: Presse Universitaire de France, 2000.

Biavati, P. *Diritto processuale dell'Unione europea.* 5th edn. Milan: Giuffrè, 2015.

Biavati, P. 'Processo dell'Unione europea', in *Enciclopedia del diritto, Ann. I*, 2007, 990 et seq.

Billard, J.N. *Droit du contentieux communautaire: système et marché intérieur.* Paris: Ellipses, 2006.

Boulouis, J., M. Darmon & J.G. Huglo. *Contentieux communautaire.* 3rd edn. Paris: Dalloz, 2009.

Condinanzi, M. & R. Mastroianni. *Il contenzioso dell'Unione europea.* Turin: Giappichelli, 2009.

Czubinski, A. & C. Pellerin-Rugliano. *Dictionnaire de la Cour de justice de l'Unione européenne et de son contentieux.* Paris: Larcier, 2017.

Dehousse, R. *La Cour de Justice des Communautés européennes.* 2nd edn. Paris: Montchrestien, 1997.

Fuenteteja Pastor, J.A. *El proceso judicial comunitario.* Madrid: Marcial Pons, 1996.

Gundisch, J. *Rechtsschutz in der Europäischen Gemeinschaften.* Stuttgart: Boorberg, 1994.

Jung, H. *Das Gericht erster Instanz der Europäischen Gemeinschaften.* Baden-Baden: Nomos, 1991.

Leanza, U., P. Paone & A. Saggio. *Il Tribunale di primo grado delle Comunità europee.* Naples: Editoriale Scientifica, 1994.

Mahieu, S. (ed.), *Contentieux de l'Union européenne – Questions choisies.* Brussels: Larcier, 2014.

Migliazza, M. *Il doppio grado di giurisdizione nel diritto delle Comunità europee.* Milan: F. Angeli, 1993.

Pechstein, M. *EU-/EG-Prozessrecht*, 3rd edn. Tübingen: Mohr Siebeck, 2007.

Plender, R. (ed.). *European Court Practice and Precedents.* London: Sweet & Maxwell, 1997.

Reale, M.C. & M. Borraccetti. *Da giudice a giudice. Il dialogo tra giudice italiano e Corte di giustizia delle Comunità europee.* Milan: Giuffrè, 2008.

Rengeling, H.W., A. Middeke & M. Gellermann. *Handbuch des Rechtsschutzes in der Europäische Union.* 2nd edn. München: Beck, 2003.

Schermers, H.G. & D. Waelbroeck. *Judicial Protection in the European Union.* 6th edn. The Hague: Kluwer, 2001.

Tizzano, A., et al. *La Cour de justice de l'Union européenne sous la présidence de Vassilios Skouris (2003–2015). Liber amicorum Vassilios Skouris.* Brussels: Bruylant, 2015.

Tizzano, A. & B. Capponi. 'Il Tribunale di primo grado e la Corte di giustizia delle Comunità europee: le nuove regole di procedura'. *Foro it.* (1991): IV, 438 et seq.

Vandersanden, G. & A. Barav. *Contentieux communautaire.* Brussels: Bruylant, 1977.

Villagómez Cebrián, M. '*La cuestión prejudicial en el derecho comunitario europeo*. Madrid: Tecnos, 1994.

Waelbroeck, M., et al., 'La Cour de Justice', in *Le droit de la Communauté Economique Européenne*, edited by J. Megret et al. 2nd edn. Brussels: Editions de l'Université de Bruxelles, 1993.

Selected Bibliography

Index

The numbers given here refer to paragraph numbers.

Index

www.ingramcontent.com/pod-product-compliance
Ingram Content Group UK Ltd.
Pitfield, Milton Keynes, MK11 3LW, UK
UKHW020139290926
15471UKWH00003B/595